International and Developme

The *International and Development Education Series* focuses on the complementary areas of comparative, international, and development education. Books emphasize a number of topics ranging from key international education issues, trends, and reforms to examinations of national education systems, social theories, and development education initiatives. Local, national, regional, and global volumes (single-authored and edited collections) constitute the breadth of the series and offer potential contributors a great deal of latitude based on interests and cutting-edge research. The series is supported by a strong network of international scholars and development professionals who serve on the International and Development Education Advisory Board and participate in the selection and review process for manuscript development.

Titles:

Higher Education in Asia/Pacific: Quality and the Public Good
Edited by Terance W. Bigalke and Deane E. Neubauer

Affirmative Action in China and the U.S.: A Dialogue on Inequality and Minority Education
Edited by Minglang Zhou and Ann Maxwell Hill

Critical Approaches to Comparative Education: Vertical Case Studies from Africa, Europe, the Middle East, and the Americas
Edited by Frances Vavrus and Lesley Bartlett

Curriculum Studies in South Africa: Intellectual Histories & Present Circumstances
Edited by William F. Pinar

Higher Education, Policy, and the Global Competition Phenomenon
Edited by Laura M. Portnoi, Val D. Rust, and Sylvia S. Bagley

The Search for New Governance of Higher Education in Asia
Edited by Ka-Ho Mok

International Students and Global Mobility in Higher Education: National Trends and New Directions
Edited by Rajika Bhandari and Peggy Blumenthal

Curriculum Studies in Brazil: Intellectual Histories, Present Circumstances
Edited by William F. Pinar

Access, Equity, and Capacity in Asia Pacific Higher Education
Edited by Deane Neubauer and Yoshiro Tanaka

Policy Debates in Comparative, International, and Development Education
Edited by John N. Hawkins and W. James Jacob

Curriculum Studies in Mexico: Intellectual Histories, Present Circumstances
Edited by William F. Pinar

Increasing Effectiveness of the Community College Financial Model: A Global Perspective for the Global Economy
Edited by Stewart E. Sutin, Daniel Derrico, Rosalind Latiner Raby, and Edward J. Valeau

The Internationalization of East Asian Higher Education: Globalization's Impact
Edited by John D. Palmer, Amy Roberts, Young Ha Cho, and Gregory Ching

University Governance and Reform: Policy, Fads, and Experience in International Perspective
Edited by Hans G. Schuetze, William Bruneau, and Garnet Grosjean

Mobility and Migration in Asian Pacific Higher Education
Edited by Deane E. Neubauer and Kazuo Kuroda

Taiwan Education at the Crossroad: When Globalization Meets Localization
Edited by Chuing Prudence Chou and Gregory Ching

THE NEW FLAGSHIP UNIVERSITY

CHANGING THE PARADIGM FROM GLOBAL RANKING TO NATIONAL RELEVANCY

EDITED BY
JOHN AUBREY DOUGLASS

THE NEW FLAGSHIP UNIVERSITY
Selection and editorial content © John Aubrey Douglass 2016
Individual chapters © their respective contributors 2016
Corrected Printing 2016

First published 2016 by
PALGRAVE MACMILLAN

The authors have asserted their rights to be identified as the authors of this work in accordance with the Copyright, Designs and Patents Act 1988.

Palgrave Macmillan in the UK is an imprint of Macmillan Publishers Limited, registered in England, company number 785998, of Houndmills, Basingstoke, Hampshire, RG21 6XS.

Palgrave Macmillan in the US is a division of Nature America, Inc., One New York Plaza, Suite 4500, New York, NY 10004-1562.

Palgrave Macmillan is the global academic imprint of the above companies and has companies and representatives throughout the world.

ISBN: 978-1-349-57665-4
E-PDF ISBN: 978-1-137-50049-6
DOI: 10.1057/9781137500496

Distribution in the UK, Europe and the rest of the world is by Palgrave Macmillan®, a division of Macmillan Publishers Limited, registered in England, company number 785998, of Houndmills, Basingstoke, Hampshire RG21 6XS.

Library of Congress Cataloging-in-Publication Data

The new flagship university : changing the paradigm from global ranking to national relevancy / edited by John Aubrey Douglass.
        pages cm.—(International and development education)
    Includes bibliographical references and index.

    1. Universities and colleges—Ratings and rankings. 2. Education, Higher—Aims and objectives. 3. Educational leadership. I. Douglass, John Aubrey.
LB2331.62.N48 2015
378—dc23   2015020258

A catalogue record for the book is available from the British Library.

Contents

Illustrations

Figures

Tables

Series Editors' Introduction

We are pleased to introduce another volume in the Palgrave Macmillan International and Development Education book series. In conceptualizing this series we took into account the extraordinary increase in the scope and depth of research on education in a global and international context. The range of topics and issues being addressed by scholars worldwide is enormous and clearly reflects the growing expansion and quality of research being conducted on comparative, international, and development education (CIDE) topics. Our goal is to cast a wide net for the most innovative and novel manuscripts, both single-authored and edited volumes, without constraints as to the level of education, geographic region, or methodology (whether disciplinary or interdisciplinary). In the process, we have also developed two subseries as part of the main series: one is cosponsored by the East-West Center in Honolulu, Hawaii, drawing from their distinguished programs, the International Forum on Education 2020 (IFE 2020) and the Asian Pacific Higher Education Research Partnership (APHERP); and the other is a publication partnership with the Higher Education Special Interest Group of the Comparative and International Education Society that highlights trends and themes on international higher education.

The issues that will be highlighted in this series are those focused on capacity, access, and equity, three interrelated topics that are central to educational transformation as it appears today around the world. There are many paradoxes and asymmetries surrounding these issues, which include problems of both excess capacity and deficits, wide access to facilities as well as severe restrictions, and all the complexities that are included in the equity debate. Closely related to this critical triumvirate is the overarching concern with quality assurance, accountability, and assessment. As educational systems have expanded, so have the needs and demands for quality assessment, with implications for accreditation and accountability. Intergroup relations, multiculturalism, and gender issues comprise another cluster of concerns facing most educational systems in differential ways when one looks at the change in educational systems in an international context. Diversified notions of the structure of knowledge and curriculum development occupy another important niche in educational change at both the precollegiate and collegiate levels. Finally, how systems are managed and governed are key policy issues for educational policy-makers worldwide. These and other key elements of the education and social change environment have guided this series and have been reflected in the books that have already appeared and those that will appear in the future. We welcome proposals on these and other topics from as wide a range of scholars and practitioners as possible. We believe that the world of educational change is dynamic, and our goal is to reflect the very best work being done in these and other areas.

JOHN N. HAWKINS
University of California, Los Angeles

W. JAMES JACOB
University of Pittsburgh

Preface

In the course of many centuries, universities have survived revolutions, coups, wars, famines, reformations, societal reengineering, and economic depression. In one fashion or another, they remain. Their nearest rival in longevity: the Catholic Church. And this has occurred despite numerous predictions of obsolesces and doom—witness management guru Peter Drucker's prediction in the 1990s that bricks-and-mortar universities and colleges would soon find themselves in the dust heap of history, brought to an end by the assumption of cheaper forms of providing "educational services." We are still waiting.

Today, universities exist within an increasingly diversified and growing market of higher education providers, shaped by growing worldwide enrollment demand and the insatiable need for new knowledge. There is little prospect for the development of a singular form of higher education.

At the same time, universities continue to evolve, increasing their value to the societies they were created to serve. Universities are now more important for socioeconomic mobility, for knowledge production, for generating economic and civic leaders, and for pushing innovation and societal self-reflection than in any other time in their history. Their modern evolution has been an iterative process of external and internal forces, marked by the movement from elite to mass higher education, from institutions primarily concerned with teaching to increased focused on creating knowledge, with economic engagement, and providing a growing array of public services; from relatively high levels of government subsidies to relatively low public funding support; from relatively high levels of institutional autonomy and isolation to much closer ties to stakeholder demands, including complex accountability regimes; from institutions with regional or national orientations and distinct academic cultures, to the aspiration to be global players and significant convergence in management structures and organizational behaviors. One result: research-intensive universities of today are very different from the leading national universities of the past. And with globalization and increasing expectations by government, by the private sector, and by society in general, organizational reforms are accelerating.

Within the pantheon of a growing number of postsecondary institutions, this book argues that there is a place, indeed a need, for a group of leading national universities with specific characteristics. As defined in the following chapters, the New Flagship University model is not simply a leading national university, with historical links to preserving socioeconomic castes and elite paths to power, with the best students, the best faculty, and the first claim on resources. Most countries have these institutions, what my coauthors and I call a Traditional Flagship University to help differentiate the old from the new.

As profiled in this book, the New Flagship University is a more comprehensive institution in the range of its activities and in its self-identified social purpose. Regional and national relevance is a primary goal of its academic leaders and faculty; global rankings are a secondary concern. International engagement, in its various forms, and increased journal publication and other markers of research productivity, are valued, yet they are framed as a path toward this larger purpose—not as an end unto itself. Flagships also seek to more overtly shape their own destinies.

In much of the world, ministries are the most significant driver of reforms within universities via new resources and sometimes intrusive accountability regimes. The great challenge for the network of universities that are truly leaders in their national systems of higher education is to more overtly shape and articulate their own missions, build their internal processes aimed toward excellence in all of their endeavors, and, ultimately, to meaningfully increase their role in the societies that gave them life and purpose.

What drives much of the current waves of ministerial edicts and funding? One cause is the sense that their universities are not productive enough, in research and in their influence in socioeconomic mobility and economic development—opinions shaped mightily by relatively new benchmarks provided by global rankings of universities. Within a vacuum of other sources of information, this has led to a contemporary infatuation with rankings, and its offspring: the notion of a World Class University (WCU). Ranking regimes and WCUs are nearly one and the same. Both are characterized by a focus on a narrow band of internationally recognized indicators of research productivity. The realization that Russia, or France, or Germany, or China, did not have a top-ranked university caused immense anxiety and a subsequent search for government-formulated solutions. To be without a globally ranked university is now viewed as a distinct disadvantage in the new knowledge economy. National pride also plays a role.

As discussed in the first section of this book, the aspirational model of the New Flagship University is, in part, a reaction to this myopic yet powerful

vision of what leading universities should do and achieve. University leaders, faculty, and ministerial agents need an alternative narrative. This book
attempts this feat by providing a profile of the New Flagship University.

Four "realms" of policy and practice are discussed, including a Flagship
University's place in national systems of higher education; the expanse
of programs and activities related to their "core" mission of teaching and
learning and research; old and new notions of public service and approaches
to regional and national economic development; and governance, management, and internally derived accountability practices that form a foundation for the New Flagship model. Each policy realm provides examples of
policies and best practices—from the conceptual idea of engaged learning, to research and public-service goals and their integration into faculty
advancement, approaches to technology transfer, and models of internal
governance and management.

One important theme is that the path to increased research productivity, and improved rankings is not through surgical efforts to boost faculty
journal publications, patents, and licenses. Rather it requires a more holistic approach to shaping the mission, academic culture, and practices of
a university to, in essence, take care of the fundamentals outlined in the
New Flagship model.

Another theme is that ministerial directives and efforts to force quality
improvement and greater productivity, a legitimate concern for all national
governments, have limits for expanding the overall social and economic
impact of their universities. Ultimately, it will be the internal academic
culture and efforts to seek institutional self-improvement that will determine which universities have a greater local, regional, national, and global
impact. The New Flagship model is an attempt not only to provide a
coherent framework toward development and change, but also to communicate the mission of leading research-intensive universities to a wider
public. Admittedly, this is an ambitious goal—one with many flaws, and
with only brief descriptions of the many facets and nuances explored in
each of the policy realms.

The list of policy and practices is not meant as a litmus test for achieving the status of the New Flagship University. Many universities are
already fully engaged in many of the characteristics and programs featured in the model. And not all universities, for example, will view the
wide range of public and community service practices described as relevant
within their national culture and societal needs. Resource constraints add
another extremely important variable. The existing academic culture of
faculty adds yet another constraint along with issues related to management capacity, and the larger political and economic environment in which
universities operate. In much of the world, there is a limited pool of faculty

with the PhD, for example, and there are major challenges related to effective university management. As discussed in the Flagship profile section of the book, and in the chapters by contributing authors who focus on various regions of the world, the level of autonomy, governance structure, and management capacity, and the alignment of an institution's academic culture, are key factors for pursuing institutional self-improvement.

Taking these national and academic culture variables into account, the idea is that the Flagship model is aspirational, adoptable, and waiting for greater definition and expansion. Whether it will be powerful enough to attract adherents is, of course, an open question.

The first part of the book concludes with a discussion of the strengths and weaknesses of the New Flagship model, the contextual aspects that may determine its relevance in various parts of the globe, and an attempt to answer predicted questions—for instance, is it most relevant in developing or developed economies? Is it simply a matter of institutional self-identity or ministerial selection? This forms a transition to Part 2 of the book.

The five chapters that then follow are written by observers of global efforts to reform and reposition higher education in nation-states. Each provides a historical and contemporary window into the leading universities within their own particular country or region of the world, which they know intimately. One important question posed to each author: to what extent is the New Flagship University model relevant in Asia, in Russia, in South America, and in the Scandinavian region? Another is the extent to which global university ranking regimes, and the World Class imagery, are influencing national policy making and institutional behaviors.

In each nation or region of the world discussed, there are significant efforts at university reform and also particular political cultures, economic capabilities, and demographic shifts. John Hawkins has extensive experience and knowledge on higher education in Asia. He offers observations on what he calls the "rapidly changing ecology of higher education in the region." Ministries and universities continue to look externally for models and inspiration, with an increasing domination of rankings and vague notions of becoming World Class.

Hawkins (Director of the Center for International Development Education at UCLA, and the former editor of *Comparative Education Review*, among many other positions) observes a "predicament." University leaders in Asia are increasingly concerned with meeting, in some form, the objectives outlined in the New Flagship model—although, again, this is a relatively new nomenclature. The push toward research productivity draws leading universities away from spending resources where the impact on local and national communities might be greatest. Yet, he sees an eventual maturation for institutions that have undergone rapid growth in enrollment and programs, and that the larger ideals of the Flagship model can coexist with their World Class desires.

In their retrospective on the role of leading national universities in Russia, Isak Froumin and Oleg Leshukov trace their transformation from a set of elite universities before the revolution into the Soviet network of institutions. This included Specialized Sectorial institutions largely focused on serving the labor needs of a specific industry under a command economy model; Regional Infrastructure Universities focused on professional programs—like teacher training and medicine—under a strict national curricular framework that served a region; and what they call Soviet Flagship Universities—the Russian version of the Traditional Flagship.

Under this coherent structure of higher education, the Soviet Flagships provided a wide range of academic degrees; they had the primary responsibility to train future faculty and Soviet government leaders and to be centers for furthering Soviet ideology. Each region had a mix of all of institutions described: Specialized Sectorial, Regional Infrastructure, and a Soviet Flagship. Some Soviet Flagships, however, were more equal than others. A small group had special status and influence, including Moscow State University and Saint Petersburg University. Under the Soviet model, basic academic research in the sciences and technology became largely the purview of researchers at the Russian Academy of Science.

The Soviet higher education system was a very powerful conceptual model that fit the needs of the state and influenced other communist countries within Russia's sphere of political influence, notably China. The post–Cold War shift in Russia, explain Froumin and Leshukov, meant another dramatic shift in this system.

The path to a quasi-market economy led to a changed conception of the role of leading national universities. Under federal government policies beginning in the 1990s, selected leading universities gained the ability to set their own educational degree requirements and to develop admission criteria beyond the national examination. They also gained a larger role in basic research once largely reserved for the Academy of Science—a difficult transition for faculty. This led to a period of experimentation that the authors view as often chaotic; universities now competed for students in a period of declining demand, and with academic cultures still stuck largely in a civil-service mentality. Government policy also came to value international comparisons in research productivity and practices, and in the organization of major research-intensive universities, leading to a restructuring of the higher education system. This included a massive wave of institutional mergers and later a series of "excellence" programs to elevate a core set of universities to higher rankings and World Class status. Greater international engagement has become a cornerstone of these efforts providing a path to greater interaction and exposure to practices that may improve research productivity and the quality of degree programs.

While government policies, and pressure, focus on higher rankings, Froumin and Leshukov recognize that the larger ambitions and framework of the New Flagship model should be the larger goal. But they see significant challenges for Russia's leading national universities to adopt a more expansive mission. Froumin has a unique perspective on Russian higher education, and on education in other parts of the globe, having worked at the World Bank when it first began to push the idea of World Class Universities.

Andrés Bernasconi and Daniela Véliz Calderón trace the historical development of national universities in Chile, and more generally in Latin America. The founding of many universities in this region of the world incorporated broad mandates intended to shape national cultures, educate future government officials, and help organize political institutions and national systems of education—a process of postcolonial state building. By the twentieth century, the Universidad de Buenos Aires, Universidad de San Carlos in Guatemala, Universidad Nacional Autónoma de México, and the Universidad de Chile, among others, emerged with these assigned roles.

In their stated mission, they had similarities with their American public university counterparts. However, they remained largely the vassals of the societal elite, with limited capacity for research and without a strong sense of their role in socioeconomic mobility and economic development. Those larger objectives—often referred to as a "third mission" in many parts of the world, connoting a sense of a new role—are now drawing the interest of national ministries and university leaders. Rankings, and the World Class prestige, are a concern, providing benchmarking that indicates generally low research productivity—with some notable exceptions. But the policy debates in nations such as Chile are more focused on how the leading national universities, public and private, both of which receive government funding, can more effectively expand access equitably, and to a lesser extent engage in promoting technological innovation and boost local economies.

Bernasconi and Véliz view the New Flagship model as a useful guide. But they also see major challenges. Universities are not adequately funded, for one. One result: most universities have very large enrollments and high student-to-faculty ratios. In Chile and in other parts of Latin America, with exceptions in Brazil, governments are reluctant to create different levels of funding for different universities. Spreading few resources among many universities creates mediocrity. The low proportion of faculty with

Acknowledgments

I first started to explore the idea of expanding on the historical and contemporary role of leading national flagship universities in a 2011 presentation to the Higher Education Research and Advocacy Network in Africa (HERANA) at the University of Stellenbosch. It was apparent that there was a thirst for an alternative framework for understanding and expressing the role of major national universities beyond global higher education rankings and the concept of world-class universities. This encouraged me to further articulate the Flagship University model and to seek opportunities to present and debate its merits with colleagues and at various conferences, including presentations at a 2013 Universitas21 Symposium in Shanghai and in a keynote address at the 2014 Consortium of Higher Education Researchers' 27th Annual Conference held in Rome. A working paper published by the Center for Studies in Higher Education at UC Berkeley, another by Universitas21, and an article in *University World News* and other venues also solicited informative responses. Besides the important input of my coauthors in this volume, I gained the thoughts, advice, and criticism on the evolving manuscript from many scholars of higher education who provided constructive criticism, including Marijk van der Wende, David Palfreyman, Jeroen Huisman, Christina Musselin, Ross Williams, Bekir Gur, C. Judson King, Richard Edelstien, and Igor Chirikov. I am indebted to the support and guidance of the Palgrave Macmillan International and Development Education series editors John Hawkins and W. James Jacob.

Part I

Exploring the New Flagship University Model

John Aubrey Douglass

Introduction

Seeking an Alternative Narrative

It is a familiar if not fully explained paradigm. A World Class University (WCU) is supposed to perform highly influential research, embody a culture of excellence, have great facilities, and retain a brand name that transcends national borders. But perhaps, most importantly, the particular institution needs to sit in the upper echelons of one or more world rankings generated each year by nonprofit and commercial enterprises. That is the ultimate proof for many government ministers and for much of the global higher education community. But is this an accurate way to gauge the value, breadth of activities, and societal impact of the best universities?

International university rankings are fixated on a narrow band of data and prestige scores. Citation indexes are biased toward the sciences and engineering, biased in their focus on peer-reviewed journals published mostly in English, on the number of Nobel laureates and other markers of academic status, and tilted toward a select group of largely older universities that always rank high in surveys of prestige.

These indicators are useful and informative, supplying a global and comparative measure of productivity and status. Yet government ministries are placing too much faith in a paradigm that is not achievable, that often fails to value the broader activities and outputs of many universities, and that loses sight of the economic and socioeconomic mobility needs of their countries. They aim for some subset of their national universities to inch up the scale of this or that ranking by building accountability systems and "excellence" programs that influence the behavior of university leaders, and, ultimately, faculty. Some of this is good. These ministerial initiatives create incentives to reshape the internal culture of some national university systems that have weak internal quality and accountability policies and practices. Their global pervasiveness reflects a frustration with the academic research achievement of higher education institutions. There also is a profound distrust among most ministries about the ability of their major national universities to elevate their performance without significant external pressure and, often, interventions. In most nations, the academic community has rarely articulated a vision of how their national systems should develop, or how their institutions might best serve the societies that created and sustains them financially. Until recently, many universities showed little interest in self-induced organizational reforms—for example, moving away from civil service as opposed to merit-based approaches to faculty advancement. Arguably, they needed a push from their respective ministries.

Yet, it is also clear that rankings have become the proxy and guide for institutional productivity. The ubiquitous efforts of ministries, and now many universities, to pursue higher rankings have detrimental consequences—in essence, establishing incentives focused largely on increasing the quantity of research production at the expense of other vitally important functions of a major national university.

In the following section of this book, I attempt to advocate and describe the notion of the New Flagship University as a more relevant ideal—a model that builds on past traditions and roles of leading national universities. This updated vision of the Flagship University is not simply an institution with some of the best students, the best faculty, high research output, and claim on public financing. That older, limited view of a leading national university is more appropriately called a Traditional Flagship University—institutions that have been grounded in national service, but historically with a limited vision of their role in socioeconomic mobility, economic development, and public service, and without the devotion to institutional self-improvement that marks the world's best and most influential universities.

The New Flagship model is much more expansive, providing an updated vision of the role, practices, and activities relevant to a contemporary world where knowledge production is rapidly advancing, and the needs and demands of society are more complex and urgent than in the past. The intent is to help steer leading universities, and their ministries, beyond the confines of rankings and myopic desires for WCU status. The Flagship model does not ignore international standards of excellence focused on research productivity, yet it is grounded in national and regional service, and has a specific set of characteristics and responsibilities that, admittedly, do not lend themselves easily to ranking regimes.

The Flagship paradigm is also built on an important proposition. After a long period of ministries attempting to shape the mission and activities of universities, including various accountability schemes and demands focused on the normative WCU model, we need to enter a period in which institutions themselves gain greater autonomy and financial ability to create, build, and sustain internal cultures of self-improvement and evidence-based management. The great challenge for the network of universities that are truly leaders in their own national systems of higher education is to more overtly shape and pronounce their own missions and, ultimately, to meaningfully increase their role in the societies that gave them life and purpose. The New Flagship University profiled in the following narrative is intended as a construct for this cause. It reflects the activities of many leading universities, and is aspirational and open to adoption and interpretation.

It is important to note that top-ranked research-intensive universities, particularly the public universities in the United States, were not built on a narrow band of quantitative measures of research productivity or reputational surveys that characterizes the contemporary crop of international rankings. And while influenced at the margin by these rankings, their path to national and international relevance was, and continues to be, rooted in their larger socioeconomic purpose and internal practices. In summary, and to offer an initial sketch, Flagship's often have some combination of the following descriptives:

- Comprehensive Institutions—These institutions are generally comprehensive and research-intensive, focused on regional and national relevancy. This does not exclude institutions focused almost entirely on science and technology, for example, but they have more limited abilities to fully embrace the Flagship model.
- Broadly Accessible—These institutions are highly selective in admissions at the undergraduate and graduate levels, yet they also are broadly accessible so as to be representative of the socioeconomic and racial/ethnic demography of a country. Flagship universities have a commitment to promote socioeconomic mobility and reduce inequality in the societies they serve and, at the same time, attract and retain talented students, and faculty, from across the world. These are not incompatible goals—indeed, they are the hallmarks of the most productive universities; but they do require sufficient enrollment and program capacity.
- Educating the Next Generation of Leaders—Flagship universities are intent on educating and providing talented leaders, generally for the regional and national societies they serve, as well as on enhancing engagement with the larger and increasingly international world.

- Highly Autonomous—These institutions are sufficiently autonomous and publicly financed so that they become leaders of knowledge generation and thought, not just followers. This is admittedly hard to define; yet I offer some practical policy realms related to governance and other management aspects of Flagship Universities.
- Management Capacity—These institutions have an internal culture of evidence-based management that includes the constant search for institutional self-improvement built on internally generated quality assurance, which, ultimately, cannot be achieved by ministerial policies and directives alone.
- Economic Engagement—These institutions are broadly engaged in regional/national economic development and public service across all the disciplines, with participation by faculty, students, and staff, and organizational support by the institution. Most universities have various activities intended to boost economic development and to integrate students and faculty into community-based research and service. But for many leading national universities, this is a relatively new pursuit, sometimes referred to as a novel "third mission" not yet fully valued by an academic culture slow to adapt to a wider definition of the purpose of their institution. Flagships view this form of engagement as a core mission, and have or are in the process of integrating these efforts into a broader institutional strategy.
- Leaders in a Larger Higher Education System—These universities have a self-identity as part of a larger system of national/regional education. In this system, Flagships can provide policies, practices, and collaborations that influence the behaviors of other postsecondary institutions in their regions and in their nations, and in other ways become more connected to the larger national education system. Too many leading universities view themselves as islands, focused on their own productivity and prestige in isolation.

These characteristics are not sufficient unto themselves to describe the New Flagship University model. A more detailed exploration and reflection on the model is offered later in this narrative. Rather, they offer an initial sketch.

Figure I.1 captures the larger purpose and objectives of Flagship Universities, with only one that is valued and partially captured in the current crop of global and national rankings—the creation of new knowledge. Different types of universities throughout the world share these objectives. Yet, they have a special meaning for the modern reincarnation of the Flagship University.

Figure I.1 The Objectives of *Flagship Universities*.

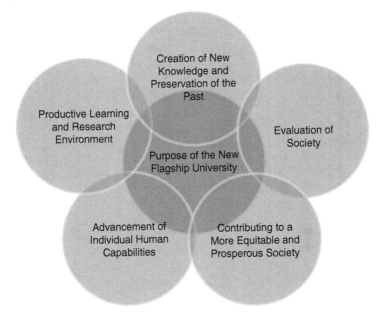

Source: John Aubrey Douglass. Center for Studies in Higher Education–UC Berkeley.

Outlining the objectives of these institutions is simply a reference point to a larger, and more challenging, question: what is the path to becoming a New Flagship University or, for those campuses that already see themselves as having such a status, for expanding on the model. The logical sequential route is from regional/national engagement, then to global influence. There probably is no shortcut. Hence, one might postulate that a WCU, defined largely by data on research productivity, does not make a Flagship. At the same time, a Flagship is more likely to be a WCU, providing the necessary environment for high-quality research productivity, but not at the expense of the larger public purpose and the soul of the university enterprise.

Before more fully venturing into the model, including goals, policies, practices, activities, and outputs, it is important to explore more fully the dynamics of the rising interest in global rankings and the notion of a WCU. What are its benefits and costs on the behaviors and success of universities and national higher education systems? Is there room for an alternative or a complementary narrative?

Chapter 1

How Rankings Came to Determine World Class

A direct correlation exists between the emergence of international rankings of universities and the pervasive rhetoric and obsession with World Class University (WCU) status. Building on a model first ventured by commercial rankings of colleges and universities in the United States as consumer guides for prospective students—notably the *US News and World Report* ranking of American colleges and universities—international rankings based on similar formulas made their appearance around 2003.[1] As government ministries focused increasingly on research-intensive universities as a path for national economic development, they quickly embraced rankings as a quantifiable source for assessing the place of their universities in the global marketplace.

Seemingly based on simple and understandable metrics, rankings reinforce an already present anxiety: that many economically developed economies, and those striving for such status, lack the best universities. There is now a widespread perception that the most competitive economies require one or more top-tier research-intensive universities to fuel innovation and economic growth—particularly in technology-driven and high-profile businesses sectors. To be without one, or a set of them, is seen as a distinct disadvantage. While economic competitiveness is arguably the primary focus of the WCU ambition, national pride plays a role as well. How could a great nation like Germany, like France, the birthplaces of so many important scientific and technological advances, survive the twenty-first century without some critical mass of WCUs? A rapidly rising China recognizes in some form that its astounding growth in its higher education system, in enrollment, in doctoral programs, and more, must also include an improvement in the quality and quantity of research output. How can it not aspire to its own network of WCUs?

Status Anxiety and Seeking Excellence

WCU anxiety, or, more accurately, the sense that Europe and most other regions of the world do not have an appropriate collection of research-intensive and quality players found prevalent in the United States and the United Kingdom, is a relatively new revelation. In the four decades after World War II, most nations, including those in Europe, sought to transform their existing network of largely elite universities that served a small and largely privileged population. They quickly built mass higher education systems focused on the equality and homogeneity of institutions. There was little or no concern for mission differentiation among universities. Institutions also clung to the notion that they should operate separately from crass commercial needs of a larger society. The result: old and new universities believed they had the same narrow ivory tower mission, the same claim to pursue research, and the same claim on funding.

With the exception of fields such as engineering, much of the research agenda of faculty, and their universities, had no strong sense of their role in economic development. Most of the academic community continued to embrace a Humboldtian model of autonomous research and doctoral training in the midst of dramatic increases in access for first-degree students mandated by governments and the thirst of a larger public for a wider vision of their engagement in society.

With many differences between nations, and among the disciplines, the macro observation is that the understandable drive to create equality of opportunity, to help reorder society, and to treat all universities the same, is one significant reason that much of continental Europe failed to support and sustain a network of highly selective, top-performing research universities. The post–World War II drive for mass higher education also led governments to see their universities as simply one among many public services, faculty as simply another brand of civil servant. Most ministries ignored the unique characteristics and organizational behaviors of the academic community. Adding to the story in Europe, in both Germany and France, existing networks of research institutes and, as in France, an elite group of small *Ecoles* all based in Paris, further eroded the ability, and interest, to create truly comprehensive research-intensive universities. In England, the 1992 elevation of the polytechnic sector to university status by the Thatcher government ended a binary system that had distinguished the mission and claim on public funding between the polytechnics and universities.

Because many parts of the world embraced over time a homogeneous model of higher education, the research-intensive university became the ideal; conversely, to be anything less, in mission and in the draw on public resources, seemed inequitable and discriminatory—a perpetuation of a division between elite and mass higher education. Reinforcing this viewpoint, other forms of postsecondary education, including vocationally oriented institutions such as the *Fachhochschulen* network of campuses in Germany, were and are viewed as not really a part of higher education, but simply an extension of a nation's secondary system.

This bifurcated vision comes in sharp contrast to the United States, where a diversity of institutional types are viewed as essential parts of state systems of higher education, including private liberal arts colleges, regional public universities that are teaching intensive, and public community colleges with a mix of vocational, liberal arts, and adult education programs. Most do not aspire to the research-intensive model and, instead, seek excellence in their own sphere of responsibility. There is always pressure for mission drift—for example, many liberal arts colleges have launched master's programs in a few fields where there is market demand. But there simply is not the status anxiety found in more homogenous systems, or expectation of most institutions to compete for research grants and the corresponding need for laboratory and other facilities found at research-intensive universities.

Informed by the American experience, and the homogeneous impulse of European ministries in the throes of a spectacular increase in the number of new universities, in 1976 sociologist Martin Trow worried that there was no ensured place for elite institutions. They were becoming an "endangered species" (Trow 1976). The egalitarian impulse of ministries saw elite institutions as incompatible with democracy, as depriving newer and more egalitarian institutions of resources and, most significantly, reinforcing socioeconomic class biases. They were being squeezed out in the rapid building of new national higher education systems. Elite institutions, Trow argued, need not be bastions of privilege. Effusing his version of the American mantra first iterated by Thomas Jefferson that America's public universities could be the breeding ground for a new "aristocracy of talent," Trow thought they instead could break class barriers. If managed in the interest of the public good, they could provide an exceptional environment for educating broadly minded and creative individuals from all walks of society. In his view, they needed not only to be preserved, but also nurtured and, by their mere output of talent, offered value for money. Influenced by California's network of public colleges and universities, Trow implied that elite institutions could be rationalized only as part of a larger coherent network of postsecondary institutions—in isolation, they were unjustified in the modern economies with democratic predilections. This was a contrarian view outside of the United States, until recently.

Many nations are transitioning from the initial stages of creating mass higher education systems, often at the expense of quality, to an understanding that successful national higher education systems must have sufficient levels of differentiation in the mission, purpose, and financing among their various institutions. Not all can be top-tier, high-performing research and doctoral educating institutions; some should be more teaching intensive or professional and vocation in orientation. The result promises a better match between the aspirations of the students and the labor needs of a particular nation, and offers a more efficient system of public funding for higher education.

The importance of a more diversified market of higher education providers is a relatively new vision. The result is that in recent years ministries, the only entities that, thus far, appear to care about the overall performance and coherence of national systems of higher education, creatively conjured indirect methods to encourage mission difference. An overt discussion was, and remains, politically volatile in much of the world. Instead, new policies emerged as part of what might be called discreet campaigns to not only foster mission differentiation, but also bolster or create a globally competitive set of universities. This includes competitions for special research funds, often called "excellence" initiatives, and new forms of national accreditation and incentives to merge specialized institutions into larger universities.

The arrival of international rankings in the early part of this century accelerated the desire for mission differentiation and further deepened growing status and performance anxiety. "The explosion of university rankings perhaps signals the reality that we live in a compared and ranked world," note Mmantsetsa Marope and Peter Wells in a 2013 report to UNESCO.[2] In the course of globalization, international agencies, such as UNESCO and the OECD, and national governments, seek new ways to judge the position of nations in the larger world. The commercial innovation of university rankings, they note, is just one part of this larger reality.

Influenced by the search for one or more WCU's, most national systems are transitioning to performance-based funding and often large-scale restructurings (van der Wende 2014; Estermann et al. 2013), with England's Research Excellence Assessment (REA) being one of the first and most influential models. In Continental Europe, for example, at least seven countries—Austria, France, Germany, Hungary, Norway, Poland, and Spain, each a member of the European Higher Education Research Area (EHEA)—had some form of an excellence program.[3] Many of these initiatives have positive influences on the resources and the culture of national universities, largely because they are competitively distributed.

Often for the first time, universities are engaged in a process of deciding where their strengths lie and what areas of research they want to expand. Even for institutions that do not "win" a government excellence grant, universities that choose to compete oftentimes are making choices about their academic programs and conjuring innovative research efforts. Although consistent funding by governments is a problem, most excellence programs have cycles for grant applications and new rounds for funding; in the case of Germany, the concept is a five-year cycle. This allows universities to return with new ideas and proposals to compete for funding. Yet, it is also important to note that excellence programs tend to reinforce existing hierarchies of institutions in national systems—an outcome that aligns with ministerial desires for greater mission differentiation.

More funding, more competition, that is all good. Academic leaders and faculty also have a long tradition of leveraging new resources, whatever their government-announced purpose, to their own priorities and uses. In the United States, the first large wave of purpose-driven external funding came in the wake of Sputnik, with fears that major universities were becoming simply research factories for the nation's defense needs. Later, increased corporate sponsorship of research led to fears of academics' subservience to commercial interests. A cavalcade of books and articles pronounced the evils and new dominance of privatization and corporate influence. But neither the dire federal nor corporate-induced consequences arrived in the force predicted. One might argue that the "excellence" initiatives focused on rankings and world-class status offer a similar opportunity to simply leverage government support.

As new and special funding schemes have become more pervasive, and the influence of rankings has accelerated, the ethos and need to compete has spread into the daily workings of universities. University administrators and academics have embraced the language of WCU and the focus on rankings, reinforcing the paradigm.[4] A survey of some 171 universities in Europe states that over 70 percent of respondents used rankings to inform strategic, organizational, managerial, or academic actions that are largely, but not solely, intended to improve their ranking. Of those who noted that rankings influenced their behaviors, some 26 percent reported changing research priorities, some 21 percent also altered faculty recruitment and promotional criteria, and many stated that they shifted funding and other campus resources, changed student admissions criteria, or closed or merged departments to enhance their standing in global and national ranking regimes (Hazelkorn 2014).

Inducing universities to be more strategic is certainly not unto itself a bad outcome, particularly among a large cadre of universities that for decades remained caught in an organization culture that avoided hard choices about resources, about faculty pay and promotion. In an era of increased global competition, "ordinal cross-border comparisons are inevitable," notes Simon Marginson.[5] Yet, there is increased recognition of the inadequacy of the ranking and WCU paradigm that, thus far and for the immediate future, focuses on a limited set of outcomes: generally, citation indexes heavily weighted to STEM fields + research income + Nobel or other internationally recognized research awards + oftentimes, reputational surveys (Marginson 2013; Hazelkorn 2011). Further, WCU advocates do not provide much guidance on what organizational behaviors and methods can lead to greater productivity in research, teaching, *and* public-service activities.

The Ranking Market

Campus rankings are not all bad, but none is particularly good—whether it is generated by a commercial enterprise, or a university-based think-tank, or the increasing phenomenon of a government entity creating its own ranking scheme. If you subscribe to the notion that the methodology to date is inadequate, biased, and overly influential, and your own national institutions rank poorly in, say, the widely cited Academic Ranking of World Universities (ARWU), then one response is to devise new ranking schemes that espouse improved methodology and, in the end, focus on tweaking the same limited set of available data.

Global higher education rankings are a growth industry. Some 50 or more countries have developed national rankings and there are ten private enterprises that claim to provide global or, in some cases, regional comparative rankings (see figure 1.1).

Dissatisfied with the poor ranking of its national universities, the Russian Federation created its own world rankings that placed Moscow State University fifth, just ahead of Harvard University and the University of Cambridge. Germany, Japan, the United Kingdom, and other countries have various forms of single-country rankings, often intended as consumer guides. But the bigger and more influential movement is global rankings that, seemingly based on quantifiable data, provide a comparative benchmark for understanding university performance.

Consternation over the poor showing of French universities, and Europe in general relative to the United Kingdom and the United States, led to a European Commission–funded effort at ranking intended to be "more objective and more favourable to European universities." Known as the "Multi-Dimensional ranking of higher education institutions," or

Figure 1.1   The Proliferation of Global Rankings.

	Year Established
Academic Ranking of World Universities ARWU Shanghai Jiao Tong University	2003
Webometrics Spanish National Research Council	2003
World University Ranking Times Higher Education/ Quacquarelli Symonds –	2004–2009
Performance Ranking of Scientific Papers for Research Universities HEEACT	2007
Leiden Ranking Centre for Science and Technology Studies, University of Leiden	2008
World's Best Colleges and Universities US News and World Report	2008
SCImago Institutional Rankings	2009
Global University Rankings Rating of Educational Resources, Russia	2009
Top University Rankings Quacquarelli Symonds	2010
World University Ranking Times Higher Education	2010
U-Multirank European Commission	2011
U21 Ranking of National Higher Education Systems University of Melbourne	2012

U-Multirank, it is intended as largely a consumer guide for prospective students and includes, unlike other rankings, student evaluations of academic programs.[6] In a recent analysis of the six major international rankings currently on the market, including Shanghai Jiaotong University's ARWU, Leiden University, QS, Scopus, the *Times Higher Education* World University Rankings, and U-Multirank, those rankings with a high dependence on research productivity indicators were viewed as strong methodologically, but weak in conveying the full mission of research-intensive universities; U-Multirank was strong conceptually but weak because of its reliance on subjective data submitted by universities and the fact that many major universities simply do not participate in providing the relevant information (Marginson 2013).

The lucrative and high-stakes business of university rankings has led to new commercial products. In search of new markets and higher profits, *Times Higher Education (THE)*, a periodical and originally a subsidiary of the *London Times*, is one of the most aggressive and imaginative purveyors. Its World University Rankings first came out in 2004 and quickly established itself as a major brand in ranking markets. Now its product line also includes a *THE* 100 Under 50 [years old] Rankings, a *THE* Asia University Rankings, and a *THE* BRICS & Emerging Economies Rankings.

Indicative of the growing complexity of the ranking industry, in 2014 *THE* announced that it would no longer contract with Thomson Reuters to use data from their Annual Academic Reputation Survey and other data-collection efforts in their products. *THE* would now do almost all data collection "in-house, carried out by a new, dedicated team of data analysts at *THE*." The exception is that research publication data would still come from Elsevier's Scopus database. Only five years earlier, *THE* ended a similar arrangement for supplying data under contract for much of its formulaic rankings with Quacquarelli Symonds, a British company, before entering the aforementioned arrangement with Thomson Reuters in 2009.

THE stated in November 2014 that it "intends to build the largest and most comprehensive database of university data in the world...to be used to develop new analyses, in response to sector demand and consultation, including new rankings and analytical services."[7] Those analytical services have already come to include "summits" related to its growing menagerie of sector-focused rankings, such as a Summit for *THE* Young Universities, that both promote their products and provide venues to guide universities on the path to higher rankings. Another summit was held in Doha in February 2015, "dedicated to addressing the development of World Class education and research in the Middle East and North Africa."[8] The so-called MENA events featured keynote speeches on university leadership, strategy, and international cooperation by Alice Gast, president of Imperial College London, along with Jean-Lou Chameau, president of the King Abdullah University of Science and Technology (KAUST) in Saudi Arabia, and Jamil Salmi, a higher education consultant and author of many WCU books and articles.

After losing its business with *THE,* Quacquarelli Symonds went on to build its own ranking product, the QS Top University Rankings, only a year later and with good success. Similarly, Thomson Reuters is attempting to no longer be simply a supplier of data for the ranking products of other companies, and has created a Global Institutional Profiles Project to generate "university profiles using multiple aspects of a university mission as a tool for consumers and governments." This Thomson Reuters project includes data from its Annual Academic Reputation Survey and information supplied by universities, along with bibliometric data from the Web of Science.[9]

Among nonprofit groups, the widely acknowledged biases in world rankings led to searches for alternative approaches. The international consortium known as Universitas21 seeks to rank the overall performance of national systems as opposed to individual campuses. This effort does not profess to find the "one best system," but seeks to add to our understanding that the national context is important, providing data on relative national investment rates in higher education and calibrating research publications in relationship to a country's total population (Williams et al. 2013). Using many of the variables included in other international rankings, such as citation analysis, plus new variables such as "connectivity"—an analysis of online interactions and similar evidence of links with the global world—the results provide a contrary view of quality and productivity. According to U21's analysis, the top five countries in terms of overall performance: the United States, Sweden, Switzerland, Canada, and Denmark.[10]

Universitas21's national rankings provide a useful view of how well national systems of higher education perform. Yet, the global campus rankings computed each year by the ARWU, and by *THE*'s World University Rankings, and to a lesser extent QS, clearly have the market advantage in influencing ministerial and campus behaviors. Their rankings of universities are not overly complicated, creating a comparative "accountability" tool that is hard to displace.

A Zero-Sum Game

There are other problems with current campus rankings regimes that are important for this discussion. Besides being methodologically suspect and narrow in their focus, global rankings generate unachievable goals for the vast majority of aspiring universities. Rankings establish what is sometimes called a "deficit model" in which no institution is ever good enough except the ones at the very top (Locke 2011).

What are the chances to move up in rankings? The top 25 universities in almost all the recognized world rankings have changed very little over the past decade, and they are not likely to change much in the future. It is a consistent bunch (see figures 1.2 and 1.3).[11] There is some movement among the various rankings between 25 and 100, but even here, it is, thus far, marginal and hard to interpret—a warning to ministries who are funneling funding into efforts intended to make large leaps in global university rankings among national universities.

Among the top 100 in the Academic Ranking of World Universities, between 2012 and 2013, the average change in rank was only 1.66—up

Figure 1.2 A Consistent Bunch: *Times Higher Education* UK-based World University Rankings 2014.

1.	CalTech
2.	Harvard University
3.	University of Oxford
4.	Stanford University
5.	University of Cambridge
6.	MIT
7.	Princeton University
8.	UC Berkeley
9.	Imperial College London
10.	Yale University
11.	University of Chicago
12.	UCLA
13.	ETH Zurich
14.	Columbia University
15.	Johns Hopkins University
16.	University of Pennsylvania
17.	University of Michigan
18.	Duke University
19.	Cornell University
20.	University of Toronto
21.	Northwestern University
22.	University College London
23.	University of Tokyo
24.	Carnegie Mellon University
25.	National University of Singapore

Source: *Times Higher Education*/Thomson Reuters World University Rankings.

or down. Shanghai Jiaotong University's ARWU was first established in 2003 at the request of the Chinese government which sought comparable information on the quality of its universities. The Shanghai ranking is largely based on citation analysis and markers of academic prestige, like Nobel laureates, and does not include the somewhat dubious variable of reputational surveys.

The average change in the *Times Higher Education* world rankings was 5.36 places and the QS average was 3.97—both are more volatile than ARWU and correlated with a much wider array of data variables, including reputational surveys. There are other reasons to trust the ARWU's rankings more than those of the other two big players. As Richard Holmes notes, "ARWU uses publicly available data that can be easily checked and is unlikely to fluctuate very much from year to year. THE and QS use data

Figure 1.3 A Consistent Bunch: Shanghai Jiaotong Academic Ranking of World Universities 2014.

1.	Harvard University
2.	Stanford University
3.	MIT
4.	UC Berkeley
5.	University of Cambridge
6.	Princeton University
7.	CalTech
8.	Columbia University
9.	University of Chicago
10.	University of Oxford
11.	Yale University
12.	UCLA
13.	Cornell
14.	UC San Diego
15.	University of Washington
16.	University of Pennsylvania
17.	Johns Hopkins University
18.	UC San Francisco
19.	ETH Zurich
20.	University College London
21.	University of Tokyo
22.	Imperial College
23.	University of Michigan
24.	University of Toronto
25.	University of Wisconsin

Source: *Academic Ranking of World Universities.*

submitted from institutions. There is room for error as data flows from branch campuses and research centres to the central administrators and then to the rankers. QS also has the option of replacing institutional data with that from third party sources."[12]

There has been some movement among the top 100 to 500, depending on the ranking enterprise, and often with small margins of cumulative scoring determining whether an institution in, say, the AWRU is ranked 150th or 180th. A number of universities in Asia, and in particular China, have moved up—an indicator of significant investments exclusively in STEM research productivity. Between 2004 and 2014, among its over 2,200 tertiary institutions, China increased the number of its universities from 8 to 32 in the top 500, and from zero to six in the top 200.

Considering the short time in which China has pursued mass higher education and the development of a core set of top institutions, this is a sign of improvement, but really only in the realm of research productivity, and specifically citations. At the same time, it is important to note that citation indexes, seemingly the gold standard for assessing research productivity and influence, may be of diminishing value. A big factor is the continued proliferation of new journals and articles facilitated, in part, by the relative ease to establish new journals, mostly online open access publications, many with open calls for contributions by authors. Many of the new publications are established in developing economies. The overall growth is correlated to the increased pressure for academics to publish, and for universities to improve their publications records and, ultimately, their rankings. Since 2008, the growth in recognized scientific journals and articles used in citation indexes has averaged just above 3 percent a year; in 2012 alone, there were 28,100 active peer-reviewed journals publishing some 1.9 million articles (Ware and Mabe 2012).

Two other forces influence the proliferation of scholarly journal articles and books and, in turn, drive up citations. One is the general growth in knowledge and the establishment of new fields, including an explosive growth in multidisciplinary research, particularly in the hard sciences, medicine, and technology. One estimate is that global scientific "output," as measured by academic articles, doubles about every nine years.[13] The other force is the growth in the number of active scientists and engineers in academia and in the private sector. For largely professional reasons, and as never before, they seek to publish, often with a dizzying array of coauthors. The inevitable growth in knowledge and new forms of inquiry, more academics looking to publish in recognized journals, more journals and new technologically driven forms of publishing and delivery—all are changing the nature of research generation and dissemination that does not always favor quality over quantity.

But beyond this and other limitations in the methodology of global university rankings, there is a conceptual limitation that is not fully appreciated by ministries and universities. Assuming that a WCU is an institution that ranks among, say, the top 50 or even 100, universities on some recognized world ranking, then it is a zero-sum game, analogous with rating universities on a bell curve. Yet, many governments and many universities strive for the WCU status under the assumption that one or more of the current global ranking enterprises will decipher that moment in time. They have bought into the bell-curve model and the concept that research productivity and citation indexes determine a global hierarchy. Married to this concept, European governments complain, as noted previously, that there are not enough European universities in the top 50 and many are spending money to do something about it. There is also a sense by governments of failed potential, or what has been called by the European Commission the *European Paradox*: "whereby Europe has the necessary knowledge and research, but fails to transfer this into innovation and enhanced productivity and economic growth" (van der Wende 2009).

To encourage greater engagement with the economy, and improve rankings, Germany's federal Ministry of Education and Research launched a widely publicized national competition to identify ten among its 104 universities that have the potential of becoming elite universities—the Excellence Program with an initial budget of €1.9 billion.[14] Under president Sarkozy, and extended by his successor, President Hollande, France launched a similar initiative to help boost the research productivity of its national universities. Despite austerity plans to cut some €50 billion in general government spending over three years, in 2014 Hollande pledged €2 billion for the creation of new regional university research centers as part of a second wave of "*Initiatives of Excellence*," or Idex (Marshall 2014).

Having fueled the ranking frenzy, China plans on having 20 top universities that aspire to match MIT in productivity. As part of that effort, but also in an attempt to improve the research and teaching quality of some 100 universities, the Chinese central government is spending nearly 3.68 billion euros over ten years. Before the World Class nomenclature appeared, in 1998 President Jiang Zemin famously explained that "China must have a number of top-class universities at the international level."

In Africa, Nigeria hopes for 20 or more WCUs, although seemingly under a rubric of its own making that is different from the current crop of ranking enterprises;[15] Sri Lanka wants at least one WCU and Vietnam desires one in the top 200 by 2020. Japan's ministry of education, known as MEXT, has a target of 30 universities becoming "World Class" institutions beyond the University of Tokyo, with five in the top 30 in global ranking, and at least one breaking the top ten mark.[16]

In 2013, the Russian government announced a plan to have at least five of its National Research Universities in the top 100 WCU by 2020. They have designated which ones, besides Moscow State University, that are assigned to achieve this goal, providing special financial subsidies: Tomsk Polytechnic University, the Higher School of Economics—Moscow, the Engineering Physics Institute, the Moscow Institute of Steel and Alloys and the National Research University of Information Technologies, Mechanics and Optics.[17]

However, ambition cannot outpace reality if rankings in the shape of a bell curve are the standard. Eventually, ministries and universities will need to recognize that the math simply does not add up for all to claim WCU status if they remain fixated on this or that ranking and the values they exude.

Recipes for Attaining World Class

The construction of international and national campus ranking regimes led to the question of, and subsequently advice on, how to achieve WCU status. In an early critique of the emerging WCU frenzy, Philip Altbach noted that "the problem is that no one knows what a World Class University is, and no one has figured out how to get one." At that time, he argued, "that it is just as important to have 'national-' or 'regional-class' academic institutions as to emulate the wealthiest and, in many ways, most elitist universities" (Altbach 2003).

As the currency of the various ranking systems increased, however, ministries and a literature emerged to do just that—essentially defining world class as a metric of certain research productivity measures and prestige indicators. Perhaps no agency has been more engaged in advocating the value and proper path than the World Bank.[18] So what defines a WCU? According to the World Bank, and others, there are three rather generic but informative traits: a *high concentration of talented* faculty and students, *abundant resources*, and a *favorable governance organization with a high level of autonomy.*[19]

Indeed, these are important, but they are not sufficient unto themselves.[20] To some degree, the WCU audience is those universities, and officials in national ministries, who rank poorly; certainly, the advocates garner little interest from the research universities with the greatest productivity. And the advocates are largely outsiders peering into the workings of major research-intensive universities, seeing certain productivity outcomes and making some general observations, yet failing to attempt to decipher the culture, organizational behaviors, and building blocks to achieve their advocated goals: higher rankings.

With the emergence of the WCU model have come worries over its influence, including shifting the priorities of universities.[21] In an earlier 2006 analysis of the WCU movement that is still relevant today, Henry M. Levin and his coauthors noted, "The subjective nature of world class status means that institutions will attempt to address those dimensions that are considered in assessing reputations and that are visible. In this respect, research activity, publications, citations, and major faculty awards are highly visible and measurable while the quality of the educational process is not" (Levin et al. 2006). Within the context of Asia, Ka Ho Mok has also complained of the one-dimensional, research productivity focus of rankings (Mok 2011). More recently, Marijk van der Wende has noted a desire for "the inclusion of the quality of teaching" (van der Wende 2014). Altbach and Jamil Salmi, while noting "different pathways" to WCU status and caution regarding overzealous national efforts and a narrow focus on rankings,[22] reiterate that such institutions should be embedded in some form in local and national needs—although what this might mean remains vague.[23] Over time, Altbach and Salmi, both keen observers of global trends in higher education, have shifted from being critics of the WCU model to what might be termed qualified advocates, publishing articles and books and giving speeches on the pathway to such a status. Indeed, the literature on WCU is large and growing, in part fostered by various consultants and conferences on how to get there, often organized by the ranking industry.[24]

Ministries pouring funding into special initiatives intended to induce higher research productivity and higher scores on citation indices might take heed of one conclusion by those studying how universities can achieve WCU status: it seems that most nations without a highly ranked university will find the fastest path toward having one is by starting a new institution from scratch, rather than attempting to shape, and fund, existing ones.[25] This implies that the organizational behavior of existing universities, and academics, is in many instances beyond repair; that internal cultures needed for high performance are elusive and limited. It also seems to imply that a route not likely to succeed are ministerial efforts to induce and sometimes require the merger of existing universities to create more comprehensive institutions, consolidate management, and improve rankings and reputations.

Yet, the concept that established universities cannot easily, or ever, make the transition to higher research productivity, or more importantly for this discussion, greater relevancy, is not a vision shared by most ministries. They are pursuing a variety of policies to change the standing of their universities. One simple observation is that many national systems of higher education suffer in the ranking metrics, and World Class race, because they have too many small institutions. Scale matters in assessing the research output of institutions and perceived prestige. Germany has significant and globally recognized research conducted in many of its specialized centers, notably the Max Planck Institutes. But they operate separately from large universities. One result is that Germany has few high-profile and highly ranked universities in any global rankings.

Increasingly, ministries and institutions themselves have sought institutional mergers based on the premise of improved university management and finances, altering academic cultures to push greater productivity, as well as improving the international standing of reconstituted universities. This is not only part of the rationale behind the merger frenzy in developing economies such as China, Russia, and Brazil, but also the modern incarnation of the University of Manchester with the absorption of the University of Manchester Institute of Science and Technology. One recent study on university mergers in Finland points to the "world class" objectives of ministries as the primary motive.[26]

Many mergers, particularly in those countries that at one time pursued the Soviet model of specialized institutions, including China, have helped improve the quality and performance of institutions, after a painful first period of reorganization. Universities that once had a limited and specific link with a segment of a planned economy, such as railroads, or telephone communications, merged to include a broader array of disciplines.

In yet another consequence of the emergence of the WCU model and ranking criteria, and also due to the general concern over the quality and productivity of academics, many ministries have adopted pay incentives for faculty who publish journal articles. Low pay for academics remains a significant problem in most parts of the world, shaping behaviors, including academics who work outside of their home universities to make a higher income. On the basis of criteria formulated often at the ministerial level, faculty can raise their low level of pay substantially by publishing in international journals that the ministry has chosen as sufficiently eminent and correlated with citation indexes—an injection into the process of faculty advancement that indicates distrust of universities and assumptions regarding what constitutes academic rigor and quality in publishing. In some instances, the number of publications in international journals figures into funding for individual academic departments and for general ministerial funding for a campus. Government-derived incentives exist in many Asian countries, including Japan, Korea, and China, and in parts of Europe, Turkey, Russia, Norway, and elsewhere. "Chinese researchers who place in the top half of colleagues in terms of bibliometric measures can earn three to four times the salaries of co-workers," note Chiara Franzoni and coauthors in an article in *Science*, "and also can be rewarded by access to better apartments. Some Chinese and Korean institutes pay cash bonuses to authors who publish in *Science, Nature* and *Cell*" (Franzoni et al. 2011).

The push for international publications is most prevalent in the sciences, but affects the social sciences as well. In England, and beginning in the 1980s, the Research Assessment Exercise (RAE) ranked academic departments based largely on citation analysis, then determined the flow of general-support funds for research, past performance thereby determining future funding. This process was modified in 2014 under a new "Research Excellence Framework" that is a more complicated formulation. The REF now attempts to also calculate the "impact" of research on the "economy, society, public policy, culture and the quality of life"—a high-stakes evaluation process that might best be called a work in progress (Atkinson 2014).

There are some indicators that these financial incentives have led to greater instances of plagiarism, a greater focus on quantity, rather than quality, of publications, and a further push for academic researchers to seek conventional lines of inquiry in order to get published (Butler and Mulgan 2013). In their study on ways to gauge the "connectivity" of universities with regional and national needs, Gaétan de Rassenfosse and Ross Williams note that the incentives to publish encourage researchers toward topics that appeal to an international audience, rather than local community needs. "Worldwide citation are larger if the research is of interest to an international audience," they state. In their analysis of some 50 national higher education systems, they note an "inherent conflict" between the emphasis of ministries on rankings, and citation analysis, and the desire and need for greater engagement with local communities, particularly in smaller-populated countries that increasingly view international interaction as key to their economic development (de Rassenfosse and Williams 2015).

However, it is also true that many universities had low expectations for faculty, linking their pay and status to a civil-service mentality that focused on years in employment as opposed to actual productivity. And, while intrusive, these policies are having a positive effect on the number, if not necessarily the quality, of journal publications, refocusing the time and effort of faculty, departments, and campuses (Franzoni et al. 2011). Faculty are incentivized to seek international collaborations, bolstering the trend that researchers view their most important colleagues in a discipline, or a field, as global.

As the ranking competition has heated up, universities in some parts of the world have attempted to game the system via key faculty, and sometimes temporary, recruitments, just in time for government ranking exercises—a known practice in England. There is also speculation that some global ranking agencies have been offered remuneration to help a university creep up a bit higher. In the United States, some institutions manipulate data, or seek international students with, on average, higher standardized test scores, to help bolster their domestic rankings, which focus largely as consumer guides for prospective students. Reporting on student-to-faculty ratios by American universities and colleges, for instance, is becoming increasingly unreliable—a major factor in the *US News and World Report* college ranking.

Since rankings are here to stay, some seek avenues to materially improve ranking methodologies and include other data; with the proliferation of global rankings, might policy makers and university leaders incorporate more nuanced interpretations of their meaning? I sense there are significant limitations on the availability of data to adequately broaden our understanding of what universities do in their respective societies. Research productivity will remain the primary focus. The proliferation of rankings may induce a more healthy understanding of the limits of their meaning, but to date most nation-states and universities look to only one to two global rankings—essentially providing a gold standard.

To return to the main theme of this chapter, there is room, indeed a great need, for more innovative and broad thinking on what a leading university might or should be—indeed, a thirst for an alternative or revised conceptual model that is distinctly separate from global rankings. At least among a cadre of leading national universities, might the ranking paradigm, and the sometimes narrow thinking and gaming it induces, be altered?

Notes

1. In the United States, there has been a long history of academic efforts at ranking the quality of institutions, or graduate programs. Commercial rankings arrived in 1985. That year, seeking new forms of income, the *U.S. News & World Report* published its first "America's Best Colleges" report—the most widely quoted of their kind in the United States. In the UK, the Higher Education Funding Council for England (HEFCE) first created "League Tables" in 1986 via the development of the Research Assessment Exercise (RAE), and as part of a process to allocate research funding to top-performing universities—a somewhat self-reinforcing approach. Since 2003, Shanghai Jiao Tong University has produced the *Academic Ranking of World Universities*, analyzing the top universities in the world on quality of faculty (40%), research output (40%), quality of education (10%), and performance versus size (10%). Its ranking is exclusively of research universities, mainly in the empirical sciences. The *Times Higher Education* published its first annual *Times Higher Education–QS World University Rankings* in November 2004. On October 30, 2009, *Times Higher Education* broke with QS, then its partner in compiling the Rankings, and signed an agreement with Thomson Reuters to provide the data instead.

2. P. T M. Marope, P. J. Wells, and E. Hazelkorn, eds. 2013. *Rankings and Accountability in Higher Education: Uses and Misuses* (Paris: UNESCO Publishing).

3. Ricardo Bascaia, Pedro Teixeira, and Vera Rocha, "Excellence Schemes in European Higher Education: Rewarding the Best?," paper presented at the Consortium of Higher Education Researchers' 27th Conference, Rome, September 10, 2014.

4. Francisco O. Ramirez and Dijana Tiplic. 2013. "In Pursuit of Excellence? Discursive Patterns in European Higher Education Research," *Higher Education*, published online, November 16, www.link.springer.com/article /10.1007/s10734-013-9681-1.

5. Simon Marginson. 2013. "University Rankings and Social Science." *European Journal of Education*. doi: 10.1111/ejed.12061: http://www.cshe.unimelb .edu.au/people/marginson_docs/European_J_of_Education_2013_univer sity%20rankings%5B1%5D.pdf.

6. U-Multirank is based on a proposal in the Commission Communication on modernisation of Europe's higher education systems COM 2011 567 final [1] accompanied by Staff Working Document SEC 2011 1063 final, p. 5–6 and is implemented by a consortium of research organizations—CHERPA Network Consortium for Higher Education and Research Performance Assessment under a two-year project funded by the European Commission. A preparatory study, "Design and Testing the Feasibility of a Multidimensional Global University Ranking," concluded in June 2011, demonstrated the feasibility of this project.

7. *Times Higher Education* announces reforms to its World University Rankings. November 19, 2014 Announcement: www.timeshighereducation.co.uk/world -university-rankings/news/times-higher-education-announces-reforms-to -world-university-rankings.

8. www.timeshighereducation.co.uk/world-university-rankings/news/times -higher-education-mena-universities-summit-programme-details-released.

9. "[A]s the world continues to flatten and specialize, profile databases must broaden in scope, deepen in content, and become increasingly flexible," states Thomson Reuters project website. In some ways this reflects a similar effort to move away from the computational rankings of institutions toward program and other subunit forms of analysis for the European Higher Education Area noted previously. See www.ip-science.thomsonreuters.com /globalprofilesproject/.

10. Universitas21 and the Melbourne Institute of Applied Economics and Social Research, *U21 Ranking of National Higher Education Systems 2013*, University of Melbourne, May 2013: www.universitas21.com/article/projects /details/152/u21-ranking-of-national-higher-education-systems.

11. The *Times Higher Education* World Rankings claim that it is, "the only global university performance tables to judge world class universities across all of their core missions—teaching, research, knowledge transfer and international outlook. The top universities rankings employ 13 carefully calibrated performance indicators to provide the most comprehensive and balanced comparisons available, which are trusted by students, academics, university leaders, industry and governments."

12. Richard Holmes, 2014. "The Noise," University Ranking Watch Blog, July 9: www.rankingwatch.blogspot.com/2014/07/the-noise.html.

13. Bibliometric analysts Lutz Bornmann, at the Max Planck Society in Munich, Germany, and Ruediger Mutz, at the Swiss Federal Institute of Technology in Zurich, think they have a better answer. It is impossible to know for sure, but the real rate is closer to 8–9 percent each year, they argue. That equates to a doubling of global scientific output roughly every nine years. http://blogs .nature.com/news/2014/05/global-scientific-output-doubles-every-nine -years.html.

14. Germany's Excellence Program, see: www.germaninnovation.org/research -and-innovation/higher-education-in-germany/excellence-initiative.
15. Ibikunle H. Tijani, "Developing World Class Universities in Nigeria: Challenges, Prospects and Implications," paper delivered at the 2nd FUNAI Leadership Development Seminar, Federal University Ndufu-Alike Ikwo, Ebonyi State, Nagieria, June 5, 2013; "Guidelines for Raising Nigerian Universities to World Class Status," Report submitted to the National Universities Commission NUC and the Association of Vice Chancellors of Nigerian Universities AVCNU, September 27–29, 2010.
16. Charles Jannuzi, 2008. "Japan Aims for 'World Class' Universities," Japan Higher Education Outline, February 5, 2008: www.//japanheo.blogspot.jp /2008/02/japan-aims-for-World Class-universities.html; Kenglun Ngok and Weiging Guo, "The Quest for World Class Universities in China: Critical Reflections," *Policy Futures in Education* 6, no. 5 (2008).
17. Eugene Vorotnikov, "Government Approves Universities for World Class Bid," *University World News*, September 11, 2013 Issue No. 287: www .universityworldnews.com/article.php?story=20130911144451887; Ann a Smolentseva, 2010. "In Search for World Class Universities: The Case of Russia." *International Higher Education* 58: 20–22.
18. Among the publications sponsored by the World Bank is a professed "guide" to build a "research university from scratch." See Philip G. Altbach and Jamil Salmi, *The Road to Academic Excellence: The Making of World Class Research Universities*, Directions in Development Series (Washington, DC: World Bank, 2009).
19. Jamil Salmi, *The Challenge of Establishing World Class Universities,* Directions in Development Series, World Bank: Washington DC, 2009; R. Deem, Mok K. H., and Lucas L., 2008. "Transforming Higher Education in Whose Image? Exploring the Concept of the 'World Class' University in Europe and Asia." *Higher Education Policy* 21, no. 1: 83–97.
20. In a paper presented in 2006 attempting to help define what a World Class University is, Henry M. Levin, Dong Wook Jeong, and Dongshu Ou, at Teachers College, Columbia University, noted the subjectivity of the title, noting, for example: "Although teaching, service to society, and research are all emphasized in the statements on what makes a great university, reputational ratings seem to be limited largely to the research dimension on the basis of our statistical analysis." Henry M. Levin, Dong Wook Jeong, and Dongshu Ou, "What Is a World Class University?", paper presented at the Conference on Comparative & International Education Society, Honolulu, Hawaii, March 16, 2006: www.tc.columbia.edu/centers/coce/pdf_files/c12.pdf.
21. *Ibid.,* Jamil Salmi, a major proponent of the WCU model, writes warnings: "Avoid overdramatization of the value and importance of World Class institutions and distortions in resource allocation patterns within national tertiary education systems. Even in a global knowledge economy, where every nation, both industrial and developing, is seeking to increase its share of the economic pie, the hype surrounding World Class institutions far exceeds the need and capacity for many systems to benefit from such advanced education

and research opportunities, at least in the short term. Indeed, in some countries where the existing tertiary education institutions are of higher quality than the economic opportunities available to graduates, excellent tertiary education may exacerbate existing brain-drain problems."

22. Jamil Salmi, and Alenoush Saroyan, 2007. "League Tables as Policy Instruments: Uses and Misuses." *Higher Education Management and Policy* 19, no.2: 31–68.

23. There are examples of serious discussions within major universities on how to absorb the meaning of rankings and the WC nomenclature. Danie Visser and Marilet Sienaert outline how "the University of Cape Town has taken a rather 'soft' approach. Aware of the university community's varied reactions and opinions to university rankings, the university helped its faculty to understand the emerging global university rankings, including goals and philosophies behind the rankings, biases, strengths and weaknesses, as well as rankings' impact on funders and policy makers. The university actively engaged the faculty in identifying relevant issues and indicators in their specific departments, and prompted them to understand that rational analysis of rankings provides the means of evaluating their own performance in relation to the university's goals. Through this practice, the university decided upon four strategies and principles that will specifically enable it as a university in the global south to achieve excellence in an increasingly globalized and competitive world, these being an increasing focus on its specific location in Africa, increasing international collaboration, increasing research visibility and increasing support to researchers at all levels." See Danie Visser and Marilet Sienaert, "Rational and Constructive Use of Rankings: A Challenge for Universities in the Global South," in *Building World Class Universities: Difference Approaches to a Shared Goal*, ed. Qi Wang, Ying Cheng and Nian Cai Liu (The Netherlands: Sense Publishers, 2012).

24. Held in Shanghai and supported by the Academic Ranking of World Universities based at Shanghai Jiaotong University, the 5th International Conference on World Class Universities occurred on November 3–8, 2013. Participants generally come from campuses that do not rank among the top universities under the ARWU ranking. See: www.shanghairanking.com/wcu/cp.html.

25. Philip G. Altbach and Jamil Salmi, 2011, *The Road to Academic Excellence: The Making of World Class Research Universities*, Directions in Development Series. (Washington DC: The World Bank).

26. Hanna-Mari Aula and Janne Tienari, "Becoming 'World Class'? Reputation-Building in a University Merger." *Emerald: Critical Perspectives on International Business* 7, no. 1 (2011): 7–29: www.academia.edu/508739/Becoming_World Class_Reputation-building_in_a_university_merger.

Chapter 2

The Origin of the Flagship Idea and Modern Adaptions

The notion of the public Flagship University has its origins in the early development of America's higher education system in the mid-1800s. It included a devotion to the English tradition of the residential college as well as the emerging Humboldtian model of independent research and graduate studies, in which academic research would, in turn, inform and shape teaching and build a stronger academic community. But just as important, the hybrid American public-university model sought utilitarian relevance. Teaching and research would purposefully advance socioeconomic mobility *and* economic development. As part of an emerging national investment in education, public universities also had a role in nurturing and guiding the development of other educational institutions. For these and other reasons, America's leading state universities were to be more practical, more engaged in society than their counterparts in Europe and elsewhere, evolving and expanding their activities in reaction to societal needs.

By the 1870s, most states had established one or more public universities—the first step in developing the world's first mass higher education system. In their mission to educate and train virtuous citizens and economic and political leaders, they also played a key role in supporting America's experimental democracy. For only an educated citizenry, it was believed, could properly carry out the civic responsibilities of a participatory form of government. In his effort to establish the University of Virginia, Thomas Jefferson noted the importance of higher education in a young nation with no monarchy or apparent class structure. As noted previously, universities could generate an "aristocracy of talent"; they could be the primary means of promoting science and learning useful to a land of yeomen farmers and merchants. In a very real sense, universities were to be the American embodiment of the Enlightenment: a progressive institution devoted to reason, to individual empowerment, to pragmatism.

As state-chartered public universities grew in their numbers and influence, the words "Flagship University" emerged in the United States, drawing on the nautical term in which the flagship or lead ship in a navy provided the primary means of coordinating naval maneuvers by an admiral or his staff. Usually one university attained a leadership position in a growing network of public institutions.

Reflective of the New Flagship University descriptive offered previously, the American public university purposefully opened their doors to a wide range of citizens from different economic, social, religious, and geographic backgrounds—a marked contrast to the array of private colleges and universities that were linked to sectarian communities and social classes. They were also distinctly secular although not godless, reflecting the establishing principles of America as a nation: the first secular and constitutionally based government in the world. Although severely hampered by overt racism and other forms of discrimination, the ideal was that public universities needed to be open to all who had the interest and abilities to benefit from a course of study.

Leading state universities were also developed as comprehensive institutions. They incorporated traditional liberal arts fields of the era *and* professionally oriented programs with a direct service to local and regional economies. Teaching and research in areas such as agriculture and engineering, along with programs providing outreach and educational services to farmers and local businesses, helped fuel economic development and socioeconomic mobility. This remains an ingrained component in the mission of America's public universities. Public service and engagement in economic development is now called a "third mission" by ministries and universities in most parts of the world, as if it were a new adventure and a departure from the traditional, and more comfortable, spheres of teaching and autonomous forms of research. This was never a "third mission" of universities in the United States, but part of their "core" purpose.

America's public universities took responsibility for setting standards and developing other sectors of a state's evolving education system—from the elementary and secondary schools, to other public tertiary institutions. State and local governments have the responsibility to build and regulate their education systems, and most initially invested in "common schools" (what today are elementary schools) and in one or more universities and colleges, but not in secondary education. State Flagship universities were central players in helping to develop the public high school as part of their assigned role to increase educational attainment rates.

Each of these distinct missions remains a component of the modern American university and forms a foundation for the New Flagship model— broad access, a wide array of academic programs, purposeful engagement with local economies, and leadership in developing public education. There were geographical differences, however, in the emergence of the American public university. In the eastern seaboard, where the US population first settled, private institutions dominated, and state governments were extremely slow to develop public universities. In the Midwest and throughout the West, however, states rushed to create new educational opportunities and established these key institutions.

Under the US constitution, states have the responsibility for organizing and coordinating their education systems; there is no equivalent power at the federal level in the United States of a higher education ministry found in most other parts of the world. But the push toward the Flagship model had an extremely important impetus from Washington. In 1862, and in the midst of the American Civil War, Congress passed and President Abraham Lincoln signed the Agricultural College Land Grant Act. It offered the one thing the federal government had lots of: land largely in the expansive West, given to each state to sell and generate income to establish or build existing universities, and, specifically, degree programs and research that would support local economies.

The "Land Grant Act" significantly bolstered the Flagship University movement. Without excluding "classical studies," or military training, and emerging scientific fields, the subsequent largess provided funding, "to teach such branches of learning as are related to agriculture and the mechanic arts, in such manner as the legislatures of the States may respectively prescribe, in order to promote the liberal and practical education of the industrial classes in the several pursuits and professions in life." In accepting the funding from Washington, states and their universities were required to have education and research programs configured to promote agriculture, mining, and civil engineering, fields vital to the nation's economy.

The United States was not alone in desiring universities with a utilitarian purpose. The notion, if not the title, of the Flagship University emerged in other parts of the world. In England, for example, Jeremy Bentham articulated the concepts of individual freedom and the need for English society to build public institutions that were utilitarian, secular, and egalitarian. Established in 1826, University College London espoused many of Bentham's ideas, becoming the first university in England to be entirely secular, admitting students regardless of their religion and gender. But within the landscape of British universities, University College's charter was unique.

Much later, England developed a set of "civic" universities that espoused similar egalitarian ideals. This included Birmingham University in 1900, followed by Liverpool in 1903, Manchester in 1903, Leeds in 1904, Sheffield in 1905, and Bristol in 1909. Each was founded in cities experiencing a boom in commerce, trade, and industry. England's existing set of universities and colleges was distinctly elitist, reinforcing an existing rigid social class structure, and seemingly far removed from the educational needs of these emerging commercial centers. Business interests merged with civic leaders to build, fund, and support these new institutions; they admitted largely sons of merchants and bankers, and focused on providing students with "real-world" skills such as in engineering, medicine, law, and business (Eggins 2014).

Later these "civic" universities, bound to a specific city, became known as "red-bricks" as they were relatively new, compared to the ancients in Oxford and Cambridge. They, along with a group of colleges that called themselves Polytechnics that focused on vocational education, marked an important innovation, but distinctly less progressive or as broad a vision of purpose as the public universities in America. They offered training, but little applied or developmental research or the range of public engagement and active involvement in local economies that were essential roles of the great publics in states like Michigan, Wisconsin, Minnesota, Texas, California, and Washington.

There are other national examples of universities established and nurtured to be, in some form, transformative institutions. As Andrés Bernasconi and Daniela Véliz discuss in their chapter in this book, there is a long history of chartering Latin American universities to improve the socioeconomic conditions of their respective nations—what is termed their "social mission." Often written in the midst of their postcolonial transition, these mission statements tended to focus on cultural preservation and enhancement, socioeconomic access, and, as stated in the charter for the Universidad de Buenos Aires, paying "particular attention to Argentina's problems," or in the case of Universidad Nacional Autónoma de México founded in its modern form in 1910, to "conduct research primarily on national problems and spread as widely as possible the benefits of culture."

Similar language can be found in the chartering of major public universities in the United States. The University of California's charter of 1868 included the charge, "A general diffusion of knowledge and intelligence being essential to the preservation of the rights and liberties of the people, the Legislature shall encourage by all suitable means the promotion of intellectual, scientific, moral, and agricultural improvement."[1] In the admission of students, the criterion was secular (religion being one of the great divides in early American society), with wide geographic representation, and, soon after its founding, open equally to women—although with ingrained biases on what studies they could pursue (Douglass 2007).

The University of Michigan, for example, was to provide an "uncommon education to the common man," as stated by its president Henry Tappan; and the University of Wisconsin, along with most other state universities chartered in mid-1800s, saw that its ultimate mission was to serve every corner of the state and every citizen in some way. And in both the United States and Latin America, the leading public universities were, at some point, also granted significant levels of autonomy—at least in law, if not always in practice. But the desire and rhetoric, I sense, of a larger social and economic role in nation building in Latin America was often louder than the actual effect, and for many complex reasons. With a few exceptions, the major public and catholic universities in Latin America focused narrowly on access and, to some degree, social programs, and less on the broader role of research that benefited economic development that characterizes the history of America's major public universities.

The Flagship University nomenclature has been used in various parts of the world, but never with a clear sense of its definition or meaning. In the post–World War II era and into the 1960s, the South Korean government established what it called "Flagship National Universities" in each of its eight provinces and two independent cities. In this era of nation building, and for a time in the midst of the Korean War, most of these institutions were the result of mergers of existing, smaller regional colleges. Today, each of these ten institutions have medical schools and like other designated national universities in Asia, they have the most competitive entrance exams. As noted, there was no clear description of what a Flagship University should be in Korea and the term was no longer used after about 1968.

Some European nations, in particular Hungary after the end of communist rule, explored using the Flagship title to distinguish a number of its leading universities. But an inherent political and organizational challenge of designating one or more existing institutions as a leading and perhaps favored university, particularly within the context of a national system with politically powerful universities with equal claim on public funding, essentially ended the reform drive. The need for mission differentiation, and with only a select few truly research-intensive universities adequately funded, is now widely understood by ministries and those who study higher education systems. Yet achieving this, either as a government directive as originally attempted in Hungary, or indirectly by competitive and selective funding of certain institutions, is politically difficult.

A new research project based at the University of Oslo uses the Flagship title to explore how some European universities are adapting to the demands of ministries and businesses to become more engaged in economic development and social inclusion. In that project, funded by the Research Council of Norway, the investigators state that a Flagship University "is defined as a comprehensive research-intensive university, located in one of its country's largest urban areas... [that is] in general among the oldest and largest institutions for higher learning of its country."[2] The project seeks to explore the activities and goals of a variety of existing departments in some 11 northern European universities—in essence, an inductive approach in which case studies will help define what it means to be a Flagship University.

Another example of the use of the Flagship moniker is a project focused on collecting data and supporting the development of eight sub-Sahara African universities by the Centre for Higher Education Transformation. Based in Cape Town, researchers at CHET have used the Flagship title to help outline the current vibrancy, goals, and challenges facing these institutions (Bunting et al. 2013). Under the title the Higher Education Research and Advocacy Network in Africa (HERANA), the project initially pursued the hard work of gathering comparative data among the universities and, via a collaborative mode, outlined the idea of the need for an Academic Core of variables—for example, student-to-faculty ratios, goals, the percentage of faculty with doctoral degrees, and correlations necessary for top-tier national universities to pursue institutional improvement.[3]

It is clear from these examples that the Flagship University title means different things to different people, and is often influenced by national context. Internationally, it is only now coming into vogue. As the reader will see in the contributing chapters to this book, observers of higher education have a view that a Flagship institution is, generally, simply a leading national university with sanction and funding from national governments, one with the best students, the best teachers, high research output, and some influence on regional politics and economic activity.

But that is an incomplete, indeed severely limited and not a very meaningful description, much like the title of World Class University. For the Flagship title to be relevant, the following chapter seeks to explore and articulate its purpose and characteristics. This includes the internal culture of a Flagship University, and what policies, practices, activities, and outputs define it and make it relevant in the modern world.

NOTES

1. California Constitution Article 9 Education Section 1, 1879. This is a reiteration of the charge originally passed in 1868 as a statutory law that established the University of California.

2. Based at the ARENA Centre for European Studies at the University of Oslo, the research project is titled European Flagship Universities: Balancing Academic Excellence and Social Relevance. See: www.sv.uio.no/arena/english /research/projects/Flagship/.

3. The HERANA project is supported by funding by the Ford Foundation and the Carnegie Corporation and includes the University of Botswana, Cape Town, Dares Salaam Tanzania, Eduardo Mondlane University Mozambique, University of Ghana, Makerere University Uganda, Mauritius, and the University of Nairobi Kenya. Beyond developing comparative data and analysis, it has the goal as, "to disseminate the findings of the research projects, better co-ordinate existing sources of information on higher education in Africa, develop a media strategy, and put in place a policy dialogue via seminars and information technology that facilitates interactions between researchers, institutional leaders and decision-makers." See www.chet.org.za /programmes/herana/.

Chapter 3

Profiling the New Flagship Model

What are the contemporary characteristics, values, and practices of a group of institutions we can identify as Flagship Universities? This chapter provides an initial profile of the model, framed by the tripartite mission of research-intensive universities: teaching and learning, research and knowledge production, and public service.[1]

Leading national universities are now more important for socioeconomic mobility, for producing economic and civic leaders, for knowledge production, and for pushing innovation and societal self-reflection than in any other time in their history. They are constantly expanding their activities in reaction to societal demands, generating new avenues of research and discovery, and expanding their reach into most aspects of modern life. The net result is that the Flagship Universities of today are significantly different from the leading national universities of an earlier era.

The descriptive that follows offers a way to capture and comprehend the modern reincarnation of what is, in essence, an ancient institution transformed. Much of the profile will be familiar; but for some engaged in building anew or reforming their universities, the true breadth of the New Flagship University's purpose and pursuits, and contemporary innovations, may come as a revelation.

To state the obvious, different nations and their universities operate in different environments, reflecting their own national cultures, politics, expectations, and the realities of their socioeconomic world. The purpose here is not to create a single template or a checklist, but an expansive array of characteristics and practices that connects a selective group of universities—an aspirational model. However, many institutions and ministries may see only a subset as relevant, or only some aspirations as achievable in the near term. Universities that practice the general ideals of the New Flagship will also see that this brief chapter does not include all the activities and roles universities play in their distinct political and economic environment.

Finally, the New Flagship University profiled is not, and could never be, a wholesale repudiation of rankings and global metrics, or of the desire for a global presence. The model is compatible with the World Class University (WCU) focus on research productivity but aims much higher to help articulate a larger purpose. And national and regional relevance and international engagement are mutually compatible goals—indeed the markers of the best universities.

Noting these caveats and qualifications, there are a few key universal conditions that allow the New Flagship University, whatever its manifestation, to exist and mature:

Mission differentiation—National systems of higher education require mission differentiation among their networks of postsecondary institutions. There can be only a limited number of research-intensive universities, some of which might be Flagship universities. Under this rubric, Flagship universities are different from most other major universities in the nation in that they are:

- Highly selective in admissions, yet also broadly accessible—At the undergraduate and graduate levels, admissions criteria need to include objectives calculated to assess the probability of a prospective student's academic success as well as their engagement and potential contribution to a university's larger purpose.
- Faculty teaching, research, and public service responsibilities—Faculty have roughly equal responsibilities for teaching, research, and public service, broadly defined duties, and clearly stated objectives, course workload requirements, and a process of evaluation that also reflects the larger purpose of the university.

A comprehensive array of academic programs—Flagship universities provide or aspire to offer degree programs across the disciplines, including professional fields such as engineering, law, medicine, and teacher training. This does not exclude campuses that are heavily or entirely focused on science and engineering; but institutions without a broad array of disciplines, including the social sciences and humanities, have a more limited ability to, for example, support interdisciplinary research or to meet regional and national socioeconomic needs.

A sufficient "academic core"—Universities that exude the values of the Flagship model can do so only if they have sufficient funding and a baseline of core characteristics. This includes manageable student-to-faculty ratios, a significant population of permanent faculty with doctoral degrees, sufficient numbers of master's and in particular doctoral students, and evidence of sufficient graduation rates and research productivity.

The Center for Higher Education Transformation (CHET), based in Cape Town, first outlined the Academic Core concept (Cloete et al. 2011; Bunting et al. 2013). CHET's baseline criteria focused on the developmental needs of African universities; but they provide a useful framework for all universities that are early in the stages of maturation.[2] In the following, I adopt criteria from CHET, with some additions:

- *Proportion of academic staff with doctoral degrees*—More than half of the faculty with teaching responsibilities should be full-time permanent faculty (positions with identified funding and a long-term contract of some form); of those, at least 40 percent of the permanent academic staff should have doctoral degrees, and at least 25 percent of the permanent faculty defined as full-time should be in the senior ranks, defined as a full or associate rank or equivalent.
- *Academic staff-to-student ratios*—Counting undergraduate and graduate students, the ratio should not exceed 25 to 1, with a preferable target of about 16 to 1.
- *Postgraduate enrollments*—Research-intensive universities require a healthy balance of postgraduate students to undergraduate students, with a floor of at least 20 percent of students in master's and doctoral programs, and a preferred ratio of approximately 30 percent or more.
- *Research funding per academic*—Research requires government and institutional funding and "third-stream" external sources such as industry and donors; Flagship institutions seek diverse funding sources for faculty-directed research activity.
- *Balanced Enrollment Portfolios*—Although the historical purpose of an institution and the needs of the society it serves may vary, generally a goal is to have 30 to 50 percent of students in science, technology, engineering, and math (STEM) fields.

These are baseline requirements for a Flagship. The Academic Core concept has particular relevance for universities in developing economies which often have a low number of faculty with doctoral degrees with adequate training in research methodologies, or experience with mentoring students, and where faculty salary levels often do not afford what would be considered a middle-class lifestyle.

These are challenges found in many part of the world.[3] The important point is that there is a healthy balance in the various ratios of first-degree and graduate students, permanent faculty, and a general assessment of productivity in graduates and research output.

Institutionally driven quality assurance—While ministries of education can influence the quality of university academic programs and activities, ultimately, top-tier institutions require sufficient independence to develop internal cultures of quality and excellence. This must include merit-based academic personnel policies. If there is any one major theme that determines what are the most productive universities, it is the quality of the faculty. Universities need to have high expectations regarding their talents, responsibilities, and performance, driven by a process of regular peer review—an important topic discussed later in this chapter.

An ancillary observation: government policy regimes and induced efforts to improve the quality and performance of all or a select group of national universities reflect doubt about the ability of their universities to become top, globally competitive institutions, and often with good reason; but ministries should view such government requirements and often one-size-fits-all policies related to academic advancement as simply an initial stage in the goal of achieving high-performing Flagship universities, with the next and more important stage focused on sufficient autonomy to support a culture of campus-based institutional self-improvement.

*   *   *

The following New Flagship University profile is organized in four categories or realms of policies and practices, summarized in figure 3.1. Each relates to the institution's external responsibilities and internal operations. Within the context of a larger national higher education system, the idea is that Flagship institutions have a set of goals, shared good practices, logics, and the resources to pursue them. Generally, the sequence is from the larger external context, to the mission of the institutions and goals, to the management structure to make it happen. Put another way, my effort here simply attempts to help create coherency, and to provide some guides and examples, for what many universities are already doing.

Figure 3.1 Flagship University Realms of Policies and Practices.

National HE System
• Position in HE System
• Defined Service Area
• Selective Admissions

Core Mission—Teaching/Learning and Research
• Undergraduate Education
• Graduate Education
• Research
• International Engagement

Public Service and Economic Engagement
• Engaged Scholarship and Service
• Regional Economic Engagement/Tech Transfer
• Lifelong Learning
• Relations with Schools

Management and Accountability
• Institutional Autonomy
• Governance
• Academic Freedom
• Quality Assurance
• Leadership

At the same time, it is important to note that universities are complex organizations that purposefully pursue mutually supportive activities that do not lend themselves easily to separate categories—in a vibrant university, teaching, research, and public service are symbiotic activities, built on a model of institutional revenue sharing and mutual support. Hence, there is some redundancy in this profile.

Profile I: Flagship Universities and National Higher Education Systems

1. Position within a Larger National Higher Education

As noted previously, the idea of the New Flagship University assumes that national higher education systems require mission differentiation among an often growing number of tertiary institutions. Most nation-states have come to realize that it is neither cost-effective nor possible to develop high-quality higher education systems in which all universities have the same mission and programs. Within a larger, hopefully coherent network of public and private tertiary institutions, it is in fact vital that there exists a subgroup of leading national universities that can help nations most effectively pursue economic development, improve socioeconomic mobility, provide measures of academic quality and support for other educational institutions, and produce political and economic leaders and good citizens. Hence, the actual number of "Flagship" universities in a nation may vary, determined in part by geography and population density, socioeconomic needs, and financial resources.

2. Defined Service Area

Most public universities have a sense of their responsibilities in regard to student admissions by some defined geographic area, with a caveat related to international students. But they often have a vague understanding of their role in economic development and public service. Greater and overt definition of a distinct "service area"—without exclusion of larger regional and international activities—is an important framework for directing or encouraging activities of universities and for evaluating their effectiveness.

3. Selective Admissions

Flagship universities draw most of their students from a national and regional pool of talented students. But this should not be to the exclusion of drawing talent from a continental and international pool—with different goals at the first-degree, graduate, and professional levels. At the first-degree level, admission standards are often regulated by national policies focused on a single national test. Flagship universities need greater flexibility for determining the talent and potential of prospective students and to balance their selection of an entering class with other considerations, including the socioeconomic background of their student body, geographic representation, and exceptions for students with special talents. [See section 13 on the "Four Essential Freedoms" of Flagship universities.]

Profile II: Flagship Core Mission—Teaching/ Learning and Research

1. First-Degree/Undergraduate Education Goals

An essential goal of the New Flagship University is to provide first-degree students with an education that is engaging, that promotes creativity and scholarship, and that results in high-order skills that are useful in the labor market, for entry possibly into graduate education, for good citizenship, and for a fulfilling life.

Pedagogical research has generated the concept of *engaged learning*. This includes two observations: (1) The amount of time and energy students put forth in academic and other pursuits (e.g., community service) is positively correlated to learning and other desired outcomes of undergraduate education; and (2) Institutional policies and practices can influence the level of student engagement. Our universities strive not to produce passive students who meet some minimum floor of knowledge and skills, but innovative and creative students who are ambitious and talented. In shaping the undergraduate experience, universities need to seek the following opportunities and learning outcomes for students:

- Inquiry-based learning
- Experiential learning
- Research engagement
- Interdisciplinary opportunities
- Integrative knowledge
- Collaborative learning and problem solving
- Diversity/global citizenry
- Ethics/responsibilities
- Quantitative literacy
- Communication skills
- Digital literacy

One important concept is that there are many different student experiences and learning processes, shaped by the socioeconomic background of students; their mental health, social support systems, and sense of belonging at a large university; their different intelligences, abilities, and interests that may change overtime; their field of study; opportunities for engaging in research, and for being mentored.

At the same time, with their wide array of disciplines and faculty, and existing and potential links with local communities, universities must assess and view the student experience holistically, and beyond the narrow confines of the traditional classroom. The Student Experience in the Research University (SERU) Consortium with survey data from top-tier research-intensive universities has explored how these experiences inside and outside of the classroom shape student engagement and learning outcomes.

With the benefit of SERU data, research-intensive universities can conceptualize *Five Spheres of the Undergraduate Student Experience*: curricular engagement (including courses as well as interaction with faculty and graduate students, learning communities etc.), research engagement (faculty directed or mentored, paid and unpaid), public and community service (voluntary or integrated into requirements or credits toward a degree, often termed service learning), cocurricular activities, and their social life and conditions (comprising a wide array of factors, including their living arrangements, financial needs, working full-time or part-time, and sense of belonging).[4]

In the accompanying Figure 3.2, the size of each of these spheres of the student experience is representative, reflecting the relative importance for a generic student. Curricular engagement is at the core of the student experience. It is therefore shown as a larger sphere. However, the student experience is not a singular model, but nuanced and varied, within a university itself, within a disciplinary field of study. The socioeconomic

Figure 3.2   Five Spheres of the Undergraduate Student Experience.

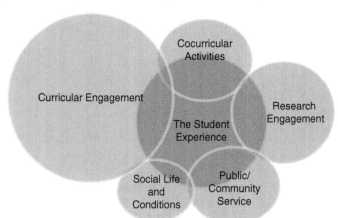

background and interests of students are a variable. At the same time, there are academic cultures, and norms in different nations, that may value certain spheres over others.

Based on this model, the following focuses on three of these spheres—curricular engagement, research engagement, and cocurricular activities. Each provides concepts and policy examples related to supporting the undergraduate experience at a Flagship University.

Curricular Engagement

Research-intensive universities, and Flagships in specific, are increasingly focused on creating a robust environment for faculty and students to be active learners and producers of knowledge. This is in sharp contrast to outmoded, yet still prevalent in many parts of the world, practices of rote teaching and learning—essentially, teaching facts and theories in lecture formats and readings without encouraging or seeking higher-order critical thinking. Flagship universities should be in the business of creating engaged and innovative thinkers. This requires the engagement of faculty in that cause—for some faculty, a relatively new concept. Too often, universities, and their faculty, have been passive in their fundamental role of mentoring and shaping the learning outcomes of undergraduate students.

This is an expansive topic. The following briefly discusses only a few concepts and programs intended to positively shape the curricular experience of students in research-intensive universities—in part, an attempt by these institutions to recalibrate their internal cultures that have increasingly valued research productivity over undergraduate education. This includes the two innovations: Learning Communities and Learning and Professional Development Goals.

Learning Communities

Large research-intensive universities need to seek curricular-focused opportunities for students to find or be invited into small, university-supported communities of students and faculty intended to promote active learning, provide greater curricular coherence, and promote interdisciplinary learning and interaction between students, undergraduate and graduate, and faculty. This can include:

- Linked courses: Students take two connected courses, usually one disciplinary course such as history or biology and one skills course such as writing, speech, or information literacy.
- Learning clusters: Students take three or more connected courses, usually with a common interdisciplinary theme uniting them.

- Freshman interest groups: Similar to learning clusters, but the students share the same major, and they often receive academic advising as part of the learning community.
- Federated learning communities: Similar to a learning cluster, but with an additional seminar course taught by a "Master Learner," a faculty member who enrolls in the other courses and takes them alongside the students. The Master Learner's course draws connections among the other courses.
- Coordinated studies: This model blurs the lines among individual courses. The learning community functions as a single, giant course that the students and faculty members work on full-time for an entire semester or academic year.
- Special University Colleges: Many US universities have what are called "honors" colleges within their universities that provide a specialized number of courses and opportunities for interaction with faculty and fellow honors students. There are also a growing number of "university colleges" that are semi-independent entities of major research universities. They often offer a liberal arts curriculum and multidisciplinary degree programs, have their own faculty and facilities, and have separate admissions practices that are significantly different from the larger university they are part of. They usually include in their curricular design a general education course progression. Amsterdam University College, a joint project of the University of Amsterdam and Vriej University, is an example of a growing movement to create alternative academic programs and environments for undergraduate students (Tinto 2003).

Figure 3.3 provides examples of institutional programs that relate to the concept of learning communities. Some are institution-wide and others are specific to academic programs or student populations such as entering first-degree students.

Learning and Professional Development Goals

Many universities are now engaged in a relatively new collaborative process that involves outline learning and professional development goals for students, and assessing outcomes. At UCLA, a recent initiative outlines campus-wide goals that are influenced by the notion of engaged learning and that are, at first glance, extremely ambitious. In the course of their studies, students are to:

- Demonstrate progressive growth of intellectual and academic competencies, including analytical and critical thinking skills as well as the

Figure 3.3 Case Examples: Honors Programs, Colleges, and Learning Communities.

- **University of Oregon—Departmental Honors Program and Honors Colleges.** Department Honors programs are offered by nearly every department. Each involves extensive course work, a final thesis or research project, and close mentoring by a faculty advisor. For example, The Lundquist College of Business Honors Program provides challenging, stimulating and enriching opportunities for learning, experience and opportunity. Each year via a highly selected admission process, a new learning community with a cohort of thirty-five dedicated students is formed. Working together with a select group of faculty, these students take classes that have been specifically designed for the Honors Program. They engage in experiences available only to Honors students. Oregon also includes the Robert D. Clark Honors College, a highly competitive, small liberal arts college of approximately 800 students admitted in their 2-year at the University of Oregon. The Clark Honors College features small classes and close interaction between students and faculty. It emphasizes interdisciplinary scholarship and independent research in a tight-knit, dynamic community of students and faculty. The College is made up of students from every department and school at the University of Oregon—from architects and musicians to biology and business majors—with classes designed to foster intense and creative exchange among different approaches and viewpoints.

- **Amsterdam University College—A Liberal Arts Program in a Large European University.** University Colleges are a major movement in Europe and elsewhere, usually providing within the venue of a larger comprehensive university a liberal arts program with its own admissions criteria and curriculum. Amsterdam University College was founded in 2009 as a joint venture of the University of Amsterdam and Vriej University. AUC offers a three-year honours degree in three very broad majors in science, social sciences, and humanities. Students can choose between approximately 200 courses across eight fields in the sciences, nine in the social sciences, seven in the humanities, as well as the academic core. As part of AUC's interdisciplinary orientation, students have to pursue 'tracks' in at least two fields within their major. Interdisciplinarity is also emphasized by AUC's themes, which link fields across majors. The college emphasizes a strong academic core, which includes academic writing and basic calculus or statistics, but also more unusual courses such as logic or 'identity and diversity', which are compulsory for students of all majors. Furthermore, students are required to take two to three language courses.

- **University of Wisconsin—Residential Learning Communities.** The campus has some ten Residential Learning Communities that group students around academic and professional fields such as biotechnology, green technologies, multicultural learning, entrepreneurialism, creative arts and women in sciences. For example, the Entrepreneurial Residential Learning

Figure 3.3   Continued

Community (ERLC) has 64 residents living in Sellery Hall. The ERLC's mission is to teach students to put their ideas into action through the entrepreneurial process. Whether a student is undecided, or thinking of majoring in art history, engineering, business, or something else the ERLC can benefit them by teaching the entrepreneurial process. All ERLC residents are asked to enroll in the 3-credit, MHR Course Entrepreneurship and Society which fulfills general education requirements, counts towards the Undergraduate Certificate Program in Entrepreneurship and provides students with access to faculty and community members on a personal basis.

- **Rutgers University—First Year Interest Groups.** First-Year Interest Group Seminars (FIGS) are one-credit seminars taught by upper-class students to aid first-year students in their transition to college while exploring an academic interest area. Every FIGS seminar is graded Pass/No-Credit. FIGS are offered to first-year students in the School of Arts and Sciences, School of Environmental and Biological Sciences, and Rutgers Business School. The course meets for 10 weeks in the Fall semester to provide opportunities to explore an interest area, topic or field of study. Additionally, students in each FIGS practice problem-solving skills, gain insight into the pursuit of academic/career interests, and learn how to tap into the resources of the University. Each FIGS section is limited to 25 students in order to facilitate an intimate educational experience, lively participation in class, trips/tours around campus, and group projects.

acquisition of knowledge, and identify the relevant academic success skills and strategies to facilitate this development.

- Develop an understanding of what a research university is and the purpose and aims of the university's curricula and how common spaces of learning across disciplines can be used to further the student's academic, personal, and professional development.
- Develop basic knowledge of university requirements and pursue opportunities to survey and explore potential majors, minors, and other programs of study that can further their academic, personal, and professional development.
- Develop skills to make decisions regarding career goals, demonstrating awareness of the factors that influence career success and satisfaction.
- Engage in a process of self-reflection to identify and continue to refine personally meaningful reasons and goals for attending the university.
- Engage in a process of identity exploration and development, including exploring personal issues and decisions based on sex/gender identity, sexual orientation, race and ethnicity, socioeconomic status, faith and spirituality, disability, and other factors.

- Demonstrate increasing levels of multicultural competence, specifically acknowledging the importance of successful interaction with people of diverse perspectives and backgrounds through respectful discourse. Students will also develop strategies related to conflict resolution and engaging in difficult dialogues.

- Demonstrate progressive growth of the self-management skills necessary to lead emotionally, physically, and fiscally healthy lives, including the ability to effectively utilize health, financial planning, and other resources.

Many universities have developed similar objectives for their students. In some form, these campus-wide objectives provide a tool for focusing faculty deliberations on the shape and structure of the curriculum at the discipline level and, at the same time, providing students with a sense of what they should get out of their degree program. With a similar set of campus-wide learning outcome goals, academic departments and schools at Berkeley have developed their own set of goals for their first-degree students (see figure 3.4).

Figure 3.4 Case Example: Learning Objectives for Electrical Engineering and Computer Sciences, University of California—Berkeley.

- An ability to apply knowledge of mathematics, science, and engineering.
- An ability to configure, apply test conditions, and evaluate outcomes of experimental systems.
- An ability to design systems, components, or processes that conform to given specifications and cost constraints.
- An ability to work cooperatively, respectfully, creatively, and responsibly as a member of a team.
- An ability to identify, formulate, and solve engineering problems.
- An understanding of the norms of expected behavior in engineering practice and their underlying ethical foundations.
- An ability to communicate effectively by oral, written, and graphical means.
- An awareness of global and societal concerns and their importance in developing engineering solutions.
- An ability to independently acquire and apply required information, and an appreciation of the associated process of lifelong learning.
- A knowledge of contemporary issues.
- An in-depth ability to use a combination of software, instrumentation, and experimental techniques practiced in circuits, physical electronics, communication, networks and systems, hardware, programming, and computer science theory.

At the same time, it is important to note the difficulty of assessing the actual ability of students and the "learning gains" they experience over the course of their university careers. This is because higher-order knowledge and thinking skills are not easily quantifiable—despite the promises of learning assessment tests (Douglass, Thomson, and Zhao 2012). Universities are in the business of helping student transition from home life to being productive citizens. The curricular structure, along with opportunities for community service, internships in local businesses, and cocurricular activities, are all components in their professional development. Beyond these core components of the student experience, universities are increasingly developing programs and links with local and regional employers and with professional associations. Professional programs such as medicine, business, and engineering programs have long had such connections with employers, including internships and on-going relationships with faculty. Preparation for the job market—local, national, or global—for students studying in the social sciences and humanities is more complex. Yet, in most developed economies, unemployment rates are much lower for students with a bachelor's degree five years or fewer after graduation—with some notable exceptions in the aftermath of the Great Recession. Further, career paths are much more nuanced with the growth of the service sector and, for example, of technology companies that rely on broad skill sets.

At the same time, universities need to recognize significant changes occurring in labor markets, reflecting the growth in the "knowledge economy." Particularly in developed economies, to be prepared and competitive in the labor market, more and more undergraduates are entering graduate education after their first degree. In many cases, this places greater value on their broad skill sets than on their knowledge of a particular field.

Undergraduate Research Engagement

In his famous manifesto on the symbiotic relationship of faculty and students, Wilhelm von Humboldt stated, "The goals of science and scholarship are worked towards most effectively through the synthesis of the teacher's and the students' dispositions. The teacher's mind is more mature but it is also somewhat one-sided in its development and more dispassionate; the student's mind is less able and less committed but it is nonetheless open and responsive to every possibility" (Humboldt, 1825).

Humboldt's vision influenced all universities that sought to be productive generators of new knowledge. But most of the focus was on graduate education, and to a lesser extent the role of undergraduates. In the

United States, a 1998 report titled *Reinventing Undergraduate Education* focused in earnest on the idea of the undergraduate "student as scholar." Building on one of the main concepts of the research university, its main author, Earnest Boyer, emphasized the ideas of "research-based learning" and engaged scholarship, in and outside of the classroom, as an important component of the student experience (Boyer, 1998).

What followed is an elevated sense by many universities globally that undergraduate research engagement in various forms should be promoted. Today this includes credit-bearing courses, funding support, and organizations to help open opportunities for faculty-directed research. It is now widely recognized that opportunities for research experience are important for students to expand their networks of professional relationships, key for deciphering their career goals, generating job opportunities, and making choices about graduate school (Douglass and Zhao 2013). Among the benefits of various forms of undergraduate research experience:

- Skills development, including study design, data collection, computation, analysis of findings, and communication of results.
- Positive attitudes, habits, and intentions, including research ethics, perseverance, and professionalism.
- Clarification or confirmation of career plans including postgraduate studies.
- Enhanced career preparation or preparation for postgraduate studies.
- Greater networking opportunities—exposure to the world of active learning and potential career paths.
- Promoting links with regional economies and public services.

Figure 3.5 offers examples of campus-supported undergraduate research programs.

Cocurricular Activities

Cocurricular refers to student activities, programs, and learning experiences that are supported in some way by a university, but that are voluntary, usually with no course credit, and reflect the students' own interests. They may be connected to or mirror the academic curriculum; some may be supported directly by the university through funding or facilities. This can include a wide range of activities in the form of student clubs and organizations, including but not limited to student government, newspapers, musical groups, reading clubs, fan clubs, environmental awareness associations, sports teams, art shows, debate competitions, and mathematics,

Figure 3.5   Case Examples: Undergraduate Research Programs.

- **University of Michigan—UG Research Opportunity Program.** This program creates research partnerships between first and second year students, and faculty, research scientist, and staff from across the University of Michigan community. Begun in 1989 with 14 student/faculty partnerships, today, approximately 1100 students and over 700 faculty researchers are engaged in research partnerships.

- **MIT—Undergraduate Research Opportunities (UROP).** MIT's program cultivates and supports research partnerships between faculty and undergraduates, with funds provided via faculty and stipends up to $4,880 offered to students to then find faculty mentors. UROP offers the chance to work on cutting edge research—whether established faculty research projects or to pursue student derived and proposed projects.

  An associated project, International Research Opportunities (IROP) is designed for MIT undergraduates who want to conduct mentored research in an international setting. The overseas research opportunities provide many of the same benefits offered through conventional study abroad experiences—including the chance to connect with individuals from diverse cultural backgrounds who share similar intellectual goals. In addition, IROP experiences help students enhance communication and leadership skills and refine collaborative and decision-making skills, while increasing understanding and awareness of ethical issues. IROP projects generally take place over the summer and mirror the traditional campus-based UROP model: qualifying projects must have the approval, mentorship, and guidance of an MIT faculty member.

- **UC Berkeley—Undergraduate Research Apprentice Program and SMART Program.** Undergraduates can apply for semester or year-long opportunities to gain skills working on faculty-led research projects under URAP; more than 1200 students from all majors participated yearly.

  Administered by the Graduate Division, the SMART (Student Mentoring and Research Teams) program enables doctoral students to provide mentored research opportunities for undergraduate students at UC Berkeley and is designed to broaden the professional development of doctoral students and to foster research skills and forge paths to advanced studies for undergraduates. Graduate mentors who work under the guidance of a faculty adviser receive a stipend of $5,000. Doctoral students selected as SMART mentors must complete a one-unit course, Mentoring in Higher Education GSPDP 301. Each undergraduate mentee will be funded in the amount of $3,500 for approximately 200 hours of work.

- **University of Campinas (Unicamp)—Brazil—Undergraduate Research Scholarships.** The office of the Vice President for Research is responsible for selecting the best undergraduate students who wish to engage in scientific research projects under the supervision of faculty members, an activity for which they receive a monthly scholarship. The program,

Figure 3.5   Continued

which exists since 1992, is supported by funds from Unicamp and from the Brazilian federal research agency. In 2010 about 1,000 students were supported through these funds. Coupled to the independent program of the state research agency FAPESP, which provides about 500 other scholarships each year, approximately 10 percent of all undergraduates are engaged in formal supervised research activities in all areas while doing their studies. At least a quarter of these students go on to pursue graduate studies, highlighting the nurturing role played by this program.

robotics, and engineering teams and contests. These activities can be provided virtually. But much more often, they provide an avenue for the personal and real-time interaction of students who are drawn to a particular interest and seek opportunities to meet and work with their peers.

Cocurricular activities may occur with a university's direct or tacit support, or simply may exist largely on the volition and drive of individual students. But in some form, they exist in all universities. Within the American context, most, if not all, of these activities outside the classroom do seem to provide substantial personal benefits to student development—particularly for students who lead a club or organization. They purport to enhance reflective thought, a capacity to apply knowledge, and what has been termed "civic skills" (Verba et al. 1995; Brint 2014).

There is wide variation in how universities, and their students, value these activities. In a nation often termed a society of joiners, and among public universities that are members of the prestigious Association of American Universities, there is on average one official student organization for approximately every 39 students. The Berkeley campus alone has over 1,700 student clubs and organizations. Steven Brint notes that students at engineering schools (those who are promoting online everything) were the most active joiners: Brint found one student organization for every nine students at MIT and Cal Tech (Brint 2014).

There is a need for further research on the different patterns of cocurricular activities in various parts of the world and their influence on student behaviors and development—including their role in developing networks that appear to sometimes influence job opportunities and career paths. There are also questions on whether a high level of engagement in these activities, seemingly removed from the formal curriculum, either benefits or detracts students from their progress toward a degree. Whatever the conclusion, Flagship universities consider the role of these activities as a component of their overall strategy for promoting engaged learning and capable graduates.

Social Life and Conditions

Many other factors influence the student experience, their academic performance and development as individuals. These include, but are not limited to, the nature of their housing arrangements (on-campus versus off-campus private housing), their income (financial aid or not), their work status (part-time or full-time work either out of necessity or cultural habit and family demands), and family responsibilities.

But just as important is the socioeconomic background of students. Flagship universities seeking to enroll students with diverse backgrounds need to better understand their needs and desires to best help them gain the most from their university careers and to help them progress toward degree completion (Douglass 2007).

Universities, and the societies that support them, vary in their perceived need to take into account the practical aspects of a student's socioeconomic background, the cultural biases within and outside the university community, and the realities of their living conditions and mental state. In some form, however, Flagship universities must have a breadth of programs to support students through their university careers, including academic tutoring and remedial instruction, career counseling services, support with student housing and residential life, student orientation, and health care provisions. More generally, campus support services help give coherency to the student experience, help to monitor students' academic progress, and attempt to support a "campus climate" that encourages inclusion, tolerance, and a sense of belonging—important at Flagships that have as part of their mission enrolling a broad spectrum of society.

2. Graduate Education

Flagship universities have special responsibilities for graduate and professional education. Reflecting their role as generators of new knowledge and as leading producers of professional talent in the societies they serve, approximately 30 to 50 percent of all student enrollment at Flagship universities should be in graduate education, and within an array of master's, doctoral, and professional degree programs.

In all nations, graduate education is a critical component in developing and supporting professional expertise required for knowledge-based economies. Increasingly, and as noted previously, undergraduate education is no longer the end of formal education, but the required entry into further formal training and, ultimately, an influential catalyst for economic growth and generating the expertise for alleviating a multitude of challenging social issues, from human health, to poverty, transportation, social services, and urban planning.

Historically, there has been a great diversity in the approaches to graduate education, in terms of what type of students enter graduate programs (e.g., natives versus international students), how they are educated, what professions they are trained for, and how they find employment. But the elevated role of graduate education has brought an increased focus on the structure and quality of graduate education.

Similar to the graphic representation of the various activities shaping the student experience at the undergraduate level, Figure 3.6 depicts the graduate student experience. Here, six spheres reflect the complexity of graduate education and training: curricular engagement, cocurricular activities, research engagement, teaching experience, and professional development (including employment and internships in business and government), public and community service, and the social life and conditions in which students pursue their degrees—from master's and professional programs, to the doctorate. In this portrayal of the graduate experience, the size of the sphere illustrates the world of a doctoral student that is not only dominated largely by developing research expertise and preparation for the job market, but is also heavily influence by their personal life.

Figure 3.6   Six Spheres of the Graduate Student Experience.

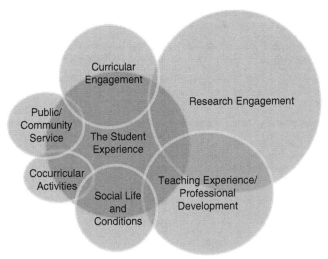

Again, universities, and their various disciplines and professional fields, will vary tremendously on what components influence the student experience. For example, cocurricular and public and community service are not always associated with graduate education; yet, degree programs in medicine, social welfare, and law often have significant components related to public service; and STEM fields also can have robust cocurricular activity and forms of social networking.

This is a period of tremendous change in graduate education. Like undergraduate education, graduate education has grown tremendously in the number of programs and enrollment. Throughout much of the developing world, graduate education is a relatively new enterprise. For instance, China now has the largest number of graduate students in the world; yet, only three decades earlier only about 19 doctoral degrees were granted annually in all of China (Ma 2007). In other parts of Asia, in Africa, and in nations attempting a rapid improvement in educational capital, there is an urgent need to expand doctoral programs to, in part, help meet the need for new faculty in their rapidly growing national systems of higher education. Globally, there is a shortage of doctorate recipients. The quality of doctoral programs, and their output in terms of degrees, is a critical role for Flagship universities that can, ultimately, shape the willingness of top talent, both students and faculty, to stay, work, and live, in a particular region of the world.

Similar to reforms in undergraduate education, there is significant global movement to improve the quality of graduate programs (Nerad and Evans 2014). This includes but is not limited to:

- More deliberately structured curricular requirements geared toward the array of professions the program is intended to serve.
- Increased use of English in courses and for master's theses and dissertations in programs attempting to attract and retain international talent, and for preparing future academics and business leaders whose professions are increasingly global in context.
- Clearly stated skills students are to acquire and expectations on their academic performance.
- Articulating the mentorship responsibilities of faculty.
- Coordination with the professions and business to better match training with labor needs.
- Collaboration with the private sector in providing internships as part of graduate training and integrating graduate students into faculty-led university–industry research activity.
- Assessments of the quality of life of graduate students and efforts to support their financial and social needs to make them productive members of the academic community.

- Improved integration of graduate education into the larger purpose and operations of the university.

Universities, in general, and Flagship universities in particular, must view graduate education as a complementary and symbiotic part of their teaching, research, and public service mission, and as a key component in their financial model. While some professional fields, such as business, may be income generators, graduate education, and doctoral programs in particular, are expensive in both time and money.

For doctoral students being trained for academic professions, this means not only the development of research skills, but also training and experience in undergraduate teaching and, when possible, supporting undergraduate engagement in research and public service (see examples in the previous sections). Reflecting their mission to serve the socioeconomic needs of the societies that sustain them, New Flagship Universities must offer professional-oriented master's and doctoral programs that are devoted to fulfilling specific labor and social needs.

3. Research

High levels of research productivity are a significant characteristic of Flagship universities, a responsibility that should be roughly equal to teaching in terms of time and effort of permanent faculty. The types of research output from academic institutions can be outlined in the following modes:

- Discovery—basic or blue-sky research that has no immediate application, commercial or otherwise.
- Integration—synthesis of information across disciplines, across topics within a discipline, or across time.
- Engaged scholarship—rigor and application of disciplinary expertise with results that can be shared and that connects the intellectual assets of the institution, that is, faculty expertise, to public issues, such as community, social, cultural, human, and economic development. (The characteristics of engaged scholarship is more fully discussed in Profile III).
- Teaching and learning—systematic study of teaching and learning processes. It differs from scholarly teaching in that it requires a format that will allow public sharing and the opportunity for application and evaluation by others.

While these are widely recognized distinct modes of academic research, it is important to note changing notions in how research is being undertaken and defined. A relatively new research culture has emerged, which increasingly seeks transdisciplinary approaches to inquiry and recognize the extensive social distribution of knowledge. Knowledge and data are now so diffuse that many researchers are required to work interactively. This creates both challenges and opportunities for Flagship universities to support research in the various disciplines, and to effectively evaluate its quality and influence. A key component in the Flagship model is regular peer evaluation of faculty research (a topic for later in this chapter). However, as noted, research activities, and knowledge production, are not simply the realm of faculty. Having graduate and undergraduate students engaged in knowledge production has always been a value in American higher education, an antecedent to the Humboldtian model of the modern university as a learning and research-focused community.

Graduate students are formally engaged normally through the process of coursework and, particularly at the doctorate level, through the dissertation and other forms of research production and dissemination. The structure and quality of doctoral programs is a concern in all major research-intensive universities, with a trend away from the once-common continental Europe model of no or negligible coursework and often minimal mentorship and supervision until the near completion of the doctoral thesis.

Research engagement for first-degree students, as noted previously, has a positive influence on a student's maturation and overall academic and social experience. Further, and to reiterate, research experience is important for expanding the development of professional relationships and networks that can be important for deciphering students' career goals, generating job opportunities, and making choices about graduate school.

International Engagement

All Flagship universities have goals and programs related to various forms of international engagement—from student enrollment and support to curriculum and research activity. The range of this activity and focus, however, will and should vary depending on the geographic location, language, political considerations, national policies such as granting travel visas, and the "brain gain" or "brain circulation" needs of a nation or region. A more expansive outline of the types of international engagements among universities is offered later in this chapter.

While the emphasis in the Flagship model offered here is on regional and national responsibility and relevancy, it is also true that, as noted in a recent study of international research engagements among Latin American nations, "International cooperation is not only a trend, but it is almost

Figure 3.8 Traditional Views on Academic Scholarship versus the Scholarship of Public Engagement.

Traditional Scholarship	Scholarship of Public Engagement
Breaks new ground in the discipline	Breaks new ground in the discipline and has a direct application to broader public issues
Answers significant questions in the discipline	Answers significant questions in the discipline, which have relevance to public or community issues
Is reviewed and validated by qualified peers in the discipline	Is reviewed and validated by qualified peers in the discipline and members of the community
Is based on a solid theoretical basis	Is based on solid theoretical and practical bases
Applies appropriate investigative methods	Applies appropriate investigative methods
Is disseminated to appropriate audiences	Is disseminated to appropriate audiences
Makes significant advances in knowledge and understanding of the discipline	Makes significant advances in knowledge and understanding of the discipline and public social issues
	Applies the knowledge to address social issues in the local community

- *Improve diversity, student retention, and progress to degree.* A university that more fully integrates community engagement into its research and teaching develops stronger ties to multiple communities and may be better able to attract and engage a diverse student body. In addition, research shows that engaged students remain in school and progress to degree at a greater rate than students who are not engaged.
- *Reenergize faculty around engaged scholarship.* Creating a civic engagement initiative and providing a supportive infrastructure may reenergize faculty teaching and research by providing a fresh perspective on the value their work brings to society.
- *Connect the university to policy makers.* Universities are being questioned about their relevance, lack of transparency, and high costs. Community-based teaching and research is one way to "live" the

public mission and reinforce the important role that the university plays in serving the public good.

- *Build transdisciplinary and interdisciplinary research capacity.* The problems of society are complex, and addressing them requires expertise and research that cross disciplinary lines. These capacities should be supported among faculty and nurtured in students.
- *Building a research community around societies' most challenging policy issues.* Focusing on issues that are of local and national public concern brings the unique strengths of a research university to bear on the most pressing challenges that face the state. This can enhance public knowledge of and appreciation for the university system, thereby making more tangible the return on public investment in higher education.
- *Bringing in new resources and funding.* Both government and private funders are calling for more collaborative approaches to projects as a condition of funding. In addition, local and regional funders who may not normally contribute to other university endeavors may have greater interest in investing in projects with clear public purposes and applications.
- *Build social capital among students, faculty, and communities.* Academic inquiry not only addresses critical research questions but also enhances the ability of students, faculty, and communities to take action and build ongoing relationships that yield multiple benefits. The development of such social capital has been shown by research to strengthen communities, making them more resilient and healthy. New networks of trust and cooperation are likely to emerge and create academic partnerships for scholarly work.

Regional Economic Engagement

Regional economic engagement is an important mission of the modern Flagships—essentially, one avenue for making university-generated basic and applied research and intellectual property relevant. To a significant extent, although not solely, Flagship universities must have teaching and research programs that specifically support local industry and businesses, and that promote entrepreneurialism. The following discusses two major forms of economic engagement: fulfilling labor needs in local markets, and technology transfer.

Labor Needs

While Flagship universities are engaged in the education and training of talent for national, indeed global, labor markets, they must include a conscious effort to support local economies. This is a dynamic process with two general routes:

- Supporting local labor markets and the needs of businesses and municipal and regional government via public service activities, research engagement usually via faculty-directed projects, and by part-time work. Public service and research engagement activities, in particular, can act as apprenticeship opportunities and often help guide student career interests and shape local economies.

- Education and training for specific professional careers such as engineering, law, and medicine, but just as often via students entering the labor market with high-order skills, such as writing and analytical abilities.

How best to build and guide university efforts to educate first-degree and graduate students for labor markets is a complex challenge. In some fields where institutions have enrollment capacity, the need may be very clear—particularly in professional fields with such shortages as nurses, doctors, or engineers. But labor markets are increasingly diversified and nuanced. In developed economies, the link between a specific university degree in a discipline with employment, particularly at the first-degree level, is often not linear. Graduates of universities often change employers. This is why Flagship universities with a broad range of academic programs, including in the social sciences and humanities, must provide opportunities for students to gain skills and knowledge that make them adaptable in the labor market.

At the same time, universities have or need to develop close associations with major employers. This can be at the programs level. Engineering programs have a long history of close interaction with business and industry, with faculty engaged in applied research, students working in related internships, faculty and postdoctoral students spending significant periods of time in formal private sector employment, and engineers in local businesses having appointments in academic departments. One sees similar patterns of close collaboration among certain science fields—particularly those related to biotechnology.

Another form of collaboration related to local, regional, and national labor needs is the establishment of, and participation of university faculty and officials in, business forums. This is sometimes organized around specific industries, such as energy or education. It can also be simply a regional business forum, seeking avenues for economic development.

Reflecting the emphasis of the Flagship model on evidence-based management, universities need to develop longitudinal data on the employment of their graduates. They should also conduct surveys on the skills and knowledge desired by, and expectations of, regional employers. More broadly, universities need to regularly assess their overall regional and national economic impact.

Until recently, in many parts of the world ministries sought to make frequently crass assessments of the needs for specific degrees for regional and national labor markets, and to then make budget allocations accordingly—a predilection for central planning that was largely a failure. Flagship universities need to engage in a rigorous process of analysis and assessment of how they can best meet labor needs and the career path, and interests, of their graduates.

Technology Transfer

Flagship universities are actively engaged in a process of technology transfer. There are many complex policy issues involved for universities. Institutions need to protect the independence of academic research, yet also form and leverage university–business partnerships that effectively bring university-generated ideas and technology into the market.

Technology transfer is process of disclosure, patenting, licensing, and enforcement of these patents and licenses. But it is also about consciously promoting economic development and making ethical choices. Among the key policies are the following:

- Goals of technological transfer—While the specter of substantial and steady income from patents and licenses, or university-associated businesses, is often a goal of universities, this is rarely a reality. Costs can be high for getting university inventions into the marketplace, and to then protect them against infringement. Much more importantly, tech transfer is part of a larger effort to promote economic development and interaction of faculty and students with local and regional business and industries—a major route for brain circulation between the public and private sectors. It is important to note that patent and licensing activity and the number of spin-offs is not necessarily the most important evidence of the key role of universities in promoting economic development.
- Technology Transfer Modes—The flow of information between university and business sectors and, perhaps most importantly, the movement of personnel to and from the academy are often cited as the critical factors for promoting a vibrant business climate.[6] The structure of a nation's economy, along with a stable government and legal framework for businesses and universities to operate in, are

also important influences on the ability of universities to strategically increase their role in the economy. University–industry relations consist of a wide variety of activities, including:

- Direct funding of research costs through contracts and grants.
- Formal licensing to industry of university-owned patents and technology.
- Gifts and endowments including endowed chairs designated for colleges, schools, departments, or individuals.
- University–industry exchange programs and student internships.
- Specialized programs designed by the university for continuing education and training of professionals, primarily through university extension programs.
- Participation of industry representatives on campus and university-wide advisory groups.
- Cooperative research projects, some of which include government participation and the use of specialized facilities.
- Use of unique university facilities on a fee-for-service basis.
- Research and development facilities of industries housed on university-property industrial parks.
- Activities of cooperative extension.
- Faculty consulting.
- Research activities of the Agricultural Experiment Station and its affiliated field stations.

• Ownership of intellectual property (IP)—Policies are generally set at the national and institutional level. Increasingly, national governments are allowing university researchers to share in the ownership of intellectual property and in any resulting income, with the university, and sometimes with the source of research funding—often a government agency. The structure and ratio of ownership may vary, but the driving principle is self-interest by the inventor and the university to get IP into the market, and to facilitate "spin-off" businesses.

The following discusses two key areas related to effective tech-transfer policy: first, setting the rules of engagement, and second, providing support mechanisms to encourage entrepreneurialism an interaction between university researchers and students with the private sector and government entities.

Rules of Engagement

A paramount concern is that universities develop rules of engagement with the private sector and other outside agencies seeking research collaborations and the development of intellectual property. Many universities do have policies shaped by years of experience in fields such as engineering. But many do not, and close ties with industry in areas such as biotech, energy, and nanotechnology are relatively new. Properly devised, these rules can provide guidance for the academic community and a university to develop ethical relationships with the private sector and government, and criteria for when to decline interactions that are inappropriate.

With a growing role of university-based research and education in economic development, there is a learning curve on how best to manage relationships with private sector, and government, interests. The following provides an example of guiding principles at the University of California for technology transfer:[7]

- Open academic environment—All university research, including research sponsored by industry, is governed by the tradition of the free exchange of ideas and timely dissemination of research results. The university is committed to an open teaching and research environment in which ideas can be exchanged freely among faculty and students in the classroom, in the laboratory, at informal meetings, and elsewhere in the university. Such an environment contributes to the progress of teaching and research in all disciplines. Reasonable steps should be taken to insure that commercial pressures do not impede faculty communication among colleagues or with their students about the progress of their research or their findings. Indicators of possible problems include the disruption of the informal exchange of research findings and products, the lessening of collegiality, and the rise of competitive and adversarial relations among faculty.
- Freedom to publish—Freedom to publish and disseminate results is a major criterion of the appropriateness of any research project. University policy precludes assigning to extramural sources the right to keep or make final decisions about what may be published. A sponsor might seek a delay, however, in order to comment upon and to review publications for disclosure of its proprietary data or for potentially patentable inventions. Such a delay in publication should normally be no more than 60 to 90 days.
- Outside professional activities—Faculty should be encouraged to engage in appropriate outside professional activities. Each year, faculty should submit an annual report on outside professional activities to the department chair. This information is included in the faculty member's record and evaluated in the academic review process. It is the responsibility of each faculty member to assure that such outside activities do not interfere with obligations to the university in

teaching, research, and public service; and that no portion of time due to the university is devoted to private purposes.

- Responsibility to students—Universities need to protect the academic freedom of students, and responsibility for adherence to these principles rests with the faculty. Students who have reasons to believe they are in situations that violate those principles should be able to discuss the issue with a third party, such as the department chair or campus ombudsperson. Students must be able to choose research topics for educational reasons without being overly influenced by the need to advance investigations of direct interest to a particular firm; they must be protected against the premature transmittal of research results; and they must be advised objectively on career choices.

- Patent and licensing policy—Universities recognize the need to encourage the practical application of the results of research for the public benefit and need to balance several objectives in both patenting and licensing intellectual property: (1) facilitating prompt and effective development of useful inventions; (2) preventing the inappropriate use of public funds for private gain; (3) maintaining good relations with industry to make the best use of opportunities for education and research funding; and (4) obtaining appropriate revenues for the university from the licensing of patents. For these purposes, the University Patent Policy provides for: (1) mandatory disclosure to the university of potentially patentable inventions by employees or those who otherwise use facilities or research funds of the university; (2) assignment of patent rights to inventions developed in the course of university employment, or with use of university research facilities, or university funds; (3) sharing of royalties with inventors; and (4) transferring of technology to industry for the public benefit.

Terms and conditions for licensing agreements should consider the nature of the technology, the stage of development of the invention, the effect on the research endeavor in question, the public benefit, and the marketplace. Agreements are negotiated on a case-by-case basis. If a company needs time to evaluate a research result, an option agreement may be negotiated to allow a limited time for a review for licensing purposes. A university can grant the right of first refusal to the sponsor for an exclusive or nonexclusive license, based on the level of sponsor support. Any license of a patentable invention must at least provide for diligent development by the licenses and, in most cases, for the payment of royalties. Reproduction of copyrightable expressions may be separately licensed. Agreements, options, nonexclusive licenses, and exclusive licenses must not interfere with the principle of open dissemination of research results.

Tech Transfer and Entrepreneurial Support

Most major universities have an office of technology transfer with varying levels of authority and effectiveness, and targeted programs to support entrepreneurialism among faculty and students (see figures 3.9 and 3.10 for examples).

Figure 3.9   Case Examples: Technology Transfer Offices.

• **University of California, Berkeley—Office of Intellectual Property &
  Industry Research Alliances.** IPIRA was created in 2004 to provide a
  "one-stop shop" for industry research partners to interact with the campus.
  IPIRA's mission is to establish and maintain multifaceted relationships
  with private companies, and thereby enhance the research enterprise of
  the Berkeley campus. These relationships include sponsored research
  collaborations, and intellectual property commercialization sometimes
  referred to as technology transfer. This office reports to the Vice Chancellor
  for Research and consists of two groups: the Office of Technology Licensing,
  and the Industry Alliances Office. OTL's primary objectives:
  ○ Pursue public benefits from UC Berkeley IP including improvements
     to quality of life and economic development by leveraging the IP rights
     of UC Berkeley innovations in ways that help catalyze the fast, broad
     application of those innovations.
  ○ Establish IP terms of research partnerships by reconciling the IP policies
     and practices of the University with the IP rights that sponsors want in
     their research agreements.
  ○ Provide IP-related guidance, education and feedback channels for the
     campus community, and also as pertinent to UC Berkeley for the public,
     industry, government and press.
  ○ Lead Fiduciary Stewardship of UC Berkeley IP by obtaining fair
     compensation from companies for access to IP rights, and prudently
     managing the campus's financial costs in securing IP rights.
• **ETH Zurich—Industry Relations.** The ETH Industry Relations team
  provides a gateway for industry and matches interested companies with
  research skills available at ETH Zurich and focused on creating and
  strengthening mutually beneficial relationships between ETH Zurich and
  corporations worldwide. This includes arranging meetings between companies
  and ETH Zurich research groups and organize workshops and laboratory
  visits and supporting ETH Zurich "Competence Centres" in Energy
  Science, Education, Materials and Proccesses, Integrative Risk Management,
  and World Food Systems, and with other institutes and national industry
  associations Across various platforms and initiatives, ETH Zurich and the
  ETH Zurich Foundation invite partners from industry to support and sponsor
  visionary projects, talented students and young entrepreneurs.

Figure 3.9   Continued

- **University of North Carolina—Office of Technology Development.** The University of North Carolina at Chapel Hill's Office of Technology Development is charged with facilitating the process of connecting the fruits of University research to the companies best equipped to bring them to the public, and in doing so, to tap into new sources of income to encourage innovators and help support additional research. the University holds public access and societal benefit to be the primary goals of technology transfer and recognizes that the patenting, licensing, and publication of its health-related innovations present opportunities to increase their global accessibility and improve the condition of human life. OTD evaluates the innovation for its commercial potential; takes steps to obtain appropriate protection for the intellectual property represented by the innovation; identifies strong prospects for commercial partnership; and negotiates an appropriate licensing agreement.

Figure 3.10   Case Examples: Entrepreneurial Support Programs.

- **University of California, Berkeley—Student Entrepreneurial Support Programs.** Berkeley's Center for Entrepreneurship and Technology (CET) includes the Berkeley Method of Entrepreneurship claims a unique pedagogy for undergraduates offered in three interconnected layers of theory, entrepreneurial mindset, and new venture networks. A seminal aspect of the BMoE is the use of a game-based learning approach to develop the entrepreneurial mindset and social behaviors needed to develop successful new ventures. The curriculum embeds games and exercises within an experiential and competition-based journey of venture creation. CET's courses leverage on the BMoE and incorporate fundamentals in entrepreneurship, leadership, and product management, combined with the latest trends in cutting-edge technology such as mobile, web 2.0, and big data, turning simple group exercises into interesting projects that often result in real world companies.

  Another Berkeley program, Skydeck, is an engineering and MBA-focused incubator to create new digital technology focused businesses Skydeck, is a joint program of the Hass School of Business, the School of Engineering, various research institutions, and with Berkeley's affiliated Lawrence Berkeley National Lab. The focus is to promote new start-ups, some student directed and driven, and to keep more of them in and around the city of Berkeley. One program is focused on supporting student start-up ideas via a dedicated team of Haas MBA students who offer direct support to startup, helping to generate financial modeling, marketing strategies, impact analysis, customer relations, project management, sustainable business development.

Figure 3.10   Continued

- **University of Washington—Venture Capital.** The Commercialization Gap Fund is a partnership between UW's Center for Commercialization and the Washington Research Foundation to help promising innovations reach the level of development at which they can attract seed stage investment.
- **ETH Zurich—ETH Innovation und Entrepreneurship Lab.** The programmes and services offered by the ieLab for young entrepreneurs and researchers are designed to help make the results of scientific research carried out at ETH Zurich available to business and society more quickly and to fully exploit their commercial value. This includes:
  - ○ Individual coaching by successful serial entrepreneurs.
  - ○ Intensive networking to establish links with experienced business figures.
  - ○ Support for forging partnerships and alliances with industry at an early stage
  - ○ Help with finding out about the wide range of funding programmes available for young entrepreneurs in Switzerland.
  - ○ "Matchmaking" through contacts with trainees, postdocs and students at ETH Zurich.
  - ○ Access to all the services offered by ETH transfer, e.g., legal matters, contracts, patents.
  - ○ Help with finding follow-up financing for setting up a business.
  - ○ Office space in an open-plan environment, including IT infrastructure.
  - ○ Specialist workspaces in the Life Science area with BSL-2 laboratories.

The trend is for universities to first set up a centralized office for a campus to connect with faculty, help assess the value of ideas and inventions, help in the process of patenting and licensing, and provide links with venture capital and potential business partners. But large universities with robust research programs in science and technology fields tend to evolve by creating technology transfer staff that work in specific disciplines.

Continuing Education and Extension Programs

A critical component in the strategy to extend university- and research-based knowledge is to offer nonformal educational programs and services within a defined service area. Continuing Education refers to courses offered beyond a university's normal curriculum and to nonregistered students; Extension is a term used in the United States and relates to a wider array of program activities, including public lectures and demonstration projects, field research, and publications intended to bolster local economies or improve water conservation and similar activities.

Dating back to the 1890s, Extension has been an extremely important part of the mission of Flagship universities in the United States, with a focus on agriculture and food, home and family, the environment, and community economic development. The innovation of online courses (often nondegree credit) and certificate programs also significantly expands the potential reach of university programs and engagement with local and global economies.

Continuing Education and Cooperative Extension exists throughout the world; but it is often not organized and financed in a way that places it more centrally into the array of university activities. Figure 3.11 offers case examples of this important activity—a fundamental service to society for Flagships.

Figure 3.11 Case Examples: Continuing Education and Extension Programs.

- **University of Cambridge—Institute of Continuing Education.** Established in 1873, the University of Cambridge's Institute of Continuing Education offers a wide array of career development part-time and short term courses that lead to certificates and diplomas up to the masters level, and including online courses.
- **University of Wisconsin—Extension.** Wisconsin's extension programs date back to 1882. The University of Wisconsin works in partnership with the 26 UW System campuses that includes community college, regional institutions and other public research university campuses, along with 72 Wisconsin counties, three tribal governments, and other public and private organizations to fulfill its public service mission. Through statewide outreach networks, UW-Extension also connects university research to the specific needs and interests of residents and communities, including:
  - Cooperative Extension—Works with individuals, families, farms, business and communities, applying university knowledge and research to address issues in rural, suburban, and urban settings. Locally based Cooperative Extension staff collaborates with University of Wisconsin campus specialists to provide educational programming in Wisconsin's 72 counties and within three tribal nations. The Wisconsin Geological and Natural History Survey and Leadership Wisconsin are part of this division.
  - Continuing Education, Outreach and E-Learning—Provides continuing education services through all 26 UW System campuses, including these leading-edge new online degrees: Bachelor of Science degree in health and wellness, bachelor of science degree in health information management and technology and bachelor of science degree in sustainable management.

Figure 3.11   Continued

> ○ Entrepreneurship and Economic Development—Supports the Broadband & E-Commerce Education Center, Center for Technology Commercialization and the Wisconsin Small Business Development Center, with locations at the University of Wisconsin System four-year institutions.
>
> ○ Broadcasting and Media Innovations—Responsible for Wisconsin Public Radio and Wisconsin Public Television as well as distance-learning and conferencing technology services.
>
> • University of Campinas Unicamp—Brazil—Extension and Outreach. An essential element of Unicamp's pedagogical and social mission, the initiatives aim at bringing the institution closer to the community is the responsibility of the Office of the Vice-President for Extension and Outreach. The office is responsible for receiving and stimulating proposals for university extension activities and implementing these with the joint efforts of technical, administrative and operational staff using the institution's own funds or funds obtained from partnerships with other teaching institutions, public bodies, non-governmental organizations or public or private companies. Initiatives have focused popular culture; the history and memory of social movements; restoration of citizenship to street dwellers and indigenous people; social inclusion of individuals with special physical needs; socio-environmental education; sustainable agriculture; socially responsible economics; and the appreciation of culture as a tool for promoting health and well-being.
>
> • University of Cape Town—Health and Welfare Outreach. The Students Health and Welfare Centres Organisation, is a student-run, non-profit community outreach organisation based at UCT. Its mission is to improve the quality of life of individuals in the developing communities in the Cape metropolitan area. It is divided into two main service sectors: Health and Education.
>
> ○ Health relies on volunteer doctors, medical and allied health science students in all years of study to deliver primary health care in under-resourced communities. It co-ordinates six clinics either from permanent health facilities or from SHAWCO Health's three, fully equipped mobile clinics. These clinics often serve as the only port-of-call for community members who work during the day, or who cannot make the trip to the neighboring day hospital.
>
> ○ Education has over 10 student projects running in four community centres, Khayelitsha, Kensington, Manenberg and Nyanga, schools and children's homes. Volunteers are transported to and from the centers where they engage with learners with structured curriculum. Junior projects focus on literacy and numeracy whereas intermediate and senior projects focus on English, Maths, Physical Science and Life Skills.

While fully online courses leading to a degree or certificate may have some limitations as a curricular tool for enrolled undergraduate and graduate students at a university, they have perhaps the most potential impact as Extension programs. Many leading national universities are expanding their efforts in this area, often using virtual platforms provided by commercial and nonprofit enterprises such as Coursera and Udacity. Figure 3.12 outlines online course definitions developed by The Sloan Consortium—a think tank that studies online education.

Some universities have also provided online access to course materials gleaned from their own curriculum and for use by other institutions and by individuals—another example of the public services activities of universities.

Figure 3.12   Definition of Traditional, Hybrid, and Online Courses.

Proportion of Content Delivered Online	Type of Course	Description
0%	Traditional	Course where no online technology is used—content is delivered in writing or orally
1–29%	Web Facilitated	Course that uses web-based technology to facilitate what is essentially a face-to-face course. May use a course management system (CMS) or web pages to post the syllabus and assignments
30–79%	Blended/Hybrid	Course that blends online and face-to-face delivery. Substantial proportion of the content is delivered online, typically uses online discussions, and typically has a reduced number of face-to-face meetings.
80–100%	Fully Online/ MOOCS	A course where most or all of the content is delivered online. Typically have no face-to-face meetings

Relations with Schools

Flagship universities can play a large role in helping to influence and support schools in a university's service area. This includes the following:

- *Shaping curriculum standards*—Through its admissions criteria, for example, required courses, or creating or participating in national/regional curricular standards, or special courses in subjects such as math and composition via Cooperative Extension, Flagship universities can and should have a significant influence on school development—particularly at the secondary level.
- *Teacher training*—All Flagship universities should operate teaching training programs that are selective in admissions. They need not be large, but should be viewed as setting standards in teaching education. Historically, many Flagship universities have also established "Laboratory Schools" owned or jointly owned and operated by the university, creating a school that can employ innovative curricular ideas and unique training opportunities that should also reflect socioeconomic realities of the societies they serve.
- *School principal education*—As part of their critical role in supporting local schools and the path to a postsecondary education, many Flagship universities have distinct graduate programs for current and future heads of schools, often with a focus on secondary schools.
- *School and student outreach*—Faculty, staff, and students should provide opportunities for students from designated service-area schools to visit and be introduced to what it means to be a tertiary student via formal programs.

Relations with Other Postsecondary HEIs

The Flagship model assumes formal and informal forms of coordination and mutual support with other major tertiary institutions. Admittedly, this runs counter to the political culture of many major research universities where national norms tend to view each institution as an island, seemingly disconnected from the operation and welfare of what are sometimes viewed as competitors. Among the forms of institutional coordination:

- *Regional and national course coordination and articulation.*—In some instances, Flagship universities may develop programs at the first-degree and professional level jointly with other usually nearby institutions. See figure 3.8 for examples.

• *Transfer programs*—Course articulation can also lead to formal programs between institutions in which students matriculate at a designated stage at one institution to the New Flagship University. Beginning as early as 1907, California led the United States in the development of a state-wide effort at course articulation for the purpose of promoting what are today known as community colleges. Community colleges were to provide vocational training and adult education courses. But they also provided the first two years of a liberal arts program leading to the Associate of Arts degree, replicating the first two years of a bachelor's program at the University of California. Then as now, students with the AA degree can then matriculate to any UC campus at the third-year level to complete a four-year bachelor's program.

Today, approximately 28 percent of all undergraduates at the University of California are transfer students; nationally in the United States, some 35 percent of all students who earn a bachelor's degree attend and gain course credits in more than one institution on the path to that degree. There are other examples of a nascent attempt in other parts of the world at promoting national and regional course articulation and pathways for students who transfer (see figure 3.13).

Figure 3.13 Case Examples: Regional and National Higher Education Coordination.

• **KU Leuven Association Belgium.** Founded in 2002, the KU Leuven Association is an open and dynamic network linking eleven university and colleges across Flanders and Brussels with the KU Leuven, but with a focus on the institutions in the Leuven regional area, and with the purpose of forming cluster of centres of excellence in areas such as teaching, research and the arts. Its members strengthen each other by exchanging expertise and pooling resources, which enables them to improve the quality of both education and research. One example of institutional coordination: the Association's common digital learning platform, Toledo, creates several possibilities for multi-campus education. Toledo offers a number of online teaching facilities to students and lecturers: making course materials available, communicating with lecturers and fellow students, posting tests and assignments, creating a wiki or blog, offering tools for assessment. Because all Association members use Toledo, it is easy for lecturers to teach the same course at different institutions or to interact with lecturers on other locations, and for students to enroll in courses at partner institutions.

Figure 3.13   Continued

> • **Intersegmental Public Higher Education Course Articulation in California.**
> The ten campus University of California system and the twenty-four campus
> California State University system work with the 110 public California
> Community Colleges to maintain "intersegmental" course articulation
> agreements. There are two kinds of articulation agreements administered:
> ○ Intersegmental General Education Transfer Curriculum IGETC
>   articulation identifies courses that may fulfill lower division general
>   education requirements at UC or CSU campuses.
> ○ Campus-specific articulation determines whether CCC coursework will
>   satisfy major, breadth or other requirements at each UC campus. Each
>   campus manages the following:
>   – Campus-specific general education/breadth agreements
>   – Course-to-course agreements by department
>   – Lower division major preparation agreements

• *Joint community outreach efforts*—Flagship universities should lead and
collaborate with other tertiary institutions in efforts to expand access
to higher education for lower-income and other disadvantaged groups
at the secondary and lower levels of education. This can include providing secondary students information and personal contacts on what
it will take to enter a higher education institution and not just the New
Flagship University, and programs at the Flagship and other postsecondary institutions in which targeted students come to a campus, are
exposed to its environment, and gain a sense that they can aspire to a
university degree within a supportive academic community.

Profile IV: Flagship Universities—the
Building Blocks for Management,
Accountability, and Quality

Institutional Autonomy

The organization and management of national higher education systems
are changing globally. Most are moving toward greater levels of autonomy
while demanding expanding accountability requirements. In 2003, for
example, Japan passed the National University Corporation Act that made
all national universities legally autonomous with greater powers delegated

to the president and a governing board. Two years later, Singapore passed similar legislation giving three universities autonomous status as nonprofit private corporations (Felden 2008). France has pursued a significant reformulation of the authority of their national universities, granting new rights for academic leaders to manage university land and finances and the process of faculty advancement.

Yet in much of the world, a dynamic still exists where national universities are still subject to significant operational and financial management dictates from ministries and, at the same time, maintain a decentralized structure of academic decision making characterized by a university rector or president (titles vary) with weak management powers. In many universities, faculty authority remains linked to the historic role of faculty as self-regulating enclaves. They are largely devoid of accountability to the university as a whole; the rector or equivalent position is elected for a relatively short term, sometimes solely by the faculty, and sometimes with voting by students and staff—although usually with faculty vote having a higher weight. The voting process and short-term tenure of the rector can be influenced by intense domestics and campus politics, pitting groups against each other and encouraging wholesale changes in a university's upper management. The new leadership tends to have a lack of interest in prior policy initiatives.

The lack of sufficient management capacity is one of the reasons that many national governments have moved toward greater levels of legal autonomy for their universities. Ministries aim for improved leadership and greater institutional accountability, quality, and productivity. But this is not an easy transition for many universities. They owe their existence and much of their management culture to a dependence on ministerial direction and, often, remain dependent on a civil-service culture that is not performance based. Once granted greater autonomy, universities often lack a clear understanding of the relative roles and authority of rectors and other top-level university managers and faculty, students, and staff. It is uncharted territory that has caused great consternation in many national higher education systems.

Flagship universities need a strong conceptual model of governance to assert their leadership role and shift their focus away from a dependence on ministerial demands. This should include the following three operating principles:

- *Academic autonomy*—Flagships should have "Four Essential Freedoms" focused on the academic operation of an institution[8]:
  - The right to select students—within some general framework of national and sometimes regional policy.
  - The right to determine what to teach.

- ○ The right to determine how it will be taught.
- ○ And the right to determine who will teach.
- *Fiduciary autonomy*—Flagship universities require a sufficient level of independence for the effective and efficient use of resources. This should include significant budget authority: for example, the ability at the university level to shift some or all allocated funds and resources, such as land and buildings, to identified needs, and to redistribute personnel, including reallocating faculty positions.
- *Public accountability*—Governments that fund and give life via chartering of universities, whether public or private, must monitor and assess institutional performance, preferably assisted by a university governing body with representatives from government and civil society that can hold academic leaders accountable for achieving institutional goals.

At the same time, a high level of institutional autonomy via government provision is not sufficient in itself to support the goals of a Flagship. It must be accompanied by a governing and management structure that allows for decision making with relatively clear lines of authority and rules on shared governance with faculty.

Governance and Management

The level of autonomy provided by governments and their ministries varies tremendously, although it is generally characterized by greater levels of freedom in financial and academic management for university administrators. Governance and management capacity are a significant variable for institutions that, properly structured, allow a university to fully pursue the Flagship model.

Governing Board

Common to all Flagship universities in the United States, and increasingly at major, top-tier research universities throughout the world, is some form of a governing board. Such boards include members from the larger society that the university serves. They are sufficiently autonomous from national ministries, and government in general, to set broad institutional policies and hire and fire the top university administrator.

Depending on its legal authority and the process for selecting members, the board should provide a crucial combination of public accountability and, at the same time, a buffer between the occasional political vacillations of ministries and other forms of political pressure that may not benefit the university's long-term mission and public purposes.

If properly constituted, governing boards act as conduit and forum for major policy decisions that balance the academic values necessary for the internal life of universities while responding to the external needs and multiple demands of stakeholders. See figure 3.14 for an example of the general principles for a university governing board's operation, developed by the Association of Governing Boards based in the United States.

Figure 3.14 Case Example: Outline of General Principles for a University Governing Board Association of Governing Boards (AGB).

- **The ultimate responsibility for governance of the institution rests in its governing board.** Boards are accountable for the mission and heritage of their institutions and the transcendent values that guide and shape higher education; they are equally accountable to the public and to their institutions' legitimate constituents. The governing board should retain ultimate responsibility and full authority to determine the mission of the institution within the constraints of state policies and with regard for the state's higher education needs in the case of public institutions or multi-campus systems, in consultation with and on the advice of the president, who should consult with the faculty and other constituents.

- **The board should establish effective ways to govern while respecting the culture of decision making in the academy.** By virtue of their special mission and purpose in a pluralistic society, universities have a tradition of both academic freedom and constituent participation—commonly called "shared governance"—that is strikingly different from that of business and more akin to that of other peer-review professions, such as law and medicine. Faculty are accorded significant responsibility for and control of curriculum and pedagogy. This delegation of authority results in continuous innovation. Board members are responsible for being well informed about and for monitoring the quality of educational programs and pedagogy. Defining the respective roles of boards, administrators, and faculty in regard to academic programs and preserving and protecting academic freedom are essential board responsibilities.

- **The board should approve a budget and establish guidelines for resource allocation using a process that reflects strategic priorities.** Budgets are usually developed by the administration, with input from and communication with interested constituents. The board should not, however, delegate the final determination of the overall resources available for strategic investment directed to achieving mission, sustaining core operations, and assuring attainment of priorities. Once the board makes these overarching decisions, it should delegate resource-allocation decisions to the president who may, in turn, delegate them to others.

Figure 3.14   Continued

- The governing board should manifest a commitment to accountability and transparency and should exemplify the behavior it expects of other participants in the governance process. From time to time, boards should examine their membership, structure, policies, and performance. Boards and their individual members should engage in periodic evaluations of their effectiveness and commitment to the institution or public system that they serve. In the spirit of transparency and accountability, the board should be prepared to set forth the reasons for its decisions.
- Governing boards have the ultimate responsibility to appoint and assess the performance of the president. Indeed, the selection, assessment, and support of the president are the most important exercises of strategic responsibility by the board. The process for selecting a new president should provide for participation of constituents, particularly faculty; however, the decision on appointment should be made by the board. Boards should assess the president's performance on an annual basis for progress toward attainment of goals and objectives, and more comprehensively every several years in consultation with other constituent groups. In assessing the president's performance, boards should bear in mind that board and presidential effectiveness are interdependent.
- Boards of both public and independent colleges and universities should play an important role in relating their institutions to the communities they serve. The preceding principles primarily address the internal governance of institutions or multi-campus systems. Governance should also be informed by and relate to external stakeholders. Governing boards can facilitate appropriate and reciprocal influence between the institution and external parties in many ways.

Source: Statement on Board Responsibility for Institutional Governance, AGB, 2010.

Most major universities also have an affiliated "Foundation" or "Development" corporation with a board to solicit donations and gifts, with funds that are managed outside of the legal framework and restrictions of the university itself. This provides a means to generate additional income and fund-targeted projects, like buildings and scholarships, and sometimes operating funds. But this is very different from the larger policy and financial accountability role of an effective governing board that optimally would charter and regulate a university's foundation.

Executive Leadership

In many countries, the role of the president or the equivalent title of rector, vice chancellor, warden, etc., has been extremely weak, largely either a ceremonial position or a temporal, elected position in the university community with limited authority to manage an institution. Similarly, the extensive, often invasive, authority of ministries and rules and regulations generated by national governments has provided little room for effective institutional management to arise. This is changing in most parts of the world, with formal government policies creating broader authority for university presidents, including greater authority in budget management and administrative authority.

As noted, growing executive authority is a source of significant tension and confusion among faculty. On one extreme, too much authority can, as Michael Shattock states, give rise to a managerial model that can "push academic participation to the periphery" and lead to "a loss of academic vitality and distinctiveness" (Shattock 2013). Yet the other extreme is more common: a lack of organizational capacity to effectively shape university activities and output.

Faculty and Shared Governance

To help navigate the proper balance in authority, universities need to clearly define the role of administrative leaders and faculty in university management under a model of "shared governance." These relative and shared roles are summarized in the following:

- Academic administrators should, generally, have the primary roles in all issues related to budget decisions, and effective management of university operations that support academic activities. They should act as the primary liaison with governing boards, government authorities, and other stakeholders. Executive leaders can also provide a strategic vision for universities and ideas for new initiatives, yet always in a consultative manner with university faculty and other members of the academic community.
- A representative body of the faculty (such as a "faculty senate") should have direct or shared authority regarding all academic activities of a university, including oversight of academic programs and curriculum, shared authority with the university's rector or president over faculty appointments, generation of admissions standards and practices where there is institutional discretion, and consultative rights for major budget decisions related to academic programs.

Most universities have never fully articulated and codified the role of faculty in formal university policies, instead relying sometimes on government laws or more informal modes of behavior and precedent. The University of California, a multicampus system with ten campuses, provides an example of policies on shared governance that arguably is one reason for its status as one of the great university systems in the world. It includes delegated authority by the university's Board of Regents to its Academic Senate—the representative body of the faculty—in five areas of university management:

- The authority to determine the conditions for admission.
- The authority to establish conditions for degrees and to supervise courses and curricula. The Senate has the responsibility to monitor the quality of the educational programs that students must complete to earn their degrees and to maintain the quality of the components of those programs.
- The authority to determine the membership of the faculty and the process of their advancement. The Senate has a responsibility to monitor the quality of the faculty who teach courses, who develop the educational program, and who conduct research at the University of California. Faculty are evaluated under a uniform set of criteria that are intended to maintain a level of excellence on each UC campus. In order to ensure the quality of the faculty, the Senate also monitors faculty welfare issues that affect recruitment and retention of high-quality faculty.
- The authority to advise on the budget of the campuses. The University empowers the Senate to advocate budget allocations that channel resources into activities that enhance the academic programs of the university.
- The authority to conduct hearings in disciplinary charges against faculty that enforce the Faculty Code of Conduct and other policies of the university related to faculty performance in carrying out the university responsibilities.

Yet, it is also important to note that statements on the relative authority for faculty and administrators are not sufficient unto themselves for effective shared governance. The best universities have an academic community with a strong sense of their shared burden in maintaining and improving the effectiveness and quality of their institutions, and mutual respect among administrators and faculty. In their study of the changing nature of shared governance among Nordic universities, including Helsinki, Copenhagen, Oslo, Lund, and Uppsala, Bjorn Stensaker and Agnete Vabø note that while most universities emphasize leadership and governance capacity, most efforts at improving university management "overlook the cultural and symbolic aspects of governance along the way" (Stensaker and Vabø 2013). It is not simply about rules and regulations regarding management authority. It is also about relationships and a sense of common purpose.[9]

Academic Freedom

Critical to the success of the New Flagship University model is the principle of academic freedom. Many universities have their own definition of this critical organizational concept. Columbia University has the following statement:

> [Columbia provides the right] of faculty to determine the content of what they teach and the manner in which it is taught and the freedom to choose the subjects of their research and publish the results. It also guarantees that they will not be penalized for expressions of opinion or associations in their private or civic capacity.[10]

With concern among major universities regarding the freedom and rights of academics in various parts of the world, in 2013 the Association of American Universities (AAU, representing the leading public and private universities in the United States), the Group of Eight Australia, and the League of European Research Universities issued the "Hefei Statement on the Ten Characteristics of New Research Universities," The statement reads:

> The responsible exercise of academic freedom by faculty to produce and disseminate knowledge through research, teaching and service without undue constraint within a research culture based on open inquiry and the continued testing of current understanding, and which extends beyond the vocational or instrumental, sees beyond immediate needs and seeks to develop the understanding, skills and expertise necessary to fashion the future and help interpret our changing world.[11]

Similar rights should be extended to students, particularly in regard to freedom of expression. For both faculty and students, however, there are restraints in all societies in some form regarding speech—including "hate speech" or varying forms of sedition. The cultural and political environment in which Flagship universities operate cannot be ignored; yet, each should have some formal statement regarding academic freedom.

Quality/Evaluation of Faculty and Academic Programs

The model of the New Flagship University requires sufficient autonomy and academic leadership to develop and sustain an internally derived culture of self-improvement and institutional quality. There are three cornerstones for this effort: (1) a clear outline of expectations for faculty that reflects the values of the Flagship University and the broad range of faculty responsibilities—often not well thought out or articulated in many universities; (2) a process of hiring faculty *and* a regular review of a faculty members' performance throughout their careers, linked to the policies on their duties; and (3) regular review of academic departments or faculties (often called program review) intended for internal decision making.

The following outlines how a system of regular evaluation of faculty and academic programs can be pursued.

Faculty Appointment and Advancement

How faculty are hired and promoted differs in various parts of the world. Many leading national universities are still mired in a civil-service mentality in which faculty seniority, not actual performance, constrains institutional effectiveness and innovation.

Over time, leading research universities in the United States have developed a process for an initial faculty hire, a period of evaluation of a person's productivity and promise (usually five to six years), and then the status of tenure (with the initial title of Assistant Professor) with regular reviews (every two to three years) of a faculty member's performance in teaching, research and public service—a process of "post tenure" review. Faculty advancement, including pay, is determined by their performance. Failure to gain regular promotions diminishes the standing of that person in the eyes of peers, and places limits on current and future salary. It also can result in greater teaching workload and does not limit a university from firing a faculty member who is a poor performer or for budgetary considerations.

Policies, and procedures related to hiring and promotion are important, but alone do not suffice. In their study of MIT and UC Berkeley, sociologists Jean-Claude Thoenig and Catherine Paradeise note the central role of a campuswide organizational culture that values innovative thinking in the course of a faculty career—not simply the quantity of journal articles or other rudimentary gauges of productivity. At the best universities, they observe, the focus on innovative work in a wide spectrum of faculty activity sets the best institutions apart. "Performance evaluation and especially the quality of a person's research are considered vital not only for that person, but the whole local community."[12]

Other national systems, such as in Australia, provide contracts for full-time faculty, initially short term and, with evidence of academic performance, longer-term contracts that, essentially, provide a similar level of stability and peer review found in tenure systems. In both, the civil-service culture based on years served is absent.

How to evaluate faculty performance and promise within a Flagship University? It is important to recognize considerable variation in the research interests of faculty. Harking back to the previous sections, some pursue traditional forms of research and other "engaged scholarship." Further, faculty teaching, research, and public service interests evolve over time.

Figure 3.15 provides a conceptualization of the primary areas of responsibility and activity for faculty: teaching and mentoring, research and creative work, professional competence and activity, university service (including activities related to academic management at the program, discipline, and campus-wide levels), and public/community service. Like the previous depiction of the experience of undergraduates and graduate students, the size of each sphere is only an example of a faculty member with significant research productivity. Theoretically, the weighting will vary depending on faculty members' interests, abilities, and stage in their academic careers.

The University of California has a history of developing innovative academic personnel policies that have significantly influenced the quality and productivity of the institution. The accompanying Figure 3.16 provides an outline of the posttenure review policies of California's Flagship University.

Figure 3.15   Five Spheres of Faculty Appointment and Promotion.

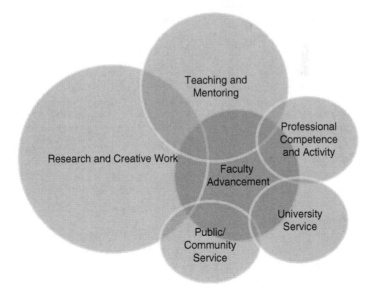

Figure 3.16   Case Example: University of California Process for Faculty Post Tenure Review.

Personnel actions for merit, promotion, and appraisal normally begin in the department. The department chair, in consultation with each candidate, assembles a review file, which, after departmental discussion and voting, is sent to the Dean or other appropriate administrative officer.

In cases of promotions the file goes next to an ad hoc review committee, which is appointed by the Chancellor or designee, from nominations provided by the Senate Committee on Academic Personnel. The majority of the ad hoc membership comes from outside the home department and the membership of this committee is kept confidential.

The ad hoc committee reviews the case and, normally, its recommendation is sent to the Committee on Academic Personnel (CAP). CAP, which is also known as the Budget Committee on some campuses, reviews the complete case, including all recommendations and documentation, and evaluates it in view of campuswide standards. Ad hoc committees are not normally used for appointments to Assistant Professor tenure track positions or for merit increases. CAP normally provides the peer review. A recommendation goes from this committee to the Chancellor or Vice Chancellor for a final decision.

If the Academic Vice Chancellor or designee makes a preliminary assessment in the case of an appointment, reappointment, formal appraisal, non-reappointment, or promotion of an individual in the Professor series, which is contrary to recommendations of the Dean or Provost, the department chair, or the Committee on Academic Personnel, the Academic Vice Chancellor informs that reviewer and asks for further information which might support a contrary decision. In the case of non-reappointment of an Assistant Professor, the candidate may, upon request, seek access to documents in the review file. The department chair shall receive documents provided to the candidate. After additional information is furnished, CAP and the Dean or Provost are given the opportunity to comment on the augmented file before the Chancellor makes the final decision.

Each faculty member understands that performance will be evaluated on campuswide criteria. The following provides the criteria for that review, as stated in the University of California's Academic Personnel Policies.[13]

Teaching and Mentoring
Clearly demonstrated evidence of high-quality in teaching is an essential criterion for appointment, advancement, or promotion that includes documentation of ability and diligence in the teaching role. In judging the effectiveness of a candidate's teaching, peer review should consider points

such as the candidate's command of the subject; continuous growth in the subject field; ability to organize material and to present it with force and logic; capacity to awaken in students an awareness of the relationship of the subject to other fields of knowledge; fostering of student independence and capability to reason; spirit and enthusiasm that vitalize the candidate's learning and teaching; ability to arouse curiosity in beginning students, to encourage high standards, and to stimulate advanced students to creative work; personal attributes as they affect teaching and students; extent and skill of the candidate's participation in the general guidance, mentoring, and advising of students; effectiveness in creating an academic environment that is open and encouraging to all students, including development of particularly effective strategies for the educational advancement of students in various underrepresented groups.

Review should pay due attention to the variety of demands placed on instructors by the types of teaching called for in various disciplines and at various levels, and should judge the total performance of the candidate with proper reference to assigned teaching responsibilities.

Research and Creative Work
Evidence of a productive and creative mind should be sought in the candidate's published research or recognized artistic production in original architectural or engineering designs or the like. Publications in research and other creative accomplishment should be evaluated, not merely enumerated. There should be evidence that the candidate is continuously and effectively engaged in creative activity of high quality and significance. Work in progress should be assessed whenever possible. When published work in joint authorship or other product of joint effort is presented as evidence, it is the responsibility of the department chair to establish as clearly as possible the role of the candidate in the joint effort. It should be recognized that special cases of collaboration occur in the performing arts and that the contribution of a particular collaborator may not be readily discernible by those viewing the finished work.

Professional Competence and Activity
In certain positions in the professional schools and colleges, such as architecture, business administration, dentistry, engineering, law, and medicine, a demonstrated distinction in the special competencies appropriate to the field and its characteristic activities should be recognized as a criterion for appointment or promotion. The candidate's professional activities should be scrutinized for evidence of achievement and leadership in the field and for demonstrated progressiveness in the development or utilization of new approaches and techniques for the solution of

professional problems, including those that specifically address the professional advancement of individuals in underrepresented groups in the candidate's field.

University and Public/Community Service

The faculty plays an important role in the administration of the university and in the formulation of its policies. Recognition should therefore be given to scholars who prove themselves to be able administrators and who participate effectively and imaginatively in faculty government and the formulation of departmental, college, and university policies. Services by members of the faculty to the community, state, and nation, both in their special capacities as scholars and in areas beyond those special capacities when the work done is at a sufficiently high level and of sufficient high quality, should likewise be recognized as evidence for promotion. Faculty service activities related to the improvement of elementary and secondary education represent one example of this kind of service. Similarly, contributions to student welfare through service on student-faculty committees and as advisers to student organizations should be recognized as evidence, as should contributions furthering diversity and equal opportunity within the university through participation in such activities as recruitment, retention, and mentoring of scholars and students.

Beyond this outline of policy on faculty responsibilities and expectations, universities need to set standards related to possible conflicts of interest, Faculty and staff are increasingly engaged in activities outside of the university, often serving the larger public-service role of the university, sometimes with additional compensation. Universities need policies that ensure these university employees are maintaining their commitments in time and service, such as teaching courses and mentoring students. They must also avoid engaging in consulting and research grants in which their financial interests may interfere with normal duties as university employees or with their impartial judgment as researchers. National or regional governments may have general policies related to ethical conduct, but universities need to have their own set of policies and the means to enforce them.

Program Review

Regular reviews of existing academic programs ensure that standards of excellence are maintained and that schools and departments plan strategically for the future. In many parts of the world, academic program review, like post-tenure review, is a relatively new concept. Increasingly, ministries of education are setting up standards and requirements for program review and for various forms of university accreditation. However, the most significant path for institutional self-improvement and evidence-based management is internal, campus-driven review processes that can offer an honest assessment of the strengths and weakness of a department, like history, or physics, or a college. Effective Academic program reviews are designed to elicit input from faculty, students, and staff of the department under review. The model at Berkeley, and similar to that at other top public universities, is to perform a review of an academic department, school, or program every eight years or so that includes the following process:

- A Program Review Committee of the Academic Senate coordinates and monitors the review process, with staff support offered by the campus' office of institutional research.
- Each department, school, or program undertakes a self-study, assessing its intellectual agenda, its programmatic goals and resources, and identifies critical challenges and opportunities facing it. The department, or unit, is supported in this effort by data provided by the Office of Planning and Analysis.
- A carefully selected external committee completes a report based on its interviews with faculty, students, and staff and relevant review documents provided by an institutional research office. The academic program being reviewed has the opportunity to respond to the committee's report and to one written by the member of the Senate's Program Review Committee. Subsequently, all review documents are submitted to the Academic Senate for response by the committees and the Executive Vice Chancellor (EVC), the head academic officer at Berkeley.
- Reviews culminate in an outcome letter that delineates action items for units, deans, and central administrators. The dean responsible for the program under review completes the EVC and Senate reports are distributed to units after the review.
- The EVC outcome letter is formally transmitted to the unit, which concludes the review. At this point, all review reports and the outcome letter become part of the public record.
- The unit is expected to take actions to address the findings of the program review. The outcome letter designates the timeline for acting on the recommendations. The unit is expected to report on actions it has taken as part of its annual request for new or replacement faculty positions to the responsible dean unless otherwise negotiated at the wrap-up meeting. The dean is expected to comment on the unit's progress in his/her annual request to gain or retain a faculty position. The institutional research office is responsible for maintaining a database of initiatives undertaken in response to the recommendations.

Diversity of Funding Sources

Most universities seek a greater array of financial sources, moving away from a funding model dependent largely on governments. In part, the diversity of funding sources for research-intensive Flagship Universities reflects the growing diversity of academic and public service activities; but it also often reflects a decline in government investment in leading national universities.

Throughout the twentieth century, for example, the state universities like Berkeley, Michigan, Texas, and North Carolina gained more than half of their operating funds from state governments. Today, declining investment rates and much expanded funding portfolios has meant that state funding is only about 15 percent of the budget for these famous universities. The other major sources of funding include tuition and fees, research grants and contracts, and income from patents and gifts.

While Flagship universities generally are diversifying their funding sources, they must retain their commitment to their regional and/or national socioeconomic role. At the same time, a diversified funding portfolio promises greater funding stability and, in most circumstances, a path to greater institutional autonomy.

Institutional Research Capacity

Institutional research (IR) is an essential activity for Flagship University. Most universities have had very limited formal policies and strategies for gathering institutional data, and for employing trained staff to generate the information and analysis required for competent and innovative management. One catalyst for increasing IR capacity is the growing demand of ministries for data to meet evolving accountability schemes; various international and national ranking efforts are also leading to relatively new campus efforts to generate and maintain databases and formulate strategies for improving citation index scores and similar measures of output.

In many research-intensive universities, however, there remains a significant lack of IR capacity and understanding, by academic leaders and by faculty, of the critical role of IR for institutional self-improvement and quality control. Flagship universities need to focus on their own data and analysis needs, including internal accountability efforts like Program Review, and not simply react to external demands. IR capability generally includes the following co-dependent functions:

- Data development and maintenance on core university activities
- Enrollment, personnel, and financial management

- Outcomes assessment, program review, accreditation
- Institutional reporting and analysis
- Strategic planning

These are interconnected purposes, of course, that link general data collection and management with efforts at strategic planning. But how to effectively pursue them? Figure 3.17 offers a model on how an Institutional Research office at a Flagship University might be organized.[14]

All major universities need a professional IR staff. They also need to seek collaborations with similar regional or national universities, and even international partners, to help build a comparative perspective, and to bolster institutional research as a profession with common standards of data collection, research, and analysis methods.

Many universities, sometimes lacking a central campus administration with sufficient authority to direct strategic efforts, simply seek out faculty without adequate training to provide IR. Often these efforts requests are ad-hoc, and do not take into account the breadth of data analysis needs of a campus. Major universities should maintain a divide between faculty responsibilities and those of professional IR staff—although interaction is obviously important and some faculty may want to take on a full-time professional role in IR.

Information is power. It is of course ironic that most universities have extremely limited IR capabilities, partially understandable, as most universities have had a decentralized structure of decision making and, until recently, limited external accountability demands. Organizational models may differ, including the focus of IR efforts that are influenced by the varying demands of ministries.[15] Yet, all campuses need some form of a centralized IR office.

International Cooperation and Consortia

While Flagship universities should have a strong focus on regional and national needs, they must also leverage collaborations with faculty, programs, and, more generally, with universities in other parts of the world. As noted previously, the crucial strategic approach for Flagship Universities is not to see international engagement as an end to itself (or, for that matter WCU rankings), but as a component of their larger missions and pursuits. At the same time, there is significant policy convergence in the activities, and social and economic demands, being made of universities. They can learn much from each other and benefit greatly by exposure to the activities and innovations of peer institutions.[16] Indeed, international cooperation and joint activities can be transformative.[17]

Figure 3.17 Case Example: Organization of an Institutional Research Office by Functions.

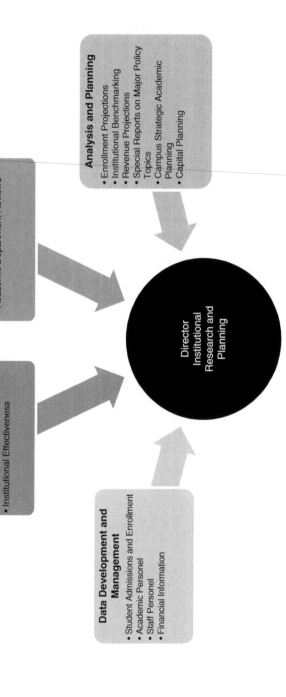

Research and Development
- Survey Research
- Outcomes Assessment
- Institutional Effectiveness

External and Internal Reporting
- National/Ministerial Data Reporting
- Academic Department Reviews

Analysis and Planning
- Enrollment Projections
- Institutional Benchmarking
- Revenue Projections
- Special Reports on Major Policy Topics
- Campus Strategic Academic Planning
- Capital Planning

Data Development and Management
- Student Admissions and Enrollment
- Academic Personnel
- Staff Personnel
- Financial Information

Director Institutional Research and Planning

There are institutions that have various international agreements and programs that are not well focused or carefully planned. The volume of engagements appears to take precedence over the value and costs to the institution—in money, but also in faculty time. High-visibility projects, like a branch campus, take shape without a substantial business plan and without strong faculty support. Sustainability in terms of funding and faculty interest and participation is often a challenge. Most international engagements cost institutions money, despite promises of income generation. This is not to discourage experimentation and risk taking, but to encourage greater introspection and analysis on initiatives.[18]

Figure 3.18 lists the ways Flagship University may pursue international engagement (Edelstein and Douglass, 2012). This includes individual faculty initiatives; the management of institutional demography; mobility initiatives; curricular and pedagogical change; transnational institutional engagements; network building; and campus culture, ethos, and leadership.

The various strategies for internationalization take different levels of institutional effort and resources. Figure 3.19 provides a general mapping of this range of institutional effort. Student and faculty exchanges are common at all leading national universities. Within non-Anglo countries, courses in English are increasingly common in selected fields, and nearly universal in business master's programs. But in many nations, there are legal and cultural difficulties, including the language ability of faculty, that pose challenges to this pathway for internationalization.

Joint courses are also increasingly common in select fields, usually driven by the interests of one or more faculty in a department or program. Joint and double-degree programs are placed as a higher order of institutional effort, conditioned by how they are organized, the ability and willingness of faculty to coordinate with faculty in other institutions, and sometimes the ability of students to physically or virtually navigate course requirements and language differences. Generally, these are degree programs with relatively small enrollments.

Joint research projects and coauthorship in academic journals with international collaborators are growing dramatically—more common than joint courses and, particularly in the sciences, can require significant resources in the form of faculty time and laboratory facilities. Curricular reforms intended to integrate global knowledge and skills into courses and degree programs are placed as a high-effort activity. As many observers of internationalization note, there is often much rhetoric around the concept that campuses are reforming and repositioning their curriculum and academic programs to be more international. Yet there are few strong examples of this happening in a coherent and pervasive manner. Particularly in

Figure 3.18   Clusters and Modes of International Engagement.

Cluster 1—Individual Faculty Initiatives
- Research Collaboration
- Teaching and Curriculum Development
- Academic Program Leadership
- Sanctioning Authority

Cluster 2—Managing Institutional Demography
- International Student Recruitment
- Recruitment of Foreign Academic and Administrative Staff
- Visiting Scholars and Lecturers
- Short Courses, Conferences and Visiting Delegations
- Summer Sessions, Extension Programs and Language Acquisition Programs

Cluster 3—Mobility Initiatives
- Exchange and Mobility Programs
- Study Abroad Programs, Internships, Service Learning, Research Projects and Practicums

Cluster 4—Curricular and Pedagogical Change
- Incremental Curricular Change
- Foreign Language and Culture
- Cross-Cultural Communication and Inter-Cultural Competence
- New Pedagogies and Learning Technologies
- Extra-Curricular and Student Initiated Activities

Cluster 5—Transnational Engagements
- Collaboration and Partnerships with Foreign Institutions
- Dual, Double and Joint Degrees
- Multi-site Joint Degrees
- Articulation Agreements, Twinning, Franchising
- Research-Intensive Partnerships
- Strategic Alliances
- Branch Campuses, Satellite Offices and Gateways

Cluster 6—Network Building
- Academic and Scholarly Networks
- Consortia
- Alumni Networks

Cluster 7—Campus Culture, Ethos, and Symbolic Action
- An International Ethos: Changing Campus Culture
- Engaged Leadership

universities that adhere to a three-year bachelor's degree and where students enter a specific field and have few or no opportunities for general education, there are limits placed on developing global knowledge and skills, including education abroad.

Figure 3.19 Mapping of University Internationalization by the Least to Most Amount of Institutional Effort.

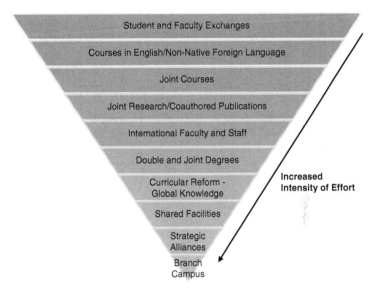

There are many purported strategic alliances among universities, either in the form of university-to-university agreements, or in various international associations. But their actual meaning and importance is often minimal. Strategic alliances in this mapping include only major and significant efforts between universities and are very rare. Perhaps the best example is the Singapore-MIT Alliance launched in 1997. Under a formal agreement, MIT and Singapore are engaged in on-going collaborations in research, education, and innovation. The relationship has yielded hundreds of joint research publications and scores of research collaborations.

Shared facilities with international partners are rare, but are a growing phenomenon. The logistics can be significant and, again, may relate to the sustained interest of key faculty and the mobility of researchers, and graduate students.

A branch campus requires the greatest level of campus time and effort and is a growing phenomenon, although with a common pattern. Almost all are small-scale, boutique experiments in a limited set of disciplines with high student demand such as business, engineering, or information systems and computer science. They are more like outposts than genuine university campuses, although with a number of exceptions. Education City in Qatar, for example, with some ten branch campuses, graduated only 243 students across all fields and institutions in 2011.

Most branch campuses also appear to be only loosely connected to their home campus, with limited impact on its core functions of teaching, learning, scholarship, and scientific research. Because of their small scale, they involve a small set of students and faculty members on the main campus. In most cases, students do not come to the "mother" institution for a period of study and home-campus students do not matriculate at the branch campus (Edelstein and Douglass 2012).

As discussed in the chapters providing case studies of Asia, Russia, Chile, and Scandinavian countries, internationalization has different levels of importance, perceived and real, among different countries. Every Flagship is expanding its international engagement; the question is in what ways and for what purpose (de Rassenfosse and Williams 2015).

NOTES

1. I realize that this effort has many biases that reflect the historical development and current mission of some of the great Flagship universities in the United States, and to some degree, my own historical research on the purpose and influence of public universities (Douglass 2000; 2007).
2. I. Bunting, N. Cloete, and F. van Schalkwyk, 2013. *An Empirical Overview of Eight Flagship Universities in Africa: 2001–2011.* Cape Town: Centre for Higher Education Transformation.
3. Andrés Bernasconi 2012. "Are Global Rankings Unfair to Latin American Universities?" *Inside Higher Education*, October 15. www.insidehighered.com /blogs/world-view/are-global-rankings-unfair-latin-american-universities# sthash.XpboINbW.dpbs.
4. SERU-based research tells us that the student experience is nuanced at major research universities—that the classroom is one component of a rich array of experiences that includes the key role of the disciplines in building learning communities, the socioeconomic background and the interaction of students, and their opportunities to engage in research, service learning, and cocurricular activities. These interactions, and the fact that there are many student experiences within each research-intensive university, are thus far not fully captured in the research literature or in the public discourse over the role of these universities in public life. See www.cshe.berkeley.edu/SERU/.
5. Marcelo Knobel, Tania Patricia Simoes, and Carlos Henrique de Brito Cruz 2013. "International Collaborations between Universities: Experiences and Best Practices," *Studies in Higher Education*, 38. no. 3: 405–424.
6. David C. Mowery, Richard R. Nelson, Bhaven N. Sampat, and Arvids A. Zeidonis, *Ivory Tower and University-Industry Technological Transfer before and after the Bayh-Dole Act.* Stanford, CA: Stanford University Press, 2004.

7. These are based on policies developed at the University of California related to both encouraging interaction with the private sector and attempting to define and avoid conflict of interest by faculty or by a department or college.

8. In 1957, Justice Felix Frankfurter set an anchor for academic freedom in the United States., drawing from language of South African educators then fighting their nation's ban on education of whites and nonwhites in the same university: *"It is the business of a university to provide that atmosphere which is most conducive to speculation, experiment and creation. It is an atmosphere in which there prevail `the four essential freedoms' of a university—to determine for itself on academic grounds who may teach, what may be taught, how it shall be taught, and who may be admitted to study."* Sweezy v. New Hampshire 354 U.S. 234 1957.

9. For a brief history of shared governance at the University of California, see John Aubrey Douglass, "Shared Governance at the University of California," CSHE Research and Occasional Papers, CSHE.1.98 March 1998 www.cshe .berkeley.edu/shared-governance-university-california-historical-review.

10. This is one sample statement drawn from Columbia University, but many similar statements can be found at major research universities.

11. "Hefei Statement on the Ten Characteristics of Contemporary Research Universities" joint statement of the Association of American Universities, Group of Eight, League of European Research Universities, Chinese 9 Universities October 10, 2013: See http://www.leru.org/files/news/Hefei _statement.pdf.

12. Jean-Claude Thoenig and Catherine Paradeise, "Organizational Governance and Production of Academic Quality: Lessons from Two Top U.S. Research Universities," pending publication *Minerva*.

13. This outline of criteria is adopted from the University of California's Academic Personnel Manual APM, section 120.

14. Fredericks J. Volkwein, Ying Liu, and James Woodell 2012. "The Structure and Functions of Institutional Research Offices," in *The Handbook of Institutional Research*, ed. Howard, Richard D., Gerald W. MacLaughlin, and William E. Kight. San Francisco: Josse-Bass. http://books.google.com /books?id=BsbP-cZxLt4C&pg=PT46&lpg=PT46&dq=ASHE+Handbook +Institutional+Research&source=bl&ots=XVwPr_n1co&sig=nD3S7DzFN nu0Mn8HUVgI2MZJwf8&hl=en&sa=X&ei=c2BhVNLIPMKsogSQo4L YDw&ved=0CDgQ6AEwBA#v=onepage&q=ASHE%20Handbook%20 Institutional%20Research&f=false.

15. Igor Chirikov, "Research Universities as Knowledge Networks: The Role of Institutional Research, *Studies in Higher Education*, 38, no. 3 (2013): 456–469.

16. John Aubrey Douglass 2009. "Higher Education's New Global Order: How and Why Governments Are Creating Structured Opportunity Markets," CSHE Research and Occasional Papers Series, December: www.cshe.berkeley .edu/publications/publications.php?id=348; also John Aubrey Douglass, "The Race for Human Capital" in *Globalization's Muse: Universities and Higher Education Systems in a Changing World*, ed. J. Douglass, C. J. King and I. Feller. Berkeley: Berkeley Public Policy Press.

17. For a discussion of models for international consortia, see Marc Tadaki and Christopher Tremewan, "Reimagining Internationalization in Higher Education: International Consortia as Transformative Space?" *Studies in Higher Education* 38, no. 3: 367–387.

18. See Richard Edelstein and John Aubrey Douglass, "The Truth about Branch Campuses," with Richard Edelstein, *Chronicle of Higher Education*, February 27, 2012: www.chronicle.com/article/To-Judge-International -Branch/130952/.

Chapter 4

Considering National Context and Other Variables

In an often cited analogy, the university is imagined as a village—an insular and tightly knit community, focused on teaching and learning as a worthy endeavor of its own, but somewhat removed from the larger world. The modern comprehensive university is, however, more like a city. It has many subcultures and responsibilities that reflect its growing role in society. "Some get lost in the city," Clark Kerr once explained in his assessment of major American universities in the early 1960s, "while others, both faculty and students, find communities within the larger institution." The "city," continued Kerr, "is more like the totality of civilization" (Kerr 1963).

Fast-forward to the beginning of the twenty-first century, and the mission and activities of the most ambitious universities is even more complex and expansive, the link between teaching, research, and public service more symbiotic. In some aspects, core values remain, like the mentoring relationship between faculty and student. But in many other ways, the university of the past and today are very different places, their once insular character dissipating in response to the growing demands of major stakeholders—national and regional governments, the private sector, and citizens seeking tertiary education.

Like no other institution in our modern world, universities service the needs of the increasingly expert-driven society. Higher education provides a key source of human capital; it is an increasingly crucial tool for bolstering socioeconomic mobility, and for providing a transition for talented young people moving from home to the working world.

Graduates then flow into the labor market, becoming entrepreneurs, professionals, good citizens, and community leaders. Some devote themselves to public service; some become the next generation of researchers and faculty.

The explosion in knowledge is another reason universities play an increasingly central societal role. The world's academic community steadily creates new fields of inquiry, innovative ideas, and new technologies. Virtually every major technological advance in the past six or more decades, for example, relates in some form to academic related research—from communications and computing, to lasers and health-related technologies like magnetic resonance imaging, the science behind research on climate change, and revolutionary discoveries in nanotechnology and biotechnology. Interdisciplinary and collaborative research is the contemporary mode, particularly in the sciences, in turn informing the teaching and the public service role of well-managed universities.

Globalization and advances in communication technologies have also reshaped the activities of faculty, students, and staff. In a fashion seen never before, individual researchers seek colleagues and collaborators outside their disciplines, and outside of their own universities and nations—not only with other academics, but also with those in business and government.

At the same time, it seems that many national universities, and their academic leaders and faculty, have difficulty conceptualizing and articulating the wide range of university activities and engagement with society. The Flagship model presented previously has the lofty objective of providing that updated vision. It also seeks to support an institutional culture of self-improvement and evidence-based management, rooted in an ethos of national and regional relevancy.

The best universities are those that are striving to get better, and not simply in the realm of research productivity—the primary concern of the rhetoric and policy initiatives associated with improved international rankings and attaining recognition as a WCU. It is a much broader charge that includes teaching, public service, and internal mechanisms for supporting quality and excellence.

A key assumption in articulating the New Flagship model is that there are universal policies and practices that can be adopted in different nations and regions of the world. However, there are many important contextual variables that constrain and influence institutions that might claim the New Flagship title. The following provides a discussion on some of these variables and the strengths and weaknesses of the model—a brief critique on its applicability in different parts of the globe.

History of Higher Education System Building

There is great variation regarding how nations have built and funded their higher education systems. These histories condition and shape contemporary efforts at reforming universities. If the national political culture, for instance, has traditionally supported uniformity in the funding and missions of its particular network of universities, then any effort to create differentiated missions among existing and oftentimes politically powerful universities is difficult. It hinders any official government designation of the Flagship title and the required financial resources.

However, leading universities in a region or nation, with components of the Flagship model, including a breadth of academic programs across the disciplines and a culture focused on public service, may self-identify as a Flagship. They may adopt the Flagship title, and perhaps use it in helping to shape institutional culture and to recast the discussions with ministries and the public on their role in society.

Demographic Variables, Economic Growth, and Funding Capability

Nations with growing populations, often accompanied by increased demographic diversity, including immigrant groups, are in particular need of universities that exude the ethos of the New Flagship University. Generally, but not always, universities are then operating in an environment of increased enrollment demand *and* additional financial resources. Stable or declining populations and economies create a more difficult environment for the Flagship model. Resource choices by ministries or regional governments often are then subject to difficult process of redistribution of existing taxpayer revenue among public services, or among postsecondary institutions.

National economies in developing nations also may find it challenging to provide adequate public funding for the full breadth of Flagship activities. A partial answer is that leading universities in, for example, Africa or parts of Asia, focus on certain aspects of the model, including public service, or tech transfer and regional economic development. As noted, the Flagship model is aspirational and adoptive to the national circumstance of universities that see value in it as a rhetorical and policy pathway.

Gender, Racial, and Class Discrimination

To some extent, all societies suffer the social malady of discrimination that excludes or segregates groups not by actual or potential academic ability, but based on societal biases. One extreme is gender discrimination that excludes women from some or all forms of higher education. Severe forms of formal and sometimes informal discrimination essentially bar any nation from achieving a New Flagship University. Not only are universities then limited in their ability to promote socioeconomic mobility and to progressively influence local communities and economies; attracting talented faculty and staff, and students, is restricted, as most of them seek institutions committed to international standards of equal opportunity and professionalism.

Democratic Traditions and Stable Governments

Nations that have strong democratic traditions and widespread faith in the capability and openness of government generally provide the best environment for a viable higher education system, and the Flagship model. Failed states or highly centralized and controlling oligarchies create significant limits on the ability of universities to be fully engaged in the Flagship ideal. At the same time, some nations with strong democratic traditions can also have ministries that are constantly pursuing major changes in accountability regimes and funding models. This also creates an unstable policy environment requiring increased effort by universities to adjust to external demands, as opposed to a focus on internally derived mechanisms for quality assurance and strategies for regional and national relevance.

Quality Feeder System of Students

Almost all universities, including those that are highly ranked or those that view themselves as among the elite and of best quality, have thus far largely neglected their potential to help shape and influence the quality of their respective national school systems. As outlined in the Flagship model, there is a wide array of activities in which universities can be engaged in shaping the curriculum and experience of prospective students, and generally the education of all students, and in providing outreach to regional school systems.

Open Societies

Societies that do not provide significant levels of freedom of speech and widely understood standards of academic freedom are excluding themselves from the pantheon of Flagship Universities. In the words of the Hefei Statement noted previously, the best universities exist more generally in societies with, "A tolerance, recognition and welcoming of competing views, perspectives, frameworks and positions as being necessary to support progress, along with a commitment to civil debate and discussion to advance understanding and produce new knowledge and technologies."[1]

Attracting and Retaining Talented Faculty

It is a simple truth: the quality and achievements of a university, Flagship or otherwise, is determined by the quality and morale of its faculty. From this fact come other markers of quality and excellence, including top-quality graduate students who are increasingly operating in a global market for academic degree programs. But there are many variables that make the process of recruiting and retaining high-quality faculty challenging. Particularly in developing economies, there is generally a shortage of doctoral programs and graduates trained as both teachers and researchers. Faculty with the appropriate credentials and abilities, many educated abroad in more developed economies, are more mobile. They can be difficult to retain.

A series of studies developed by the Centre for Higher Education Transformation (CHET) has outlined the capacity challenges for sub-Sahara African universities: a lack of faculty with a doctorate; a poor pipeline to supply the growing number of faculty positions; inadequate time and funding for faculty-directed research.[2] The reality is that in many nation-states in the midst of building their higher education systems, universities have little choice but to hire their own doctoral degree students as full-time faculty. This process of internal faculty development is prone to nepotism and lower levels of faculty productivity as researchers (Yudkevich, Altbach and Rumbley 2015). Faculty with experience in other university environments, and with rigorous academic cultures, tends to generate more innovative and quality academic programs. As noted, the hiring and retention of quality faculty, the existence of a clear set of expectations and a process of regular review and opportunities for promotion, and adequate salaries, are among the most important preconditions for a Flagship University.

University Management and Governance Capacity

Institutions that are constantly reacting to ministerial directives, including where and how funding should be spent or, to provide another example, that have highly decentralized organizations in which departments or schools are seemingly immune to universitywide efforts at reform and resource reallocation, experience reduced capacity to mature and expand their role in society.

Relevance in Developing Economies

The Flagship model has the greatest potential impact on nations still in the process of expanding and shaping their higher education systems. Usually within the context of a growing population enrollment demand, there are more opportunities to build academic programs, to hire new faculty, and to develop innovative outreach services to businesses and local communities.

But there are also significant challenges. Low faculty salaries relative to the cost of living are a common problem, for example, and correlate with faculty seeking other forms of income—often teaching at another institution. Without the appropriate level of institutional support and a clear understanding of their responsibilities, entrepreneurial faculty sometimes operate their research activities in an agency or institute outside their home university. Some universities also operate within cultures that have significant levels of corruption. For example, and particularly where faculty salaries are extremely low relative to the cost of living, students of means may pay for an improved grade in a class. Some regions of the world also have severe rules and customs constraining the ability of women to gain an advanced education or to enter the labor market as equals with men. Some nations have policies and practices limiting academic freedom and free speech.

Institutions that aspire to the Flagship model may also face questions related to the supply and demand for their graduates, in turn influencing ministerial decisions on funding. Many nations face a problem with providing appropriate employment opportunities for university graduates, like in China, Spain, and even the United States. This is a disjuncture that in part reflects the structure of economies. In China, for example, the service sector and other economic sectors in need of advanced education remain relatively small, although growing.[3] In Spain, there are similar challenges, with unemployment for university graduates clearly exacerbated by the downturn in the global economy and the slow pace of a recovery in business activity. Yet, one of the great stories in the growth of the US economy, and the support of socioeconomic mobility, was that most state governments sought to create a supply of higher education opportunities before there was significant demand, eventually fueling long-term economic growth. This historical lesson remains salient.

Another concern is "brain drain," the movement of educated or professional people from one country, economic sector, or field for another, usually for better pay or living conditions. We still see significant movement of academic talent from the Southern to the Northern Hemisphere. The desire is that the brain drain phenomenon is eventually superseded by the concept of "brain circulation," as talent—in the form of students, faculty, researchers, and business people—increasingly moves among nation-states and economies. Many nations with developing economies have established programs to attract talented academics, mostly scientists and engineers, to their top universities, including paths to citizenship. The Flagship model could assist in these efforts, making institutions that espouse its values more attractive.

Relevance in Developed Economies

Developed economies have generally a mature mix of existing universities and, sometimes, as in Germany and France, a network of highly productive research institutions such as the Max Planck and Leibnez Institutes and the CNRS/*Grands Etablissements* that have, thus far, operated largely separately from the public university sector—although often with links to graduate programs and, in the case of Germany, shared faculty with local universities. In this context, the Flagship model is more difficult to achieve.

Germany offers an alternative approach. There are few leading national universities; rather, good-quality universities exist across the network of nearly 100 institutions in the 16 *Landers* (or states), each with a few highly ranked academic departments. U-Multirank, which focuses on the strength of academic programs by discipline, indicates this selective strength in German universities. Combined with federally and *Lander*-funded Institutes, 13 universities of technology, including the *Fachhochschule* (Universities of Applied Sciences in the mold of a polytechnic with vocational programs usually tied directly to local labor market needs), comprise a well-defined system in Germany that is, in terms of graduates and research productivity, very successful.

Most German universities, however, and specifically their academic leaders and faculty, remain tied to an older and rather limited vision of their role in society, focused on teaching and research, and not on public service or larger concepts of institutional engagement. Federal "excellence" initiatives push at the edges of this model, but the ability of Germany's universities to pursue a more ambitious institutional profile appears limited.

Official Government Identification and Funding

As indicated previously, the Flagship model can be aspirational, helping to guide the behavior of relatively to highly mature universities that see value in its outline of public purpose, and potentially a revision or replacement for the World Class paradigm. There is a growing recognition that greater mission differentiation, in which institutions excel in their area of responsibility as members of a system of higher education, means that not all institutions are alike. The World Class race is just one example of this recognition; more common are indirect efforts at differentiation, like revised funding regimes for research found in England.

Ultimately, the preferred evolution is to have a certain number of institutions, possibly through a government-devised competition, attain the Flagship title. The aspirational, self-identified Flagship is the likely path, but perhaps a longer road to expanding the model if there are no additional general operational resources offered to institutions. Some institutions, however, could claim the Flagship mantel, offering a strategy or academic plan that appeals to ministries or other funding sources.

Private Universities and the New Flagship Model

The Flagship ideal has its historical roots in public universities with their primary responsibility, in the United States and increasingly internationally, to be inclusive and to focus much of their activity on promoting socioeconomic mobility and economic development. Yet, many private institutions, including many of the Catholic-affiliated universities, also exude or aspire to elements of the Flagship model.

How Does the Flagship Model Help Other Postsecondary Institutions?

While the Flagship model is fully applicable to only a select group of national universities, in part because it requires significant financial resources, elements of the model can provide guidance and use by other institutions that are not fully research intensive or able to focus on the large array of purposes and programs outlined in the model. A key concept in the idea of Flagships is that they are part of a larger higher education system, with institutions that have a responsibility to excel in their particular spheres of responsibility. Institutions that are more teaching intensive, or focused largely on local labor markets, or on engaging students in community service, may find elements of the model useful and with a similar goal: to constantly seek institutional self-improvement.

*   *   *

The New Flagship University is a holistic model, applicable to some subgroup of major universities. While governments and other stakeholders have a legitimate claim to influence and shape the operations and missions of their universities, the Flagship model may provide a path for some universities to explain and seek greater institutional identity, to build a stronger internal culture of self-improvement and, ultimately, a greater contribution to economic development and higher rates of socioeconomic mobility that all societies seek. For that to happen, some groups of institutions will need to embrace some version of the model on their own terms and articulate it clearly and loudly.

Notes

1. "Hefei Statement on the Ten Characteristics of Contemporary Research Universities," joint statement of the Association of American Universities, Group of Eight, League of European Research Universities, Chinese 9 Universities October 10, 2013: See www.leru.org/files/news/Hefei_statement .pdf.
2. Nico Cloete et al. 2011. *Universities and Economic Development in Africa*, Higher Education Research and Advocacy Network in Africa HERANA Centre for Higher Education Transformation, Cape Town, South Africa.

3. For a discussion of the challenges facing Chinese higher education, see John Aubrey Douglass, "China Futurisms: Research Universities and Leaders or Followers?" *Social Research: An International Quarterly*, 79, no. 3 (Fall 2012): 639–688: www.socialresearch.metapress.com/link.asp?id=bv6l4755157834u4; a version published in *University World News* December 16, 2012, Issue No 252: www.universityworldnews.com/article.php?story=20121212160450595.

Part II

The Flagship University in
Global Perspective

Chapter 5

The Predicament of the Quest for WCU Status and Seeking an Asian Flagship University

John N. Hawkins

Higher education in Asia has a long history of leading national universities that have some of the New Flagship University characteristics—primarily as highly selective institutions, employing among the best scholars and serving as the primary path for creating a nation's civic elites in the absence of other postsecondary institutions (Hawkins 2013). Historically, these leading universities were grounded in national service, but with a limited vision of their role in socioeconomic mobility, economic development, and public service. One thinks of Tokyo University, Peking University, and Seoul National University in East Asia, and on a smaller scale, their counterparts in Southeast Asia and South Asia.

In the twentieth century, several forces and factors were at work to push forward the expansion of this elite system toward what Martin Trow (2005) has called the massification phase, and which Ronald Dore termed "the diploma disease" (Dore 1997). Despite the difference in tone of these two descriptions of this movement, it can be said that the process of expansion has had three perhaps-unintended outcomes. These include:

- Because their mission was primarily "internal," these leading national universities were not necessarily concerned with competing with other higher education institutions (HEIs) outside of the national setting.

- With the rise of the complex interplay of neoliberalism, globalization, and internationalization in the mid-twentieth century (already, in the twenty-first century, these have become contested concepts—see Hawkins 2014), the "internality" changed as national higher educational systems looked "externally," seeking to achieve a new goal of joining the ranks of world-class universities (WCUs) legitimated and measured via the rise of a series of new comparative international ranking regimes.
- This, in turn, has created a "predicament" for higher education in general and historical flagship universities and newly arising research universities in particular, resulting in a rapidly changing ecology of higher education in the region.[1]

This chapter explores this ecology and the complexity of these various forces and factors in the Asia region within the critical context of massification, the rise of dominant ranking regimes, the quest for WCU status, and the contrast and predicament of policy makers who may seek to articulate and pursue the two models of the World Class and the New Flagship University.

Massification, Rankings, and the Quest for WCU Status

Higher education throughout much of the world, and certainly across the considerable differences of the Asia Pacific region, has been in one or another stage of massification (Trow 2005) for the past three or four decades. From an outside perspective, it may appear as if the general shape and dynamics of this massification movement are similar, largely irrespective of local country differences. On closer inspection, however, it seems as if the process of massification itself is highly complex and differentiated, taking a variety of shapes and pathways.

There exist at least two ways of looking at this process. One hypothesis is that increasing access through massification increases inequality. That is, as a higher education system becomes more massified, contradictions emerge. For example, massification of higher education produces institutions of significantly different quality—in the research productivity of faculty, in the preparedness and academic talent of students, in their graduate rates, and their value to the labor market. Some observers assert that the gulf between HEIs at the "top" of the quality end of the distribution and the "bottom" (however determined) has widened worldwide, year after year, as massification has progressed. Further, that it will grow more pronounced in the coming decades. What evidence is there to support this proposition?

In the case of Asia, an important consideration is to look where enrollment demand and growth has occurred and the dynamics related to that growth. Enrollments at the tertiary level globally have increased by over 50 percent in the last decade, and in Asia by a much greater percentage (Calderon 2012). The majority of the enrollment growth in coming years will be in two countries: China and India. Both have massive populations and are characterized by very significant patterns of income and social inequality. It follows that the diversity of students in higher education increases as they come from social classes and income levels with little preparation, increasing the propensity of for them to drop out; many attend low-quality and sometimes exploitative postsecondary institutions that spring up to "serve" underprepared populations (Bettinger and Long 2009).

Within "conventional" tertiary institutions, these students come at a greater cost because they require tutoring, counseling, and a variety of support services—more than the elites do. As participants within the higher education process, they simply do not have the academic background or ability when compared with those in the historically Flagship Universities. Building up overall systemic capacity is also expensive and time consuming, with the result that often expansion cannot keep up with demand, facilities become substandard (often because investment for them is all on the front end for initial construction, with little thought of or provision for on-going maintenance), which in turn leads to study conditions that are inferior, overcrowded, characterized by inadequate libraries and information and communication technologies, resulting in restricted range of the curriculum. In most of these situations, very few or no resources are made available for the continued education and training of faculty, which in turn quickly leads to the perpetuation of outdated curricula, and other challenges (Trow 1973; Altbach 2010).

The academic professionals needed to staff these expanded facilities tend to be less qualified, overworked with very large teaching loads that include large classes, low salaries, and little opportunity in time and energy to provide personal attention to students. Indeed, in many of these contemporary massified higher education systems in the Asia Pacific region, faculty at lesser-regarded institutions are often forced to hold positions at multiple institutions, a situation that leads to a downward cascade of professional preparation, timeliness of knowledge, and energy to teach effectively. This situation may be seen to approximate an under-class of this fraction of the academic profession (Chapman 2009). Massification usually means that much of the expansion is in the private sector, often leading to the proliferation of institutions that are underfunded and exploitative, and which tend to function basically as "demand absorbing" institutions, almost irrespective of the quality of the education being produced (Jiang 2011). At the same time, high noncompletion rates tend to grow with massification (especially as it moves toward Trow's final stage of "universalization" in which higher education is deemed necessary for all). Even in the United States, data indicate that it takes longer to graduate (on average 6.3 years for a BA) with many students being either unwilling or unable (often for financial reasons) to continue, and they simply drop out. In many countries, the practice is to simply fail large proportions of students to bring in more, either to meet income needs or to fulfill government-mandated quotas (Smit 2012).

Therefore, massification in many instances takes place in the absence of an increase in the quality of the secondary system and adequate-quality regimes, leading to admission of students unprepared for higher education. When massification of higher education takes place in the absence of a corresponding "reform" or "restructuring" of secondary education, the distortions of the latter are telegraphed directly into the former. The result is that many institutions (as suggested earlier) may end up in the periphery of the newly emergent system, with students fundamentally unprepared to succeed with the demands of higher education. Such institutions, however, are characteristically likely to be evaluated in terms of metrics common to the system as a whole, and thus enormous pressures are generated and transmitted throughout the system to sustain what are deemed suitable levels of graduation. These tendencies are underscored and multiplied when the processes of massification are accelerated. The most common indicators of the costs of such dynamics are often made present in professional fields in which graduates are required to take national qualification examinations where failure rates can be high. One important result of these dynamics is that the combination of all of these factors often leads to efforts to create, assure, and maintain quality by agencies (both governmental and nongovernmental) providing a quality-assurance mission, often resulting in an impossible challenge. Determining the quality of these new institutions entering the system is a daunting challenge, but often no less so than that of seeking to create and implement quality routines that can lead to sensible and verifiable data for such a wide range of institutions. One result is that "quality assurance" exercises often are empty and of dubious value.

Another important result is that elite institutions continue to dominate these differentiated systems, characterized by enrolling a highest text scores and percentage of upper-income students, the best faculty, the highest completion rates, the largest share of the public higher education budget, and other accruements. In contrast, the lower-level institutions attract those with lower (and lowest) scores and less income, who are less competitive on examinations and generally ill prepared for a "true" higher education.

Overall, however, the available data are unclear on whether a degree from one of the lesser institutions actually increases life and opportunities, although some US data suggests that, overall, a higher education degree from any institution *does* increase such lifelong income opportunities (Baum 2014). On the other hand, Korean and Japanese data, which is available, show that it does not do so, and acts instead to perpetuate inequalities. Studies by Lee (2014) show that in both Japan and Korea, despite massification and declining fertility, socioeconomic stratification in higher education remains persistent over time. The data indicate that in terms of academic preparedness, financial affordability, and investment attractiveness, massification has not ameliorated socioeconomic stratification, but rather there has been a low impact on changing the background of students and continued vertical stratification among institutions.

Another aspect of massification has been the actual scale on which many of these unintended consequences arise. Wang and Liu (2011), for example, detail many of these for China in *Higher Education News*, noting that whereas many of these occurrences have taken place outside of China, within China they have occurred on a massive scale, complete with numerous protests and other manifestations of disorder arising in large part from the unexpected and unanticipated high cost of higher education and its surprisingly low returns for a certain class of students ("Facts and Details" 2013).

To this circumstance must be added, not only for China but also increasingly for much of the developed world (e.g., Spain, Egypt, France, and Britain), the astonishing increase in the number of under- and unemployed graduates. For Xiaoyan Wang and Jian Liu, this phenomenon stands as evidence that, for China at least, its "current social, economic and political structures are not ready to absorb them" (Wang and Liu 2011, p. 2). An increasingly apparent conclusion evident to many commentators is that the well-known and remarked "alignment crisis" in higher education that is typified by the inability of graduates to find employment is a fundamental structural feature of those economies in which massification is the characteristic form of higher education. This is compounded by data that reveal that in China there are downsides for both equity and equality in postsecondary participation that can affect students' lifetime opportunities. Surveys continue to show that upper-income students are favored for access to the best and most selective universities; they receive more financial aid than lower socioeconomic students in lesser institutions, and, despite massification, have fewer lifetime opportunities as a result (Qiong Zha 2011).

A Competing Hypothesis

A second and competing hypothesis states that even conceding all or most of the above problems and issues, a massified system nevertheless increases "long-term" equity and equality prospects. Part of the apparent conflict between the two views can be explained by the reality that it just might take longer to achieve this relative social state than is thought. This proposition points to the following *kinds* of evidence that may be adduced from what in most instances must be viewed as *emerging* or *emergent* forms of massified higher education. This includes the following observations.

Massification, it is held (in a contradictory argument to that made previously), sets a tone for all further education, and raises the overall talent pool of emerging countries. In this framing, massification acts as a kind of "demand pull" that transmits signals of quality and aspiration (often drawn from global comparisons) that are held to "chip away" at the parochial and more narrowly conceived educational parameters and standards of nationalist systems prior to the onset of the massification stage (Dill 2007). Eventually, it will pay to attend HEIs and obtain a degree. This assertion accords with recent studies in the United States that find, in surveys of all members of the labor force, those with a bachelor's degree earn about 170 percent more than those who attain no more than a high school diploma, while those with an advanced degree earn about 225 percent more (Baum 2014). Whether this is an economic principle or an indication that the United States is some sort of outlier remains to be demonstrated. Recent reports from China's newly massified system suggest that recruitment is down in almost every province as parents and students opt out of attending a postsecondary institution, skeptical of the benefits they might accrue ("Tremors in China" 2014).

It seemingly is an invariable requirement that governments must increase their regulation and monitoring of these new largely private institutions that contribute to massification, to gradually increase their quality through rigorous quality assurance and accreditation processes (Dill 2007). In order for massification to result in a steady pattern of improved access accompanied by requisite quality, there must be greater transparency. Experience throughout the world continually attests to this central proposition of higher education quality assurance, namely that whether recognized or not, higher education both nationally and internationally constitutes a form of market in which various forms of symbolic currency are given value and exchanged. Transparency is a requisite requirement for the effective exchange of information in such a market, one that allows "consumers" of the higher education "product" (however defined) to make informed decisions. This has become a major task of national quality assurance activities and figures importantly into both the emergent ranking system (as one form of generating such transparency) and nascent efforts to create viable standards for international/global quality comparisons (Marginson and Sawir 2005).

It is evident that for the qualitative improvement and overall beneficial aspects of massification to occur, there must be government action to provide for cost-sharing, financial aid, and admissions practices and outreach (as outlined in the Flagship model discussed in Part I of this book), to help the low socioeconomic students with abilities gain access to the top institutions, thus increasing that pool of talent. Where such action is absent, as indicated in Hypothesis One above, higher education systems will inevitably operate to both perpetuate existing inequalities and to create new ones. This is a particularly important point on which to gather data and provide context, inasmuch as the "modal" pattern of government involvement in higher education is to provide significant support in earlier stages of massification (along with the loosening of government regulation for private institutions), but in later stages, spurred by elements of neoliberalism, to restrict government support. Current concerns in the United States focus on how declining support for higher education may reduce middle-class achievement for graduates (Quinterno and Orozco 2012) (providing evidence for Hypothesis One), whereas much evidence exists to document how, when government support *does* exist, it tends to level inequalities (Arrow 1993; Schultz 1972; 1988). This "role of the state," much maligned in the climate of neoliberalism in recent years, is being reinvigorated as a kind of "fourth revolution," with Asia as the model exemplar (Micklethwait and Wooldridge 2014).

One apparent requirement to achieve an outcome of long-term equity and equality is to construct diversified systems and alternative paths for students to climb what is sometimes termed an educational ladder. National governments need to provide coherent and stable higher education systems—as Douglass notes, a prerequisite for rationalizing the existence of more elite Flagship universities. As experience with the California Master Plan indicates, these systems can be constructed such that institutions are provided with funding appropriate to their mission, are provided access to sufficient numbers of students who have demonstrated academic competence appropriate to that institution, and where faculty, administration, and regulatory authorities (whomever they are) agree on the mission, capabilities, and limits of each institution within the system. Such explicit and self-conscious ideas of mission, combined with explicit notions of limitation, militate against "mission creep," which is invariably a source of "introduced inequality" and instability where it occurs. Here is where we see clearly the critical role that Flagship Universities can and should play in the broader scheme of a national higher education system (Douglass 2015; 2000). In the modern context of Asia, and elsewhere, they cannot and should not be independent operators, but part of a larger network of institutions.

Given the foregoing, we can then provide two "contextual" conditions for each of the two hypotheses. The first focuses specifically on issues concerning the changing economic structures, locally, nationally, regionally, and globally, and their implications for how, where, and why educational efforts are situated within these changing structures. More simply, given the dynamics of massification, how do Asian nations in particular make assessments, judgments, and efforts to create appropriate higher education capacities within the continually changing parameters of labor markets at all four levels specified above, and how do they relate to the more contemporary notion of the Flagship University discussed in this book? An important entailment of this question is how do they do so (or are expected to do so) within a climate and structure of international competition such as that generated by the pervasive focus on international rankings, a phenomenon that often generates stipulations for institutions irrespective of what some would see as the requirement to produce quality education for meeting local needs.

The second contextual condition one would wish to see addressed is the complex of implications for the growth of higher education in the ever-developing context of existing and future regional cooperation. For example, how do universities with higher numbers of students foster more regional cooperation in promoting research, in the range and nature of academic programs, and in the various pathways and processes supporting student mobility? This appears a critical consideration in many instances, since some commentators perceive that collectively we will run short of resources to invest in higher education if we continue to engage in unnecessary competition and status seeking (Hawkins and Neubauer 2014), in part influenced by the increasing influence of rankings and the notion of WCUs.

The Effects of the Ranking Game in Asia

It is understandable that along with the expansion of higher education capacity came a desire to make some sense of comparative quality out of this complex enlarged pool of institutions nationally and internationally. That, along with the competitive environment of globalization and increased student and faculty mobility, helped create an ecology that begged for comparative measures. By 2014, it could be argued that six ranking agencies dominated the higher education ranking scene: Academic Ranking of World Universities (ARWU-Shanghai Jiaotong), Leiden University, QS (Quacquarelli Symonds), Scimago, *Times Higher Education*, and U-Multirank. Despite early critiques of such regimes and their obvious shortcomings, even some of the most critical observers were forced to conclude, "…global university ranking is here to stay" (Marginson 2014, p. 45). With that in mind, it is important to remember that the evidence is sound that they indeed are quite limited in their ability to contribute to a reasonable evaluation of the quality of a university. Simon Marginson (2014) notes at least eight social science and behavioral arguments in favor of this conclusion, noting that improvements need to be made in the quality of the data utilized in the ranking schemes, the methodologies employed, and the criteria utilized to optimize behavioral effects on performance, among others.

In the Asia region, while the ranking phenomenon has clearly colonized some aspects of higher education policy, key higher education scholars have presented sharp critiques of its allure. To cite just three prominent scholars: Liu Niancai, who developed the ARWU model, nevertheless notes that most ranking systems measure only portions of university goals and objectives and that "the fundamental role of universities—teaching, and their contributions to society are not well taken into account" (Liu 2011, p. 5; 2009). In Hong Kong, Ka Ho Mok and Anthony Cheung, both of the Hong Kong Institute of Education, have critiqued the rankings as being one-dimensional, ignorant of student learning measures, methodologically biased, overly focused on citation indices, and ignorant of teaching quality, university's role and mission, and the contributions universities make toward community and human development (Mok 2011).

As discussed in this book, many basic weaknesses exist in the ranking phenomenon, whereby much is made about the value of comparisons and methods, while its limitations are also widely recognized yet largely ignored in the race for status and prestige promoted by ministries and many universities alike, particularly in Asia. Dean Neubauer (2011) observes that ranking exercises have taken over the more traditional evaluation functions common to most HEIs in the Asian region. They are basically too simplistic for the complexity that the expansion of higher education in Asia demands, thus contributing to the predicament that higher education finds itself in as it seeks to redefine itself in the twenty-first century. This stands in contrast to an increased interest in the "internally" driven academic culture of self-evaluation and devotion to institutional self-improvement that is offered in the contemporary Flagship University model.

China, Japan, Korea, Hong Kong, Singapore—all are pursuing major higher education reforms designed specifically to improve the ranking of their major universities. Constrained by the skewed viewpoint of the WCU model, most have been partially successful. The following comments are focused on the elite, research universities in these settings, since that is where the example of what constitutes research is most often defined. It is suggested that even for this level of higher education, let alone the mass of institutions in Asia, the research model historically developed in the United States and Europe may not be the most appropriate for the twenty-first century and for developing innovative universities and colleges, and may in fact drive out such other critical missions of the university as teaching and learning.

In China, roughly 150 universities have been selected through either the 211 or 985 projects and billions of yuan invested to raise the overall quality of these institutions, especially their research endeavors, to achieve WCU status and rise in one or more of the ranking regimes. In the Chinese Academy of Sciences (CAS) institutes, equally large investments have been made in mathematics, physics, chemistry, chemical engineering, biological sciences, earth sciences, and technological sciences, to bring these fields up to World Class status. Without doubt, these efforts have yielded impressive results as measured by publication rates, patent rights, and other metrics (Salmi 2009). When looked at more carefully, there remains much to be done. Evaluations of both the quantity and quality of R&D show that institutions, especially those benefitting from the two programs mentioned earlier, are now contributing around 80 percent of internationally recognized publications in China, and that China, in 2007, had a higher share of scientific publications than other East Asian nations. However, there are questions regarding the quality of the research output (NSF 2007; Simon and Cao 2009). The reasons cited for this lack in quality are several, but the main focus is on a lack of creativity and reluctance for risk taking (Simon and Cao 2009).

China has also moved quickly in the direction of facilitating university–industry linkages, away from basic research and toward applied research, so that a national pattern has emerged reflecting an increasing share of university-affiliated enterprises in S&T dominated by those universities in the 985 program (Zhu and Liu 2009). Nevertheless, the research gap between China's best and most heavily funded universities (the 211 and 985 universities) and the ranking-dominated WCU model remains large, as does the research gap between all universities that are not part of these two programs and those that are, thus leaving the system with a large contradiction and predicament whereby a small elite group receiving large investments from the central authorities defines "quality" research while not meeting this standard itself when compared with highly ranked universities elsewhere.

When taken as whole, China's higher education system is facing a number of contradictions. As in the majority of the world's countries, rankings are equated with WCU status. The incredible expansion of capacity has without doubt offered more access to higher education for increasing numbers of Chinese students (producing about 3 million graduates per year). At the same time, employment rates are declining, degrees are devalued, quality has suffered, and China appears to be facing a bubble in the number of graduates and a limited labor market (Minzner 2013). Educational leaders are reassessing state priorities, seeking to strike a more appropriate balance between the elite institutions that are seeking higher rankings and the increasingly large number of relatively "new" universities that are also expensive but producing graduates who face an uncertain future of underemployment, unemployment, and failed expectations. A 2006 evaluation of the 985 project asks the question of how much more investment it would take to successfully imitate the top research universities in the West and concluded that "it is uncertain for the Chinese government how much total financial support would be enough for helping the top Chinese universities reach the goal of a world-class university" (Chen 2006, p. 148).

Japan has taken a similar route to boost its research efforts through the so-called Toyoma Plan (Shinohara 2002) launched in 2002, and the Japan Top 30 Program (Centers of Excellence for 21st Century Plan). The Top 30 program provides 31 research universities with US $150 million per year over five-year period. Yet another program, the Global Centers of Excellence initiative begun in 2007, funded an additional 50 to 75 universities in five new fields every five years (Salmi 2009). Many of these efforts focused on the sciences, although literature and some social sciences were also included. In general, this centrally directed effort to raise the quantity and quality of research in Japanese universities and institutes had several objectives:

- Invite World Class researchers to join faculty in select universities.
- Involve doctoral-level students in joining research teams.
- Financially support such young researchers as research assistants and postdoctoral scholars.
- Increase international collaborative linkages with world-class (e.g., highly ranked) universities.
- Conduct international symposia and workshops.
- Upgrade research equipment.
- Increase research space.
- Establish laboratories overseas.
- Generally take measures to promote R&D (Shinohara 2002).

Then in 2007, Ministry of Education (MEXT) launched the World Premier International Research Center Initiative (WPI) as a further effort to meet world research standards and "...position Japan within the global flow of intellectual mobility." The stated goal for this research improvement effort was to

> provide concentrated support for projects to establish and operate research centers that have at their core a group of very high-level investigators [in science and technology]. These centers are to create a research environment of a sufficiently higher standard to give them a highly visible presence within the global scientific community—that is, to create a vibrant environment that will be of strong incentive to front-line researchers around the world to want to come and work at these centers. (MEXT 2007)

These are just the most prominent of Japan's efforts to increase research quality in a global context. Again the question remains as to the success of these efforts and whether they have also had an effect on innovation rather than simply imitating a research model that is perhaps inappropriate for the Japanese system as a whole. The government ministry responsible for higher education, MEXT, and has conducted various evaluations by other agencies or companies (such as the Mitsubishi Research Institute) on these efforts and with mixed results. The funds expended to launch and maintain these programs have produced positive results for some of the centers but questionable results for others. The general critique has been that there is a lack of information about programs such as WPI and that fewer than half of the "internationally leading scientists" are aware of the program (Mitsubishi 2009).

The quality of the research that can be tracked to the COE and WPI initiatives is mixed as well, with much room for improvement. There appears to be no discernible narrowing of the quality gap between Japan and other competing nations (Mitsubishi 2009). A final evaluation of these programs will be conducted in 2017, but it is questionable whether the expenditures can be justified, given the results so far. The research gap between those few universities that received the funds and those that did not remains and has widened. There appears to be little discussion about the nature of research and the need for alternative models for the range and diversity of higher education in Japan (Mori 2013).

In the Republic of Korea, a broad program was launched in 1999 to upgrade the research profile for the twenty-first century. Called Brain Korea 21 (BK21), this effort not only focused on the top research universities but also singled out selective regional HEIs, impacting about 50 universities overall. The Korea case is instructive because it demonstrates what a middle-income nation can accomplish in seeking to raise its research standards to approximate those of the leading world universities. The principal vehicle for this effort was BK21. With over US $ 1.2 billion invested over seven years, BK 21 focused on raising the quality of graduate students rather than making a direct investment in faculty research per se. Nevertheless, this investment had a significant impact on the research environment for Korea's top universities. The role of the national government in funding research was central: in 2003, 76 percent of all R&D funds came from the government.

Seoul National University, as the once traditional and now increasingly like the New Flagship University, has been the natural leader in Korea, influencing other universities. "Most universities in Korea are aspiring to become flagship universities like SNU," explains Kim Ki Seok, seeking to become the "Korean Harvard, or Korean 'Todai' [University of Tokyo]" (Kim 2007, p. 125). The imitative impulse is prevalent in Korean higher education, including a revised tenure and promotion system, and a related reward structure built on the publish-or-perish model. Kim (2007) provides an interesting discussion of the limits of this structure, the overreliance on the SCI index in evaluating research, and comparisons between Korea and Harvard, the University of Tokyo, and the University of California at Los Angeles, demonstrating how SNU has come close to matching the research prowess of these three comparison institutions. Kim notes, however, the limits of these quantitative approaches to measuring the quality of research and little is said about whether an "innovative" or creative outcome has been achieved that serves national as well as international goals and distinguishes between Flagship and WCU missions.

A number of evaluations on the impact of BK21 on Korean university research quality and capacity have been completed or are in progress (Shin 2009a; 2009b; Seong et al. 2008). There is general agreement that according to a variety of metrics, Korean research productivity since the implementation of BK21 has increased (as measured by the number of scholarly research articles, books, and other research outputs). But at most, these increases only kept pace with other developing or developed economies and, in some cases, such as China, fell behind their competitors. There was no narrowing of the research gap between Korean universities and those of the West, particularly the United States. A RAND study critiqued most of the other evaluations as well as structural impediments in Korean universities to increasing research innovation and capacity. This report proposes a new evaluation model to determine the effectiveness and impact of BK21. At the most, one could suggest that BK21 was very effective in bumping Korea R&D in selected universities to a new level, but given the investment and the continuing gap that exists among other advanced systems, one can wonder if it was worth the investment or if the program was too narrowly constructed toward the goal of achieving WCU status. The elite nature of the effort did not positively impact the bulk of Korean four-year universities, other than to set up a research goal not likely to be achieved by most of them (Shin 2009b).

Other universities in the region have focused on carving out a particular niche in which to excel and innovate yet largely focus on research output. Recognizing that it is unrealistic to be "good at everything," Hong Kong University, the Hong Kong University of Science and Technology (HKUST), and National University of Singapore (NUS) have deployed strategies to excel in selected areas. Recruiting the best faculty both locally and from abroad, as HKU and NSU have done, has resulted in a faculty mix that is very diverse and who "think in different ways," according to Barry Halliwell, deputy president of NUS (Thomas 2013). Building a research niche that is related to local circumstances is another such strategy. HKUST has achieved high marks from the Quacquarelli Symonds (QS) rankings because of its research program that focuses on under researched areas in the local region, its relatively new history as a university (1991), and "a hunger to be better" (Thomas 2013). These institutions appear to be pursuing strategies more in line with the missions of flagship universities, in that they are imitative (but in highly selective ways), innovative, and locally relevant.

A final look at the research environment in India demonstrates the limits of an imitative model of higher education with respect to research, and perhaps makes the case for finding new approaches to what constitutes research, allowing for some success in building an innovative university. India's colonial legacy has left it with a system of research best described by Jayaram as "retailing knowledge" (Jayaram 2007). This has left India with a research system far behind other advanced countries, both in quality and in quantity of research productivity. There is a hard distinction between teaching and research, which disconnects graduate students from the research world and provides disincentives for faculty to maintain a research program beyond their dissertation. Research remains the purview of institutes, which are decoupled from universities and thus disconnected from graduate students. So while India does not imitate the dominant model of research, it has not developed any real alternative either. India in some respects illustrates the difficulty of linking research appropriately with higher education, with the intent of creating new and innovative approaches to higher education and relevant research.

On the other hand, India has an opportunity to try new approaches to this linkage rather than be trapped in the race to develop "World Class" higher education based on the dominant model. Indiresan (2007) in some respects makes the same point by suggesting that if India has the "will" (a big "if") to establish an innovative research university, it can do so "without having to face opposition from entrenched vested interests" (p. 118). While China, Japan, and Korea are clearly on a path to imitate the dominant model of the research university, India may offer a surprise by developing a new and innovative research university, possibly at odds with current ranking regimes.

This opportunity may be realized due to the unlikely but incredibly fortunate discovery of US$22 billion in the basement of the Sree Padmanabhaswamy Temple in the capital of the state of Kerala. Inasmuch as India does not currently possess anything approaching what might be called a WCU, here is an opportunity to build an institution where money is clearly not an objective (Altbach 2012). Accomplishing this outcome, however, would require building a university that is completely out of the context of the Indian higher education experience: a governance model that is independent of the Indian government, has an independent board of trustees, isolated from government bureaucracy and capricious private-sector for-profit investors. Such a university would be both international and local-regional (thus satisfying one major criteria of the Flagship model), and it would follow a meritocratic reward structure for both students and faculty (Altbach 2012). It is unknown as of this writing whether this project has begun or is just an idea. In any case, it offers an important lesson about what a difficult and tremendous task it would be to suddenly "construct" a WCU in a setting that has not thus far nurtured the basic fundamentals for such a venture. Questions about sustainability, relevance, and quality abound and there is a hint that a focus on the Flagship model would be much more feasible and likely to succeed.

Nalanda International University is another example in India. With significant investments, high cultural status, and international linkages working in its favor, this project has much going for it, but as Altbach points out, its rural location (Bihar) and its "development" focus will make it difficult to progress in the rankings competition (Altbach 2013). One option would be to "forget about the rankings." But the risk is the alienation of public and private funding sources, which place high value on these metrics (Altbach 2013, p. 3). Again, this is a work in progress meriting close observation in the future.

Another interesting development suggests that a WCU has been formed quickly by leveraging both funding and a history of R&D. It is the recent formation of the University of Chinese Academy of Sciences (UCAS) (Zha and Zhou 2013). Described as having been "born with a silver spoon," UCAS was formed in 2012 by transforming the Graduate School of the Chinese Academy of Sciences into a university, automatically boasting a faculty, doctoral supervisors, and doctoral students exceeding those of both Peking University and Tsinghua University and conferring more doctoral degrees than the most productive universities in the United States. As Zha and Zhou note, "China seems to have had a world class university overnight" (Zha and Zhou 2013, p. 2). This follows a trend where since 2011 universities have gradually been taking on significant research roles, the primary goal of which is to achieve WCU status. Distributing CAS's various research units, laboratories, and faculty to higher education would provide a significant boost to China's university system and its quest to attain WCU status.

Is this "quick fix" through restructuring and fund allocation a reliable method of attaining WCU status? What does it mean for the idea of the New Flagship University advocated in this volume? On the face of it, the predicament remains of a disproportionate share of the budget and curriculum targeting S&T, rather than providing a comprehensive approach to the great variety of activities and purposes of universities, including the interplay of their teaching and learning at both the undergraduate and graduate levels, knowledge production, and a public service role in the societies they are intended to serve.

Challenging the WCU Paradigm

While the pursuit of improved rankings and a claim to WCU status described continues as seemingly the primary goal for most universities in the Asian Pacific region, there has been a growing debate about the value and feasibility of this vision. Alternative ways are being discussed that challenge and critique this model and suggest other more creative ways to look at the role of R&D and scholarship in higher education. Here I will outline some of the features of that debate and, returning the reader to the idea of the New Flagship University as an alternative, reflect on its applicability and nuances.

It has been difficult for universities in the region to avoid the temptation to be imitative rather than innovative. The strategy of imitation (largely of US and Western European higher education, and focused largely on research productivity) has in some respects limited the opportunities for innovation, inasmuch as imitation is costly, based on "ladder climbing," and often driven by rankings, rather than by new ideas. Striving for WCU status, high rankings, the desire to strive toward the "emerging global model" (EGM), and other policy goals that rely on what Deem, Mok, and Lucas (2008) call "copying," are typical of such strategies. This is especially true of research, which in the United States carries with it a somewhat unique history. The predominant role of government-funded research through large competitive contracts (such as the National Science Foundation, NASA, and others), firmly established this Federal model that characterized the research efforts initially of universities such as Harvard, MIT, and Cal Tech, and then was followed by other universities in the United States. It was heavily science oriented, discovery based, and while playing a positive role in those disciplines it also created a funding divide among other disciplines (social science and humanities), and set the standard for evaluation of faculty, departments, centers, programs, institutes, and the university itself. The question here is, Is this model appropriate or even feasible for universities in other national settings?

The gradual increase in dominance and stature of the research mission of universities also impacted the reward structure at most research-intensive universities, so that faculty, reflecting the explosion in knowledge and movement toward large research teams in the sciences and engineering, have focused less on the classroom and more on research productivity, including grant writing, raising funds for their research, running research labs, scholarly publications, and other research-related activities. On the other hand, there has been a trend in some national settings (e.g., the United States) to incorporate undergraduate learning with research. While the shift away from traditional classroom instruction first occurred in sciences and engineering, it was not long before this became the evaluative model for all disciplines. If university faculty are naturally drawn toward research and away from their traditional classroom teaching role, there are implications for universities in the Asian Pacific region. Is it possible to truly strike a balance between teaching and research in the modern university, or is the "research model" so prevalent in the United States and elsewhere being blindly imitated globally? This is a "predicament" facing Asian higher education, accentuated by the pursuit of the WCUs model. The New Flagship model partially addresses this by seeking a balance, including a healthy interplay of teaching and research, and public service.

One of the contradictions in imitating this research model is that, in most settings in the Asia Pacific region, as has been shown elsewhere, is that rapid increases in enrollment and related course workload are coupled with high expectations for research, fund-raising, and publication prowess. As faculty are drawn away from teaching, increasing numbers of students are left without benefitting from the presence of the very faculty they came to encounter; they are often left with junior faculty or part-time faculty teaching the basic courses. As faculty sort themselves out along the research axis (those who are successful and those who are not), another divide appears, as those faculty less able as researchers pick up the teaching load or are simply let go through the tenure process. Again, this is a model that may not be the most productive for many universities and may in fact limit the possibilities of becoming an "innovative" university. A reward structure that hinges largely on being published in the "best journals" increasingly leaves many behind in the race to become a top-ranked university, especially as the race becomes global, with an increased number of faculty seeking this status, and a fairly stable limited number of elite journals. Another divide thus appears if this becomes the imitative model, still dominated by the West.

This brings us back to the concept of the New Flagship University in the Asia region. There is place for both Flagship ideals and practices and the desire for the ranking-focused WCU model to coexist. As Douglass argues in Part I, the Flagship model can be a route to WCU status, but the WCU model as it now stands is not a model to be a Flagship University. Because of the rate of change in higher education in the Asian region, it is likely we cannot safely reach any firm conclusions about this. Indeed, a modest informal survey of some of the best academic leaders in higher education in the East Asia region generated mixed results.[2] Most interviewees agreed that there is indeed a lively debate on role and mission of Flagship Universities and WCUs. In most cases, however, it is clear that they are referencing older notions of a Flagship rather than the transformed and ambitious university presented in this book. However, the responses to this dilemma were mixed. In Hong Kong this issue has been little discussed, perhaps due to the scale of the higher education segment, and in Korea this debate is considered somewhat "old news." When pressed as to whether there is a significant difference between these two concepts, it was agreed that there is a difference, but that semantic differences with respect to these terms also exist.

In China and Taiwan more use is made of the term "leading" (*yi liu*, which means "first rate") university, rather than Flagship University. A *yi liu* is not necessarily a WCU. The Flagship University might also have little interest in rankings, which is not true for those seeking to become WCUs. Also, Flagship Universities have more defined regional boundaries and missions than do WCUs, and finally, WCU is thought to be a relatively recent phenomenon stimulated in part by an imitative desire to compete with the West. In Japan, reference is made to the former imperial universities as comprising the Flagship category including both public and private institutions (e.g., Keio and Waseda), noting that the difference between the two types has to do with their mission, functions, and funding. The WCUs, on the other hand, are typically focused much more on research. Similar remarks were made in the survey with respect to Korean higher education.

With regard to the ranking debate, there was near unanimity among the panel of experts. All agreed that rankings should *not* be of primary importance to university administrators, faculty, and other stakeholders, even though ministries support the practice. At the most, rankings should be utilized for providing some benchmarking for stakeholders but not for providing good measures on the quality of universities. Although there was also general agreement that rankings were not going to disappear from the higher education landscape, the motivation promoting and supporting such exercises ranged from self-interested officials and administrators (Korea), to pressure from industry (China, Korea, and Taiwan), and to useful benchmarking and market differentiation (Japan, Taiwan, Hong Kong, and China).

Finally, in response to the question of financial incentives (excellence programs of one sort or another) for achieving WCU status or higher rankings, the panel generally agreed that funds focused on student support (Korea) or on faculty development can be a valuable resource, but if they are focused on vague concepts such as internationalization (Japan), or commercialized outcomes (China), the likely result will be a loss of academic freedom or simply "excellence without a soul" (Japan and China).

Thus, the "predicament" for higher education in many settings in Asia remains. There are no easy "solutions" to the contradictions that emerge from the Asian experience in the past two decades or more. The ecology of higher education in that region is in a state of rapid change and transformation. By continually reexamining the costs and benefits of massification, the respective roles of historically grounded Flagship Universities, the new quest for WCU status and the limitations of ranking regimes, policy makers in Asia can perhaps begin to see a way forward toward "resolving" these predicaments and building a higher education system that serves, and is competitive for, both international and domestic needs.

NOTES

1. Hershock P. (2007). Hershock distinguishes between "problems" that can be solved, and "predicaments" that can only be *resolved*. Predicaments more closely describe the challenges facing HEIs as they encounter massification, rankings, and the quest for WCU status in a context of well-established Flagship HEIs—long-held assumptions about the purposes of HE need to be rethought; there are no easy solutions.
2. A panel of HE experts in the region was surveyed to discuss six basic issues (see appendix 1). The panel consisted of Professors Sheng-ju Chan (National

Chung Cheng University, Taiwan), Kan Yue (Zhejiang University China), Yuto Kitamura (Tokyo University, Japan), Ma Wanhua (Peking University, China), Ka Ho Mok (Hong Kong Institute of Education, Hong Kong), and Jung Cheol Shin (Seoul National University).

REFERENCES

Altbach, Philip G. 2013. "Nalanda Redux: Is a World-Class University Possible in Rural Bihar." *International Higher Education,* no. 70 (Winter): 1–3.

Altbach, Philip G. 2012. "Temples and World-Class Universities." *International Higher Education,* no. 67 (Spring): 25–26.

Altbach, Philip G. 2010. "Access Means Inequality." *International Higher Education,* no. 61.

Altbach, Philip G. and Balan, Jorge, eds. 2007. *Transforming Research Universities in Asia and Latin America: World Class Worldwide.* Baltimore, MD: Johns Hopkins University Press.

Arrow, Kenneth J. 1993. "Excellence and Equity in Higher Education." *Education Economics* 1, no. 1: 5–12.

Baum, Sandy. 2014. "Higher Education Earnings Premium: Value, Variation and Trends. The Urban Institute." Available at: www.urban.org/Uploaded PDF/413033-Higher-Education-Earnings-Premium-Value-Variation-and-Trends .pdf. Accessed on June 6, 2014.

Bettinger, Eric P. and Terry Long, Bridget. 2009. "Addressing the Needs of Under-Prepared Students in Higher Education: Does College Remediation Work?" *Journal of Human Resources, University of Wisconsin Press,* 44, no. 3.

Calderon, Angel. 2012. "Massification Continues to Transform Higher Education." *University World News,* September 2, 2012, Issue No. 237. Available at: www .universityworldnews.com/article.php?story=20120831155341147. Accessed on June 7, 2014.

Chapman, David W. 2009. "Higher Education Faculty in East Asia." World Bank. Available at: www.siteresources.worldbank.org/INTEASTASIAPACIFIC /Resources/EastAsia-HigherEducationFaculty.pdf. Accessed on June 7, 2014.

Chen Xuefei. 2006. "Ideal Orientation Policy-Making: Analysis of the 985 Process," *Peking University Education Review,* 4, no. 1 (January): 145–157.

Deem, Rosemary, Mok, Ka Ho, and Lucas, Lisa. 2008. "Transforming Higher Education in Whose Image? Exploring the Concept of the 'World Class' University in Europe and Asia." *Higher Education Policy* 21: 83–97.

Dill, David. 2007. "Quality Assurance in Higher Education: Practices and Issues." In *The 3rd International Encyclopedia of Education,* edited by Barry McGraw, Eva Baker, Penelope P. Peterson. Elsevier Publications.

Dore, R. 1997. *The Diploma Disease: Education, Qualification and Development.* New York: Institute of Education.

Douglass, John Aubrey. 2000. *The California Idea and American Higher Education.* Stanford: Stanford University Press.

Facts and Details. 2013. "Chinese Universities: Professors, Student Life and Problems," www.factsanddetails.com/china/cat13/sub82/item337.html.

Hawkins John N. and Neubauer, Deane. 2014. "The Many Faces of Asia Pacific Higher Education in the Era of Massification," Concept paper for Senior Seminar held in Hong Kong, Hong Kong Institute of Education, October 2014.

Hawkins, John N. 2014. "Globalization, Internationalization, and Asian Educational Hubs: Do We Need Some New Metaphors?" In *Rethinking Globalization and Internationalization in Higher Education*, edited by Reiko Yamada. Kyoto: Doshisha Press.

Hawkins, John N. 2013. "Education in the Asia-Pacific Region: Some Enduring Challenges." In *Comparative Education: The Dialectic of the Global and the Local*, edited by Robert Arnove, Carlos A. Torres, and Stephan Franz. 341–368. New York: Rowman & Littlefield Publishers.

Hershock, Peter. 2007. "Education and Alleviating Poverty: Educating for Equity and Diversity." In *Changing Education: Leadership, Innovation and Development in a Globalizing Asia Pacific*, edited by Peter Hershock, Mark Mason, John N. Hawkins. Hong Kong: Springer/CERC.

Indiresan P. V. 2007. "Prospects for World-Class Research Universities in India." In *Transforming Research Universities*, edited by Philip G. Altbach and Jorge Balan.

Jayaram N. 2007. "Beyond Retailing Knowledge." In *Transforming Research Universities*, edited by Philip G. Altbach and Jorge Balan.

Jiang Youguo. 2011. "The Role of Private Education in the Chinese Higher Education System." *International perspectives on Education and Society*, 15: 377–400.

Kim K. S. 2007. "The Making of a World-Class University at the Periphery." In *Transforming Research Universities*, edited by Philip G. Altbach and Jorge Balan.

Lee, Jeongwoo. 2014. "Potential Reasons of Consistent Stratification in Tertiary Education Participation in Korea and Japan." Paper presented at UCLA conference on education and development in Asia, June 2014.

Liu, Niancai. 2011. "The Phenomenon of Academic Ranking of World Universities Model: Future Directions." In Deane Neubauer and John N. Hawkins 2011.

Liu Niancai. 2009. "The Story of Academic Ranking of World Universities." *International Higher Education*, no. 54 (Winter): 2–3.

Marginson, Simon. 2014. "University Rankings and Social Science," *European Journal of Education,* 49, no. 1: 45–59.

Marginson, Simon and Sawir, Erlenawati. 2005. "Interrogating Global Flows in Higher Education." *Globalisation, Societies and Education*, 3, no. 3 (November): 281–309.

MEXT, 2007. *World Premier International Research Center (WPI) Initiative.* www.mext.go.jp/english/research_promotion. Accessed January 8, 2015.

Micklethwait, John and Wooldridge, Adrian. 2014. *The Fourth Revolution: The Global Race to Reinvent the State.* New York: Penguin Press.

Minzner, C. 2013. "China's Higher Education Bubble," *China File.* www.china-file.com/chinas-higher-education-bubble. Accessed on December 19, 2013.

Mitsubishi. 2009. *Report on the Results of the Questionnaire of WPI Initiative.* Tokyo: Mitsubishi Corporation.

Mok, K. H. 2011. "Enhancing Quality of Higher Education: Approaches, Strategies and Challenges for Hong Kong." In *Quality in Higher Education: Identifying, Developing and Sustaining Best Practices in the APEC Region,* edited by Deane Neaubauer and John N. Hawkins. Singapore: APEC Secretariat.

Mori, Rie. 2013. Correspondence with Professor Rie Mori, National Institute for Academic Degrees and University Evaluation.

Neubauer, Deane and Hawkins, John N., eds. 2011. *Quality in Higher Education: Identifying, Developing and Sustaining Best Practices in the APEC Region.* Singapore: APEC Secretariat.

Neubauer, Deane. 2011. "How Might University Rankings Contribute to Quality Assurance Endeavors?" In *Quality in Higher Education: Identifying, Developing and Sustaining Best Practices in the APEC Region,* edited by Neubauer and Hawkins.

National Science Foundation. 2007. *Asia's Rising Science and Technology Strength: Comparative Indicators for Asia, the European Union and the United States.* Arlington, VA: National Science Foundation, Division of Science Resources Statistics.

Quinterno, John and Viany Orozco. 2012. *The Great Cost Shift: How Higher Education Cuts Undermine the Future Middle Class.* Demos, March. www.demos.org/sites/default/files/publications/TheGreatCostShift_Demos_0.pdf. Accessed on June 7, 2014.

Salmi, Jamil. 2009. *The Challenge of Establishing World-Class Universities.* Washington DC: The World Bank.

Schultz, T. W., 1988. "On Investing in Specialised Human Capital to Attain Increasing Returns." In *The State of Development Economics: Progress and Perspectives,* edited by G. Ranis and T. P. Schultz. 339–52. Oxford: Basil Blackwell.

Schultz, Theodore W. 1972. "Optimal Investment in College Instruction: Equity and Efficiency." *Journal of Political Economy* 80 (May/June): S2–S30.

Seong, S., Popper, S., Goldman, C., and Evans, D. 2008. *Brain Korea 21, Phase II A New Evaluation Model.* Santa Monica CA: RAND Education.

Shin Jung Cheol. 2009a. "Building World-Class Research University: the Brain Korea 21 Project." *Higher Education* 58: 669–688.

Shin Jung Cheol. 2009b. "Classifying Research Universities in Korea: A Performance Based Approach." *Higher Education* 57: 247–266.

Shinohara, Kazuko. 2002. "Toyoma Plan—Center of Excellence Program for the 21st Century." *National Science Foundation Tokyo Regional Office.* Tokyo: Japan.

Simon, Dennis and Cong Cao. 2009. *China's Emerging Technological Edge: Assessing the Role of High-End Talent.* Cambridge, UK: Cambridge University Press.

Smit, R. 2012. "Towards a Clearer Understanding of Student Disadvantage in Higher Education: Problematising Deficit Thinking." *Higher Education Research & Development* 31, no. 3: 369.

Thomas K. 2013. "Scientific Research: How Asia Carved Its Niche." *The Guardian* (January 17).

"Tremors in China." June 11, 2014. *Higher Education Strategies Associates.* www .higheredstrategy.com. Accessed on June 11, 2014.

Trow, Martin. 2005. "Reflections on the Transition from Elite to Mass to Universal Access in Modern Societies since WWII." In *International Handbook of Higher Education*, edited by James Forest and Philip Altbach. New York: Springer Press.

Trow, Martin. 1973. *Problems in the Transition from Elite to Mass Education.* Berkeley, CA: Carnegie Commission on Higher Education.

Wang, Xiaoyan and Liu, Jian. 2011. "China: Massification Has Increased Inequalities," July 10, 2011. www.universityworldnews.com.

Zha, Q. and Zhou, G. 2013. "The Founding of University of Chinese Academy of Sciences." *International Higher Education* no. 73 (Fall): 1–5.

Zha, Qiong. 2011. "China's Move to Mass Higher Education in a Comparative Perspective." *Compare* 41, no. 6: 751–768.

Zhu, Wenjun and Liu, Niancai. 2009. "Research Performance of Chinese Research Universities: a Scientometric Study." *Journal of Higher Education* 30, no. 2: 30–35 (in Chinese).

Appendix to Chapter 5

Brief Survey Questions for Higher Education Experts in Asia

Introduction: There are currently complex national policy debates regarding the interplay between the quest for achieving World Class University status, high-level rankings in one or more of the ranking regimes, and the idea of the Flagship University.

1. Is this debate occurring in your country's HE community?
2. As an expert in HE do you see a difference between the WCU idea and the idea of the Flagship University?
3. If so, what would be the key differences (list two or three)?
4. Achieving high-level rankings is understandable, but do you think this should be a primary mission of HE in your country?
5. If so, why? What are the primary motivations of high rankings?
6. If your government has engaged in financial incentives for some sort of "excellence" program (i.e., centers of excellence and centers of global excellence), do you believe the expenditures have been worthwhile?

Please return your comments to: John N. Hawkins, Professor Emeritus, UCLA, at Hawkins@gseis.ucla.edu

Chapter 6

Latin American Flagship Universities: From Early Notions of State Building to Seeking a Larger Role in Society

Andrés Bernasconi and Daniela Véliz Calderón

Government ministries and other stakeholders are increasingly expecting and demanding that their national universities perform functions that transcend their traditional sense of purpose, including a role in innovation and economic development, the promotion of social equality, and fostering environmental sustainability. Some universities around the world have long engaged in this broad mission, including the great public universities in the United States; but for many other leading national universities, this so-called third mission is a relatively new concept. To date, efforts to become more engaged in the socioeconomic needs of nations simply mimic the more robust initiatives of some of the world's leading universities (DiMaggio and Powell 1983), or simply incorporate well-meaning rhetoric aimed at influential constituents inside the university or prominent stakeholders outside.

While this is generally true for leading universities in Latin American, there is a strong tradition that these institutions should help lead nation-building and social cohesion (Levy 1986, 1994; Schwartzman 1991). Historically, in developing countries and in nations on the periphery of the world economy, leading universities have played a central role in the political and juridical organization of the state. This has included the education of professional and bureaucratic elites and the configuration and transmission of a national identity. Perhaps as a consequence of the dearth of solid institutions in most domains of social life, and the need to "invent" traditions (Hobsbawm and Ranger 1983, Anderson 1991) to promote national cohesion and a shared identity, new countries have had a tendency to expect a lot from their universities. They have served (or have claimed to serve, or been required to fulfill) a predominant role in the creation of state bureaucracies, the organization of national systems of education, the adaptation of agricultural technologies, the legitimation of political institutions, the configuration of professions, and the like (Levy 1986). In the case of Latin America, scholars have argued that universities have been central in creating appropriate conditions for the expansion and consolidation of the state, and in its intellectual and social legitimation (Ordorika and Pusser 2006, Serrano 1994).

Frequently, the leaders of Latin American universities refer to this role as the "social mission" of the university, one that expands well beyond research, teaching, or public service, to encompass processes of socialization, democratization, and modernization. Hence, the notion of the "national" university—a public, usually large, and highly autonomous typically not more than one in each country—emerged in the nineteenth century with a very clear meaning throughout Latin American.

While far-reaching notions of the mission of a university can be found elsewhere, the establishment and history of Latin America's national universities had a particularly vibrant call for transforming the societies they were to serve. In this chapter, we discuss this history of these Latin American Flagship Universities, their more recent development and expanded missions and struggles to adapt, and then contrast them with the more aspirational New Flagship University model discussed in this book. We argue that national universities remain in a leading position in their respective countries, and in that sense they exert a "Flagship" role steeped in their historical charters. However, their allegiance to a vast and elusive "social" mission, coupled with insufficient resources for science and technology, poor governance and administration, and the general ills of underdevelopment, hinder their ability to fulfill the entire set of attributes associated with that of New Flagships.

The Latin American Flagship University

Higher education systems in Latin American, as in other systems in the world, have evolved amidst a global movement of massification of higher education, shifting from elite to mass access, and requiring increasing services to the multiple needs of ever-more diverse students. The emergence in the past four decades of numerous institutions of higher education to accommodate the expansion of enrollments led to a series of criticisms over poor quality, excess privatization, educational inequality, and social and economic segmentation. In particular, the expansion of the private sector has been regarded as undermining public higher education, as private institutions veer for a legitimacy based on different attributes than those of publics, sometimes in sharp contrast to the weaknesses of the public university. For instance, privates tout their efficiency in contrast to publics' heavy bureaucracies, or their close connection to the labor markets for their graduates, as opposed to the public university "ivory tower" mindset.

In this context, there have been a number of efforts to define the purpose and characteristics of the Latin American Flagship University, largely in historical terms. Some observers have focused their attention on describing their specific characteristics (Daniels 1996, Didriksson 2002); others have concentrated mainly on the role they play in state-building, and specifically the social relations among the state, individuals, and social groups (Ordorika and Pusser 2006). In many ways, cultural traditions, economic development, and the political sphere shape social arrangements between individuals and social groups. While the state organizes institutions that express these social relations, these relations are unequal and buttress the domination of one group over the others, often inadvertently reinforcing socioeconomic inequality.

At the same time, national universities symbolize the aspirations of developing societies, with clear connections between their history and contemporary world. As universities embrace the deep aspirations of nations, these institutions exist also in the minds and hearts of the citizenry. And with high levels of autonomy, they often have afforded students and faculty some level of freedom to openly criticize society and provide an intellectual home for national political and social thought (Ordorika and Pusser 2006). In short, they serve as an important source of ideas and influence for the political transformation of many Latin American countries—many of which suffered under dictatorial regimes in a protracted processes of transformation from colonial outposts to more democratic governing systems.

While some variation exists in this model from country to country, due to different historical paths, degrees of economic development, regional rivalries within one nation, and other factors exogenous to the universities, Latin American Flagships have had similar missions and characteristics. Some founded in colonial times, most after independence, these public institutions also have been described as having relatively high levels of autonomy from government (Bernasconi 2013b); they are the most visible universities in their countries because of the breadth of social demands they seek to serve, covering a broad range of disciplines from science and technology to social sciences and humanities, and are complex and decentralized organizations. They account for most of the research published in Latin America and have the highest concentration of graduate programs. Because they are public and autonomous, and free or almost free of charge to students, they consume the greatest share of the national budgets for higher education. Lastly, they often conserve a vast heritage of works of art, patrimonial buildings, bibliographic treasures, and music and dance traditions (Didriksson 2002).

They include very large universities with over 200,000 students, such as Universidad de Buenos Aires and Universidad Nacional Autónoma de México, both pinnacles of the public higher education sector in their countries. They also include smaller institutions, in terms of enrollment, that are also the sole public universities in their countries, such as Universidad de El Salvador, Universidad Nacional Autónoma de Honduras, Universidad de la República in Uruguay, Universidad de San Carlos in Guatemala, and Universidad Autónoma de Santo Domingo in the Dominican Republic.

In Nicaragua and Panama, the national universities are the premier institutions while sharing the higher education market with other specialized technical universities focused on fields such as engineering and agriculture. The Universidad de Chile exists today as an institutional space crowded with many other public and private universities, but retains its distinction as the first university in the Chilean republic. Similarly, Colombia has the Universidad Nacional, and Venezuela the Universidad Central, occupying analogous positions of prestige, as does the Universidad de Costa Rica. Universidad San Marcos in Peru, although steadily losing status due to politicization and poor governance and management, remains respected as the senior university in Peru, among the oldest in the region, founded in the sixteenth century.

Ecuador and Bolivia can be singled out as exceptions. Both countries have several public universities roughly equal in stature. Perhaps coincidentally, these are nations with deep-seated regional enmities between the high- and the lowlands. This makes it hard for either party to recognize the primacy of the other, even in matters such as this one. Brazil is an exception too, but of a different kind. While the most lauded universities are those in the state of Sao Paulo, they are not federal universities, but entities of the State of Sao Paulo. Hence, they are technically not national insitutions which include a dozen federal universities spread throughout the different Brazilian states. However, if the State of Sao Paulo were a country, it would be the third largest in Latin America in terms of population and the size of its economy. In light of this, one could think of the Universidade de Sao Paulo as the national university of this grand state.

To explore the role of leading national universities, we studied the institutional mission statements and statutes of many of the universities noted previously: including the Universidad de Buenos Aires, Universidad Nacional Autónoma de México, Universidad de El Salvador, Universidad Nacional Autónoma de Honduras, Universidad de la República in Uruguay, Universidad de San Carlos in Guatemala, Universidad Autónoma de Santo Domingo, Universidad de Chile, and Universidad San Marcos. We used document-content analysis techniques, primarily through an inductive approach to the analysis, which was guided by various categories (Merriam 1998)—specifically, social mission and national identity.

These mission statements clearly specified the conventional characteristics expected of consolidated universities, such as autonomy, public character, research orientation, and leadership in the system. They also reflect the extended social role we associate with the national university. For example, most of the statements emphasize the role that the university in addressing "national problems." As an illustration, we translated part of the bylaws of the Universidad de Buenos Aires (established in 1821).[1]

> The Universidad de Buenos Aires is a public corporation whose purpose is the promotion, dissemination and preservation of culture. It serves this purpose in direct and permanent contact with the universal thought and pays particular attention to Argentina's problems.[2]

In the same way, the Universidad de San Carlos in Guatemala (established in 1676) states in its current mission statement:

> In its capacity as the sole state university, it is its exclusive role to direct, organize and develop higher education in the state and state education, and the dissemination of culture in all its manifestations. It will promote, by all means available, research in all fields of human knowledge, and cooperate in the study and solution of national problems.[3]

Perhaps even more intriguing is the role that universities claim to have on the configuration of the national identity through the promotion of an intellectual and cultural heritage. Indeed, several statements emphasized the responsibility the institution has regarding the identity of their respective countries. For example, statutes passed in 2006 regarding the Universidad de Chile state, "It is the responsibility of the University to contribute to the development of the cultural heritage and national identity and the improvement of the educational system of the country."[4] The 1910 statutes establishing the Universidad Nacional Autónoma de México provide a similar announcement of purpose:

> The Universidad Nacional Autónoma de México is a decentralized public corporation of the state endowed with full legal capacity and whose purpose is to provide higher education to train professionals, researchers, academics and technicians useful to society; organize and conduct research primarily on national conditions and problems, and spread as widely as possible the benefits of culture.[5]

The connections among the knowledge-related functions of the university, the cultural heritage of the country, and the solution to national problems emerge as defining characteristics of these national universities. In this sense, the universities see national identity and social advancement as dependent on their contributions to the common good.

A New Flagship in Latin America?

Among the characteristics of New Flagship Universities discussed in this book, leading national universities in Latin American should have highly selective admission processes; most faculty should hold doctoral degrees and be active in cutting-edge research; they should have a relatively high percentage of graduate enrollments and provide a nurturing environment for doctoral students; and they should seek to educate talented leaders, usually for the regional or national population they serve, as well as for engaging with the larger world. In terms of governance, they should be highly autonomous and mostly publicly funded; and they are constantly looking for self-improvement through their own internal mechanisms for quality assurance.

Yet, there are significant differences in the context and current capabilities of the leading Latin American universities that pose challenges for their further maturation. For one, comprehensive research universities are hard to find in developing countries, and in particular in Latin America. Perhaps two or three universities in Brazil could be described as comprehensive in this way. As Philip Altbach (2007) has noted, for developing countries to join the ranks of advanced economies, research universities with comprehensive programs are a prerequisite. They provide a passage to the broader world of science, technology, and scholarship. Governments and university leaders in Latin America seem to grasp this, and there is indeed a small but growing subset of public universities evolving to such a profile, but very slowly.

And while many leading Latin American universities share some of the attributes of the New Flagship model, they come up short in many others, for reasons external and internal to the institution (Castro and Levy 2000). Adequate funding is a major roadblock. The New Flagship model provides concepts, standards, policies, and procedures and outlines the management capacity necessary for meeting the larger needs of society. But these require resources look immense in the confines of the educational budgets of developing countries (Altbach 2011). High-quality universities are expensive, and they need substantial and permanent public support to operate. From an institutional point of view, the scarcity of public and private resources in Latin America limits the maturation of these institutions that often depend solely on national public funding.

Beyond general operating funding for universities, Latin America has lagged in its funding for research and development. Investment in R&D is the key to promoting competitiveness, productivity, and long-term growth. With the exception of Brazil (and specifically the State of Sao Paulo), Latin American countries lag behind the most advanced economies and rapidly emerging economies like those in China, Israel, and South Korea. The Latin America and Caribbean region accounts for only 3.2 percent of the world's investment in R&D (RICYT 2013, p. 15), of which 63 percent comes from Brazil alone (RICYT 2013, p. 12). It is no coincidence, then, that no Latin American country appears in the first quintile in the Global Competitiveness Reports (Brunner and Ferrada 2011, p. 59). The development of higher education in the region is thus limited by a lack of investment in knowledge creation and application. Without strong investment in the capacity for innovation through knowledge creation and application, the probability of the region's higher education system, or a few national universities, achieving international status via rankings or other frameworks for determining prestige, is unlikely.

At the same time, it is difficult to make the case for further investment in research and advanced education when Latin America still faces the challenge of reducing poverty and meeting basic human needs. To be sure, progress has been made. In 1990, the incidence of poverty among Latin America's population was 48.4 percent, half of which was extreme poverty. In 2013, poverty had fallen to 27.9 percent, one-third of which was at the extreme level (CEPAL 2013, p. 18). In the long run, only the increased investment in human capital and workforce productivity brought about by more and better education, along with technological advances, all of which depend upon the capacity of universities, will usher in greater prosperity in developing societies. This has elevated the role of universities as an investment by most Latin American governments. But the realities of the pressing needs for health care, food, and shelter simply trump the efforts to increase funding for higher education to the levels needed to support top research universities.

Funding support is not the only problem separating Latin American national universities from the level of research performance and advanced training for research required of Flagship Universities. The PhD degree is still not the standard qualification for faculty, with large numbers of senior faculty hired 40 or 30 years ago at a time when the doctorate was quite exceptional outside of the fields of the natural sciences. Only a handful of universities in the region have graduate enrollments to rival their figures for undergraduate students.

Finally, a systematic quest for continuous quality improvement is alien to the ethos of governance and management at most Latin American universities. For example, university administrators are elected at every level (department, school, and university) by the faculty, with a minority vote by students and administrative staff. All key academic and economic decisions remain entrusted to university councils composed of several dozens of faculty, as well as students and administrative staff, operating under near-parliamentary political procedures of agenda setting, coalition building, deliberation, negotiation, and vote. The result is that most efforts at institutional reform never emerge or are implemented (Bernasconi 2008, 2013b).

Rankings as a Source of Comparative Positioning

While the leading universities in Latin America are the most prestigious institutions in their respective countries, they are still far from the level of performance captured in the top echelons of the research-based international rankings. Not surprisingly, global university rankings are customarily met with skepticism by the academic leaders and faculty. They argue that rankings are biased against universities that, like those in Latin America, do not take research as their sole, or even their main, mission, but are engaged instead in nation building, cultural construction, and political transformation of their countries (Balán 2012; Bernasconi 2013a).

There is some merit to this argument rankings are not "fair" to many regions in the world. Yet we live in the age of globalization. And globalization generates international awareness. When national universities do not do well in global rankings, academics recognize that they are not competitive in certain aspects while claiming Latin American exceptionalism. While leading universities around the globe are actively seeking ways to adopt best practices and recognize international standards of excellence and performance to integrate into an international system, competing for talented students and professors regardless of nationality, and projecting their intellectual might (and even campuses!) past national and continental boundaries, most national Latin American universities remain firmly local. Faculty and students are often more interested using their university as an instrument of political agendas then on the work of institutional self-improvement.

The Missing Drive for Change

There are a number of national Flagships—among which we can find the Universidad de Buenos Aires, the Universidad de Chile, the Universidad Nacional Autónoma de México, the Universidad Nacional de Colombia, and in Brazil the Universities of Sao Paulo, Campinas, and several of the Federal Universities—that are cosmopolitan national, and that exhibit some of the features of the New Flagship model. They stand out as the premier universities within their national systems of higher education, enroll the bulk of the best students in the country, house the best of the nation's research capabilities across a broad range of disciplines, conserve collections of cultural patrimony of national significance, maintain active international connections, and exert considerable clout in national politics. What is, then, still missing in these universities that separates them from fulfillment of the New Flagship ideal?

Lack of funding support for effective mission differentiation is the main flaw. It is enormously difficult for governments to single out one or two universities nationally for preferential funding and development support. Current governance of the national higher education in Latin American countries essentially rules out the possibility of targeted funding, as governments must deal with councils of rectors or university associations as their policy development counterparts (Bernasconi 2013a). In some countries in the region, for example, the budget for higher education is passed along to these councils or associations for them to apportion to each member campus. There is a built-in disincentive to alter the funding status quo: rectors do not dare disturb it lest they lose out in a new distribution scheme.

Governments, in turn, are reluctant to seek other funding rationales, especially those that would give more to the most consolidated universities, for these are the fewer, and the vast majority of the institutions would oppose. As a result, most baseline public funding is allocated fundamentally along the pattern of the historical distribution of funds across all public universities, loosely based on enrollments or faculty headcount. When overall funding for higher education is as distant from the standards of advanced economies as it is in Latin America, spreading the money so widely is tantamount to insuring mediocrity. Therefore, universities in the best position to meet a research and graduate education mission are left bereft of the resources to turn that mission into reality.

The main exception to this funding pattern is the research grants assigned competitively by national research agencies to individual researchers or research groups in universities. In Brazil, Mexico, Argentina, and Chile, these are an important source of differential funding for universities where research capacity is most heavily concentrated. As the budgets of these agencies expand, as they have since the 1990s, research-oriented universities have had access to resources to fuel their scientific endeavors beyond the baseline funding allocated to the university as a whole (Balán 2012).

Turning now to the internal academic cultures of universities, elements of the New Flagship *ethos* exist: a comprehensive array of programs, but without (with the exception of Brazil's elite research-intensive universities, the prime example of which is the Universidade Estadual de Campinas and the University of São Paulo) the reasonable student-to-faculty ratios, or the significant proportion of permanent faculty with doctoral degrees, or the sizable population of doctoral students, or graduation rates and expected research productivity.

Why are those elements absent? Part of the problem is size: some of these universities are too big, and too heterogeneous as a result. Quality across the various academic fields fluctuates. Doubtless, some departments or faculties within these universities would meet the productivity indicators of a New Flagship University, but the universities as a whole would not. As part of their state-building missions, they operate a vast array of activities: mass media outlets, hospitals, museums, secondary schools, professional sports teams, and they train tens of thousands of students in all professional fields. Granted, US Flagships have similar activities, if not the enrollments, but with more funding, and with a management structure that includes presidents accountable to a governing board, and with deans and other administrative staff accountable to a president. The centrifugal force in a Latin American university is massive, each part of the university marching to its own tune. This is not decentralization or federalism: it is closer to entropy.

As Jorge Balán notes, a "major stumbling block in the success-ful incorporation of research within the university remains the rela-tive ability of central administrations to manage their own resources, develop universitywide academic strategies, and establish differential rewards according to the achievement and potential for growth of dif-ferent university segments" (Balán 2012: 766). Leadership from the top is generally weak, or ineffective, and management is largely amateur, procedural, bureaucratic, and slow. There is no culture and practice of ongoing quality control and improvement. In this environment, man-agement is simply incapable of putting together a system for effective quality assurance and development. Even though national accreditation schemes have emerged in part to address the inadequacies of univer-sity performance, internal mechanisms of continued monitoring and improvement remain feeble, largely resistant to these external pressures (Lemaitre and Zenteno 2012).

University governance is, therefore, the premier challenge that rests mostly within the scope of responsibility of the institutions themselves. Latin American Flagships are still too tied to their traditions; they are loathe to entertain the kind of shifts in governance we have seen in Europe and Asia in the past 30 years. Lack of effective governance leads to stagnant faculty: with their votes, the incumbents wield the power to remain in the faculty, and those outside, better qualified, often younger, cannot break in. Academic cadres renovate very slowly, almost exclusively from retire-ment, as little accountability is demanded from professors by their elected authorities. At this pace, leading Latin American universities will reach the overall density of permanent faculty with doctoral degrees expected of a New Flagship in a generation or so. By then, the gap will continue to widen with those pursuing and defining the New Flagships model in other parts of the world.

Beyond funding inadequacies and governance and management capac-ity, the insufficient numbers of permanent faculty with doctoral degrees is another major cause of the output gap with the New Flagship model. The large student-to-faculty ratios are also a function of how institutions have developed their academic departments and hired faculty. From the outset in the nineteenth century, Latin American universities were meant to devote themselves primarily to the training of professionals for the development needs of nascent nation-states (Balán, 2013). There were no colleges of arts and sciences, as in the United States, devoted solely to the cultivation of the disciplines. All schools, even those in the sciences and the humanities, were professionally oriented. Practicing professionals who taught part-time, not scholars, educated students. A modification in this system came in the middle of last century. Some with research training entered the faculty to take charge of the academic departments in the sciences and the humanities. A division of labor ensued: researchers taught the foundation courses in the disciplines, and practicing professionals taught the applied arts. To this date, Latin American universities retain vast numbers of part-time lecturers who are active in their professions, do not have doctoral degrees, and are uninterested in research. But they have nonetheless political rights as citizens of the university, and count as professors in the faculty statistics.

Latin American national universities need to transform themselves. Governments may provide additional funding and induce policy reform and greater productivity; but the largest challenge is to create the academic culture and institutional mission outlined in the New Flagship model. In the meantime, it will remain more of a benchmark for most leading Latin American universities than a realized ideal.

Notes

1. The following excerpts have been translated from Spanish by the authors.
2. Statutes of the Universidad de Buenos Aires, at www.uba.ar/download/insti tucional/uba/9-32.pdf.
3. From the webpage of Universidad de San Carlos de Guatemala, at www.usac .edu.gt/misionvision.php.
4. Statutes of the Universidad de Chile, at www.uchile.cl/portal/presentacion /normativa-y-reglamentos/13805/estatuto-de-la-universidad-de-chile.
5. Statutes of the Universidad Nacional Autónoma de México, at www.dgae .unam.mx/normativ/legislacion/egunam.html.

References

Altbach, Philip. 2007. "Empires of Knowledge and Development." In *World Class World Wide: Transforming Research Universities in Asia and Latin America,* edited by Philip Altbach and Jorge Balán. 1–28. Baltimore, MD: Johns Hopkins University Press.

Altbach, Philip. G. 2011. "The Past, Present, and Future of the Research University." In *The Road to Academic Excellence: The Making of World-Class Research Universities,* edited by Philip G. Altbach and Jamil Salmi, 11–32. Washington, DC: The World Bank.

Anderson, Benedict. 1991. *Imagined Communities.* 2nd edition. London and New York: Verso.

Berdahl, Robert M. 1998. The Future of Flagship Universities. Convocation address presented at Texas A&M University, College Station, TX. Available online at: www.aasbi.com, accessed on 1 December 2014.

Balán, Jorge. 2012. "Research Universities in Latin America: The Challenges of Growth and Institutional Diversity." *Social Research: An International Quarterly*, 79: 741–770.

Balán, Jorge. 2013. "Introduction: Latin American Higher Education Systems in a Historical and Comparative Perspective." *Latin America's New Knowledge Economy: Higher Education, Government, and International Collaboration*, edited by Jorge Balán, vii–xx. New York: Institute for International Education.

Bernasconi, Andrés. 2008. "Is There a Latin American Model of the University?" *Comparative Education Review* 52, no. 1: 27–52.

Bernasconi, Andrés. 2013a. "Are Global Rankings Unfair to Latin American Universites?" *International Higher Education* 72: 12–13.

Bernasconi, Andrés. 2013b. "Government and University Autonomy: The Governance Structure of Latin American Public Institutions." *Latin America's New Knowledge Economy: Higher Education, Government, and International Collaboration*, edited by Jorge Balán, 1–17. New York: Institute for International Education.

Brunner, José Joaquin and Ferrada, Rocía, eds. 2011. *Educación superior en Iberoamérica: Informe 2011*. Santiago, Chile: CINDA-UNIVERSIA.

Castro, Claudio, and Levy, Daniel. 2000. *Myth, Reality and Reform. Higher Education Policy in Latin America*. Washington, DC: Inter-American Development Bank.

CEPAL, Comisión Económica para América latina y el caribe. 2013. *Panorama Social de América Latina*. Santiago: Naciones Unidas.

Daniel, John S. 1996. *Megauniversities and Knowledge Media*. London: Kogan Page.

Didriksson, Axel. 2006. Caracterización y Desarrollo de las Macrouniversidades de América Latina y el Caribe. Available online at: http://sic.conaculta.gob.mx /centrodoc_documentos/559.pdf.

DiMaggio, P. and Powell, W. 1983. "The Iron Cage Revisited: Institutional Isomorphism and Collective Rationality in Organizations Fields." *American Sociological Review* 48, no. 2: 147–160.

Hobsbawm, Eric and Ranger, Terence, eds. 1983. *The Invention of Tradition*. Cambridge: Cambridge University Press.

Lemaitre, María José, and Zenteno, María Elisa. 2012. Aseguramiento de la Calidad en Iberoamérica. Santiago de Chile: CINDA.

Levy, Daniel C. 1994. "Higher Education amid the Political-Economic Changes of the 1990s. Report of the LASA Task Force on Higher Education." *LASA Forum*, 25, no. 1 (Spring).

Levy, D. C. 1986. *Higher Education and the State in Latin America: Private Challenges to Public Dominance*. Chicago: University of Chicago Press.

Merriam, Sharan. B. 1998. *Qualitative Research and Case Study Applications in Education*. San Francisco: Jossey-Bass.

Odorika, Imanol, and Pusser, Brian. 2006. "La máxima casa de estudios: Universidad Autónoma de México as a State-Building University." In *World Class World Wide: Transforming Research Universities in Asia and Latin America*, edited by Philip Altbach and Jorge Balán, 189–215. Baltimore, MD: Johns Hopkins University Press.

RICYT, Red de Indicadores de Ciencia y Tecnología. 2013. *El estado de la ciencia 2013*. At http://www.ricyt.org/publicaciones. Consulted January 23, 2015.

Schwartzman, Simon. 1991. Latin America: Higher Education in a Lost Decade. *Prospects*, 21, no. 3: 363–373.

Serrano, Sol. 1994. *Universidad y nación. Chile en el siglo XIX*. Santiago de Chile: Editorial Universitaria.

Chapter 7

Scandinavian Flagship Universities: An Appraisal of Leading National Universities in the European Context

Bjørn Stensaker and Tatiana Fumasoli

In the immediate post-Sputnik era, Clark Kerr saw America's breed of universities as "multiversities," characterized by growing enrollment, an increasingly diversified academic community, and as the emerging driver of knowledge production and innovation (Kerr 2001: xi). This is now a widely shared vision throughout the world. Governments have provided additional funding, fueling further growth in academic programs and attracting talent. One result: the number of perceived stakeholders has increased, along with their expectations.

Many universities have been granted greater institutional autonomy to encourage them to become more strategic actors, and hence more productive and competitive in the global race for "scientific excellence." And many universities did become more strategic in their management, developing and pursuing objectives often for the first time, and becoming more entrepreneurial (Gibbons et al. 1994, Etzkowitz et al. 2008). However, many also developed objectives that do not align with larger national and regional policy goals and needs. In these cases, governments have seen their control over higher education fade, often with unanticipated outcomes.

Many European universities, along with their responsible ministries, are now in a new era of reframing the expectations of performance and outcomes. This development can be partly explained by the idea of the "World Class University" (WCU)—according to one definition, a university that is capable of transforming its traditional academic ethos to an entrepreneurial mode focused on research production, and on global prestige and relationships (Power 2007).

In the past decade, the WCU concept has become a reference point for universities and ministries alike (Salmi 2009). Although there is no clear definition of what it is (Altbach 2003, Li 2012), it is clear that it has been stimulated by a clear expectation: leading national universities need to improve their relative positions on one or more global rankings (Geiger 2004; Teixeira et al. 2004). With this goal in mind, a growing crop of ministerial policy initiatives reflect the ambition of significantly elevating research productivity and, hence, boosting the prestige of a group of leading national universities.

In Northern Europe, governments have funded "excellence" initiatives with this purpose in mind, usually in combination with broader aspirations to build higher education systems capable of fulfilling a range of functions and roles (Schuetze 2007, Leibfried 2009, Christensen, Gornitzka and Maassen 2014). Such initiatives include mergers of institutions and attempts to secure a more efficient division of labor between higher education institutions and greater integration of the whole system (Ritzen 2010).

In this chapter, we discuss to what extent aspects of the New Flagship University model can be understood in relation to current developments in the Scandinavian countries of Denmark, Norway, and Sweden. The leading national universities in these countries are characterized by being relatively old, comprehensive, research-intensive public universities funded largely by national governments, located in urban areas, and generally recognized as central institutions within society. Most are transitioning to a broader understanding of their roles in the socioeconomic development of their countries. They are adopting such global standards, paying attention to global rankings, and creating competitive environments for research grants, for talented students, and talented faculty. Finally, they have responded to accountability demands of national public authorities. In short, over the past decade they have become examples of institutions that exemplify many of the characteristics of the New Flagship University.

In analyzing this transition among Nordic universities toward elements of the Flagship model, the following provides a two-level analysis by considering, first, policy reforms at the national level, and second, the response and adaptation at three institutions—the University of Copenhagen, University of Oslo, and Stockholm University. The framework for this analysis comes from a larger research project funded by the Research Council of Norway, the "European Flagship Universities—Balancing Academic Excellence and Socio-Economic Relevance."

The Continuing Importance of National Higher Education Systems in the Era of Globalization

Previous studies on the history of higher education often focus is one major goal on individual institutions and their rise to fame and influence (Martin and Etzkowitz 2001, Robbins 2003); however, the expansion of higher education systems throughout the world has triggered the development of system analysis on the sector (Ben-David 1991, Clark 1983, Kerr 2001). This includes the role of nations in generating reform initiatives (Cerych and Sabatier 1986). In the past three decades, as noted previously, reform efforts focused on the deregulation of the sector, on attempts to boost institutional autonomy and to develop new intermediate governing bodies in the sector (Enders 2004). Most initially promoted the idea of the entrepreneurial university (Clark 1998, Etzkowitz et al. 2000, Clark, 2004). More recently, initiatives have promoted the ascendency of the WCU and international rankings as a benchmark (Salmi 2009, Brint 2005, Bonaccorsi et al. 2010).

While the WCU model and improved rankings of government and university reform efforts, national policy has also focused on improved university management (Wildavsky 2010, Stensaker and Benner 2013). But to what effect? Christina Musselin (2005) has argued that although there have been transformations in institutional governance and academic leadership in many national systems in Europe, fewer changes can be identified within departments, where teaching and research are conducted. Academics are generally conservative and seek to preserve or enhance their own self-interests, restricting the ability of university management to be more strategic (Whitley 2008). Research-intensive universities in particular are decentralized and somewhat unique organizations; they do not lend themselves easily to theories of how to implement organizational change (Jarzabkowski 2005, Fumasoli and Lepori 2011, Fumasoli et al., forthcoming).

The seemingly mixed effects of deregulation of higher education, for instance, with respect to diversity and division of labor among institutions (Labianca et al. 2001, Halffman and Leydesdorff 2010), can be explained also by two central characteristics of universities. On the one hand, universities have organizational cultures that are resilient to external demands (Olsen and Maassen 2007); on the other hand, increasingly autonomous universities engage strategically within their higher education systems, thus affecting them in ways that are unforeseen by public authorities (Fumasoli and Huisman 2013).

Adding to or reforming the mission of universities and constructing new identities for them is a large challenge (Czarniawska and Wolff

1998, Huisman et al. 2002, Stensaker and Benner 2013, Stensaker 2015). Reform can best described as an evolutionary rather than a revolutionary process (Martin 2012). As a result, impatient national governments in Scandinavian countries are pushing for more rapid changes in the programs and cultures of their universities. While governance reforms in recent history have tended to emphasize a more arm's-length state steering of the sector, including the development new intermediate governing bodies, evaluation agencies, and more formula-based funding schemes (Teixeira et al. 2004, Enders 2004), there is a growing interest in stronger coordination of the national higher education systems—at both the European Union (Maassen and Stensaker 2011) and national levels (Gornitzka and Maassen 2014). While research productivity, and rankings, remain on the agenda of many countries (see, e.g., Leibfried 2009), governments have begun to take a broader policy view, finding value in regional economic development, innovation, employability, and public engagement (Kyvik 2009, Ritzen 2010). This has generated renewed interest in the design and overall functioning of the national higher education system.

Hence, in assessing the expanding role of individual leading Scandinavian universities, these national and European-wide policy interests and initiatives provide an important context. In Scandinavian nations, common questions include: How should a division of labor take place within a higher education system? How should resources be allocated to achieve the many ambitions directed at higher education?

The following analysis comprises two parts: the first outlines each higher education system and the reforms undergone in the past 15 years in Scandinavia; the second part illustrates how leading universities in each country cope with demands and expectations from their national public funding authorities.

Characteristics of Higher Education Systems and Reforms 2000–2014

Our sample consists of three universities: the University of Copenhagen in Denmark, University of Oslo in Norway, and Stockholm University in Sweden. The goal is to illustrate how national and university reforms play out in a group of similar European countries with these characteristics: small to medium population size, above-average GDP per capita, well-endowed systems in research and development and public higher education, and high performance in teaching and research compared to other European countries (see Table 7.1).

Table 7.1 Characteristics of Higher Education National Systems

	Inhabitants (million)	GDP pro capita (EUR 2013)	GERD[a] (2011)	HERD[b] (2010 OECD)	Universities	Other higher education institutions
EU	505.7 Total	25,500	2.06	0.57		
Denmark	5.6	32,100	2.99	0.90	8	31
Norway	5.0	49,900	1.66	0.55	8	19
Sweden	9.6	32,700	3.41	0.90	14	16

Erawatch, accessed 16.04.2014.

[a] Gross domestic Expenditure on R&D, European average.

[b] Higher-education expenditure on R&D as a percentage of GDP.

Denmark

In recent years, Denmark has seen multiple reforms in its higher education sector. The main aim of these reforms is to improve quality, develop strategic management establish research priorities, and improve the relationships between universities and the economic and industry sectors. The most important changes comprise the governance of universities, their missions and the funding structures, the criteria for resource distribution, the linkages between science and society, and the scale and orientation of science dissemination, mainly to industry. The overall reform objectives can be summed up in three themes: quality, mergers and concentration, and interaction and synergy.

These reforms began with the implementation of a new University Act in 2003 that focused on university autonomy and on improving accountability and transparency. The Act abolished collegial and representative councils, replacing them with appointed leaders at all levels (rectors, deans, and heads of department). The Act introduced governing boards with a majority of external members and a chairman appointed by the Minister of Science. The objective was to strengthen university management, improve decision making, establish strategic goals, and promote greater economic and public service engagement. In addition, the Act explicitly stated that universities be more engaged in technology transfers and public service. As a consequence, universities expanded and professionalized their science dissemination activities, particularly by establishing new administrative positions and subunits devoted to external communication and technology transfer.

This reform was followed by a number of institutional mergers in 2007–2008. A collection of 12 higher education institutions became eight; ten ministerial agencies conducting publicly funded research were also consolidated within the university sector. The merger process between universities and governmental research institutes was intended to improve the quality of research output and its impact on Denmark, and to increase international engagement with other researchers. Mergers were partially focused on expanding interdisciplinary research and giving universities an improved ability to strategically manage their now-larger researcher portfolios. And the merger process did allow universities to become more economically engaged and to seek funding support beyond the Ministry of Science and other ministries.

Since the beginning of the millennium, government policies supported by a vast parliamentary majority helped intensify university and private sector interaction, and bolstered technology transfer and innovation. Innovation has thus been a priority in the enlarged Ministry for Science, Technology and Innovation.

Beginning in 2009, additional university funding, beyond the previous base budget, was distributed according to a formula that included the number of students (45 percent), bibliometric measures of research output (25 percent), external grants (20 percent), and number of PhD awards (10 percent). The purpose was to create greater transparency regarding public spending and productivity. Even though only additional funding is distributed on this basis, it appears to have had a significant impact on the behavior of academic staff and leadership at Danish universities. It has resulted in a more competitive environment within universities. Increasingly, the ability to attract external funding is becoming part of the evaluation of academic staff and university subunits.

Norway

Norway's higher education system has eight public universities with nearly 103,000 enrolled students. The system has undergone major changes since the Quality Reform Act of 2003, which granted institutional autonomy to universities that includes a reformed governance structure. In 2005, a law on public and private universities was approved, providing a common framework for all Norwegian higher education institutions related to accreditation, funding, and quality. The funding formula is structured around basic state funding (60%), students (credits, degrees, international students, 25%), and research (partly result-based, 15%).

Norwegian universities remain part of the public sector and their staff—both permanent and temporary—are employed as civil servants as in all other Norwegian public sector organizations. Government policies and funding focus on higher education as a producer of R&D and as key mechanisms for social stability and economic competitiveness, buttressed by Norway's substantial income from oil reserves in the North Sea.

Norway not only has a predominantly positive, optimistic view of the role of higher education in society regarding equity and democratization, but also strong external demands and expectations. Reforms in the regulative framework, governance, and organization of Norwegian universities has focused on a number of areas for improvement: student drop-out rates, time-to-degree rates, student learning, research productivity, and better European integration fostered by the Bologna process. To help set standards among all of Norway's universities, an independent quality assurance agency—the Norwegian Agency for Quality Assurance in Education, or NOKUT—was established to conduct a compulsory national quality assurance process.

Sweden

Sweden has 52 institutions offering higher education in various forms. A majority of the universities and university colleges are public, subject to the same legislation and regulations as other public organizations in Sweden, as well as statutes, ordinances, and regulations particular to the higher education sector. A number of tertiary institutions are self-governing and independent. They have greater freedom with regard to the governance and management of their affairs, but continue to operate on the basis of an agreement with the government and are obliged to follow statutes, ordinances, and regulations. In the latter part of the twentieth century, there was a major expansion of higher education. New regional higher education institutions were founded throughout Sweden to widen access to higher education. Student enrollment grew enormously.

The Parliament and government ministries have overall responsibility for higher education and research, which means that they make decisions about performance targets, guidelines on how to achieve them, and the allocation of resources. Education and research fall under the scope of the Ministry of Education and Research. The Swedish National Agency for Higher Education is the central government agency responsible for matters concerning higher education, but under legislations passed in 2011, universities and university colleges are separate government entities and make their own decisions about the content of courses, admissions, grades, organizational structure, internal allocation of funds (undergraduate levels), and other related issues. Under this law, Sweden's universities and university colleges are performing better. Among other changes, the reform provides universities and university colleges with more power to determine academic policy. However, universities are obliged to require that academic program decisions must be made by two people with scientific or artistic expertise, and that students must be entitled to representation when decisions relating to education or student issues are made.

Research in Sweden is financed and promoted primarily by the Swedish Research Council. The Swedish Higher Education Act and the Higher Education Ordinance specify that all education at universities and university colleges should be based on scientific principles. Education should provide knowledge and skills in relevant areas; develop the ability to make independent critical assessments and to identify, formulate, and solve problems; and develop the capacity to prepare for changes in the student's professional life.

A new quality assurance system is being introduced in conjunction with these recent reforms. Universities and university colleges with higher-quality degree programs will be given increased funding under an evaluation carried out by the Swedish National Agency for Higher Education. Policies enacted since 2008 have attempted to separate the funding for teaching and research to concentrate funding in a few top universities, to change the legal status of higher education institutions (HEIs) into public corporations (as in Finland), to enhance system-mission differentiation, and to strengthen institutional leadership and management. Furthermore, there is a majority of external members on the board of universities, HEIs are now responsible for quality assurance, and the cessation of staff as civil servants became effective in 2011. The minister has also promoted voluntary mergers among HEIs; some institutions are considering merging, or have merged.

Reform Ambitions of Scandinavian Flagship Universities

The three leading Scandinavian universities share many common features: they are all located in a capital, hence they have relatively high student enrollments in their national context; on average, they have slightly more than two-thirds of their budget funded by public authorities through block grants; and they all score in the top 100 of the Shanghai ranking (see Table 7.2).

University of Copenhagen

The University of Copenhagen (UC) is a self-governing unit under the state and the Ministry of Science. The board of the university is the highest authority, with the task of ensuring the interests of the university; it determines, among other things, the guidelines for university organization and its long-term activities and development. The board has six external members and five internal members. Board meetings are held relatively often, about eight times a year, and the university's senior management attends them. The meetings are open to the public.

Until 2004, a rector and a council traditionally led the university. That year, a "Board of Governors" replaced the council. The Board appoints a rector and pro-rector to head the university's management. The deans are nominated by the rector and appointed by the board to head the faculties. The deans appoint the heads of departments. The rector appoints the academic councils, one in every faculty, after recommendation from the deans. The Board appoints a university director after a recommendation

Table 7.2 Characteristics of Scandinavian Flagship Universities

	Country	Founded	Students	Staff FTE	Revenue EUR	Block grant %	Shanghai Ranking	Alliances
University of Copenhagen	Denmark	1479	36,891	9,087	1,108	67,5 (2010)	42	IARU—International Alliance of Research Universities, UNICA
University of Oslo	Norway	1811	26,923	6,066	817	73.0 (2011)	69	UNICA—Network of Universities form the European capitals
Stockholm University	Sweden	1878	29,448	4,932	458	68.0	82	UNICA

Staff includes academic, administrative, and technical.

Figures 2013, if not specified.

Change rate to EUR on www.finance.yahoo.com, accessed on August 29, 2014.

from the rector. The director is the head of the central administration. Faculties and departments have their own individual administrations, although the general budget is overseen by the central administration.

The management at UC is responsible for establishing guidelines and procedures to ensure that prudent budgeting is exercised by the administration of the institution, and that the information contained in the Financial Statements and Management's Reviews on targets and performance is documented and adequate for the activities of the university. The UC leadership reports to the Ministry of Science, with which the board of the university has entered into a development contract. This contract formulates the university's objectives and intended progress for a fixed period of time, organized around three goals: research, teaching, and dissemination of knowledge. Within this framework the development contract lists a number of intended results that do not reflect the overall profile of the university, but set out development trends within the university core activities. The ministry fixes objectives regarding the expected production of journal articles, depth of internationalization, third-party funding, research activities, and PhD enrollment and degree recipients.

For teaching programs at the first-degree level, objectives in the mid-term address student admission and enrollment, dropout rates, study-completion time, examples of the adaption of degree programs that align with the needs of the labor market, entrepreneurship, internationalization, and high-quality teaching. Dissemination of knowledge lists objectives such as cooperation with vocational schools, continuing and further education, participation and contributions to public debates, patents and licenses, and evidence of meaningful cooperation with the business community. Finally, the university is requested to achieve objectives related to public service, for example, providing scientific expertise to various ministries.

In 2007, UC merged with the Royal Veterinary and Agricultural University and the Danish University of Pharmaceutical Sciences. UC now contains one of the largest Health and Life Science Centers in Northern Europe. In 2012, the rector and the Board initiated a series of reorganizations. The Faculty of Life Sciences (LIFE) and the Faculty of Science merged into a new Faculty of Science. Similarly, the Faculty of Pharmaceutical Sciences, the Faculty of Health Sciences, and the veterinary field at the Faculty of Life Sciences merged into the new Faculty of Health and Medical Sciences.

With respect to internationalization, UC focuses on recruiting the best of the future generation of Danish and international research talent. A human resources department was established with a priority to build interdisciplinary programs for all staff and ensure intercultural competencies to meet globalization demands.

The mergers among the UC, the Royal Veterinary and Agricultural University, and the Danish University of Pharmaceutical Sciences have increased the scope for multidisciplinary research. The university's strategy document "Destination 2012" states that the university has significant scientific diversity within education and research—a capacity that has been further strengthened by the mergers.

The university has a long-standing educational and research collaboration with other universities in the Øresund region. The Øresund university network involves 14 universities in eastern Denmark and southern Sweden and provides researchers and students with improved access to expertise on both sides of the Sound. The Øresund Science Region forms an umbrella for research cooperation and operates through six research and innovation platforms integrating universities, industries, and the public sector.

With the introduction of the 2003 University Act, universities gained increased autonomy, which they administered very differently. The UC started a reorganization process during the past five years—generally a slower pace than found in other large Danish universities, such as at Aarhus University. Nevertheless, UC is undergoing physical, structural, and administrative changes, initiated and implemented by the university leadership. This has included allowing for mergers and establishing greater management authority by the Board and the rector, creating a much more centralized institution.

University of Oslo

The Strategic planning process at University of Oslo (UiO) has changed dramatically in the past decade. A five-year plan replaced a ten-year planning horizon to reflect the long-term effort and investment required to improve university programs and activities. More so than in the past, the planning process involved internal and external stakeholders, organized with an integrated approach to the core roles traditionally ascribed to the university and linked to a new budgeting process demanding performance results that includes a set of indicators. Each year, the governing board decides to focus on a special topic central to the strategy. For example, the focus was teaching quality in 2011; the following year, it was internationalization; and in 2013, the theme was innovation.

The new strategic plan also espoused the importance of academic freedom and collegiality, supporting the core university values that include the pursuit of quality, social responsibility, community, concern for the environment, breadth and support for cutting-edge teaching and research, and the campus as a high-quality and supportive learning space.

The following is stated as the overriding planning goal: "The University of Oslo will strengthen its international position as a leading research-intensive university through a close interaction across research, education, communication and innovation." UiO aims at increasing its contribution to academic research internationally and to addressing the challenges facing Norwegian society. The strategic plan outlines goals for 2020 and is structured around five objectives: promoting pioneering research, education, and communication and being sought as an international partner; offering research-based education equivalent to that offered by the foremost international places of learning; ensuring the research-based knowledge to solve the major challenges facing society in the twenty-first century; administering its aggregate resources proactively; and providing good working and learning environments such that students and staff are able to realize their potential.

In 2012, a Strategic Advisory Board (SAB) was established to develop UiO's position as a leading international research university. SAB provides external and scientifically based feedback on the position the university currently occupies, and on what will be needed to reach the high ambitions embedded in UiO's Strategy 2020. The Board has been also engaged in a discussion on how academic values and academic freedom can be protected. In a recent report from the SAB, the UiO was advised to rethink how the diverse aims sketched out in the strategic plan could be implemented in practice; to help in that cause, the SAB argued for more flexible and diverse organizing of the university. This recommendation was welcomed by the governing board and the institutional leadership, resulting in several initiatives.

Stockholm University

Stockholm University (SU)'s strategic plan (2011–2015) sets the mid-term vision of the university. "By 2015 the bulk of teaching and research activities at the university will be leading references nationally and recognized internationally," notes the plan, with academic professionalism and integrity stated as the foundation for the strategic development of the university. The central urban location of SU is also highlighted, with reference to its historical aim of becoming an open entity engaged with, and responsive to, the outside world.

SU's four faculties are the largest in the country in enrollment. It is explicitly expressed in the plan that new strategic efforts be undertaken to strengthen existing and potentially new areas of scientific excellence. Excellence in research and in teaching is to be achieved in tandem and aligned with equity goals. Economic engagement and public service are also valued, particularly in the greater Stockholm region. And the university is expanding efforts to help secure working opportunities for students and to develop ongoing contact with alumni.

The university governing board is responsible for matters concerning the long-term profile and welfare of the university. It is composed of internal (staff and students) and external representatives (public and private sectors). The university central leadership is composed of the rector, the pro-rector, two vice rectors (one for the natural sciences and the other for the social sciences and humanities), and the university director, who heads the technical-administrative structure. In addition, there are a number of specialized roles that provide strategic advice to the rector in key areas such as quality, environmental issues (sustainability), pedagogy, and equality.

Quality in the university's teaching, research, and public service activities is the major goal, in addition to equity (gender, race and ethnicity) in access and treatment of students and academic and administrative staff. Internationalization of teaching and research and strategic cooperation with other Swedish tertiary institutions are also referred to as key priorities. In the realm of research, a special focus is attributed to the establishment of a "vibrant work environment" that is capable of attracting and retaining talented researchers. All faculty are expected to dedicate a part of their work time to research, including engagement with international research projects (particularly at EU level) and, consequently, the development of international networks.

An annual follow-up of progress in each of the various areas is to be undertaken. As a result, internal plans, goals, and ambitions are to be revisited and revised accordingly. The current operational cycle sheds light on seven key strategic goals, as approved by the SU's board in December 2010. The plan is organized around three distinct parts. In the first part, the goals and objectives regarding each one of the three main functions—teaching, research, and service to society—are outlined. In the second part, the general guidelines framing the work around quality and quality-assurance mechanisms are presented. The last part includes a number of quantitative benchmarks (for 2011–2012) to provide a general picture regarding university finances and performance. The goals per specific area of activity are as follows. Teaching: (a) increasing international exchange at all levels of education; (b) varied and student-driven teaching and examination procedures; (c) active participation of students in matters pertaining to improving education and learning environments. Research: (a) a higher percentage of international researchers and doctoral students; (b) good social and economic conditions for all doctoral candidates. Impact in society (third mission): (a) good conditions that make it possible for students to enter the labor market either as an employee or as an entrepreneur (own business); (b) good possibilities for students to undertake practical training and examinations in work outside HE.

The Future of Scandinavian Flagships

The leading national Scandinavian universities in this study have made significant progress toward the New Flagship model. While they have ambitions to improve their international rankings focused on research production, they also value their broader mission and their key role in their respective national systems of higher education.

Greater institutional autonomy and other government-induced reforms have also helped turn these universities into more strategic actors and closer partners with ministries. For example, in Denmark, the relation between the ministry responsible for higher education and individual institutions has led to contractual agreements and a regular dialogue between the ministry and academic leaders that sets out terms regarding mission differentiation among universities and colleges. Institutional mergers in Denmark and Norway also reflect a broader interest in building a productive national higher education system, not simply on institutional prestige and performance.

Why is there this attention to the broader development of higher education in Scandinavian countries? Why do we sense a more strategic role by Scandinavian universities in building these systems, while they pursue reforms that form an adoption of the New Flagship model? In short, there is a *governance logic* operating within the Scandinavian region that is more collaborative than the *competitive logic* associated with the WCU and ranking paradigm that dominates the political agenda in many other countries. We observe that Scandinavian universities operate at a twofold level: a systemic level, which is mainly national but also regional; and an international level where they endeavor as single academic organizations in a competitive arena, pursuing excellence and prestige through research and ranking. The leading national universities in Scandinavia are balancing these different missions of research excellence and societal relevance by exploring possible synergies with their many stakeholders.

But it is also true that higher education systems in the Scandinavian countries are relatively small in enrollment, faculty, and academic programs. These countries have financial muscle and long traditions of scientific excellence, and, unlike some of the massive universities found in, for example, Latin America, an awareness and ability to coordinate and pursue institutional goals. Small size is a considerable comparative advantage. One might speculate whether these factors also make the Scandinavian countries more resilient to "global pressures." While the Scandinavian countries are exposed to and are very much part of the current globalization of higher education and the ranking frenzy, the healthy and ongoing dialogue between national authorities and university leaders helps provide a perspective on the many purposes of major universities.

This is not to argue that Scandinavian policymaking in higher education is better than in other parts of the world, or that the leading universities in Scandinavia behave in a more innovative way. On the contrary, we conclude that higher education in many countries is still predominantly a domestic affair, regulated and funded by national authorities who have a diverse reform agenda for higher education.

This chapter has been written in the framework of the "European Flagship Universities—Balancing Academic Excellence and Socio-Economic Relevance," funded by the Research Council of Norway (FORFI program, grant 212422).

REFERENCES

Altbach, Philip G. 2003. "The Costs and Benefits of World-Class Universities." *International Higher Education*, 33.

Ben-David, Joseph. 1991. *Essays on the Social Organization and Ethos of Science*, edited by Gad Freudenthal. Berkeley: University of California Press.

Brint, Stephen. 2005. "Creating the Future: 'New Directions' in American Research Universities." *Minerva* 43: 23–50.

Bonaccorsi, Andrea, Daraio, Cinzia, and Geuna, Aldo. 2010. "Universities in the New Knowledge Landscape: Tensions, Challenges, Change—an Introduction." *Minerva* 48: 1–4.

Cerych, Ladislav and Sabatier, Paul. 1986. *Great Expectations and Mixed Performance: The Implementation of Higher Education Reforms in Europe*. Stoke-on-Trent: Trentham Books.

Christensen, Tom, Gornitzka, Åse and Maassen, Peter. 2014. "Global Pressures and National Cultures: A Nordic University Template?" In *University Adaptation in Difficult Economic Times*, 30–51. Oxford: Oxford University Press.

Christensen, Tom and Lægreid, Per. 2007. "The Whole-of-Government Approach to Public Sector Reform." *Public Administration Review* 67: 1059–1066.

Clark, Burton. R. 1983. *The Higher Education System*. Berkeley: University of California Press.

Clark, Burton. R. 1998. *Creating Entrepreneurial Universities: Organizational Pathways of Transformation.* New York: International Association of Universities Press/Pergamon—Elsevier Science.

Clark, Burton. R. 2004. *Sustaining Change in Universities: Continuities in Case Studies and Concepts.* Berkshire: Open University Press.

Czarniawska, Barbara and Wolff, Rolf. 1998. "Constructing New Identities in Established Organizational Fields: Young Universities in Old Europe." *International Studies in Management and Organization* 28: 32–56.

Enders, Jürgen. 2004. "Higher Education, Internationalization, and the Nation-State: Recent Developments and Challenges to Governance Theory." *Higher Education* 47: 361–382.

Etzkowitz, Henry, Webster, Andrew, Gebhardt, Christiane, and Terra, Branca. R. 2000. "The Future of the University and the University of the Future: Evolution of Ivory Tower to Entrepreneurial Paradigm." *Research Policy* 29: 313–330.

Etzkowitz, Henry, Ranga, Marina, Benner, Mats, Guaranys, Lucia, Macukan, Anne Marie, and Kneller, Robert. 2008. "Pathways to the Entrepreneurial University: Towards a Global Convergence." *Science and Public Policy.* 35: 681–695.

Fumasoli, Tatiana and Lepori, Benedetto. 2011. Patterns of Strategies in Swiss Higher Education Institutions. *Higher Education* 61: 157–178.

Fumasoli, Tatiana and Huisman, Jeroen. 2011. "Strategic Agency and System Diversity: Conceptualizing Institutional Positioning in Higher Education." *Minerva* 51: 155–169.

Fumasoli, Tatiana, Pinheiro, Romulo, and Stensaker, Bjørn. Forthcoming. "Handling Uncertainty of Strategic Ambitions: The Use of Organizational Identity as a Risk-Reducing Device." *International Journal of Public Administration.*

Geiger, Roger. 2004. *Knowledge and Money: Research Universities and the Paradox of the Marketplace.* Stanford: Stanford University Press.

Gibbons, Michael et al. 1994. *The New Production of Knowledge.* London: Sage.

Gornitzka, Åse and Maassen, Peter. 2014. "Dynamics of Convergence and Divergence: Exploring Accounts of Higher Education Policy Change." In *University Adaptation in Difficult Economic Times*, edited by Paola Mattei. 13–29. Oxford: Oxford University Press.

Halffman, Willem and Leydesdorff, Loet. 2010. "Is Inequality among Universities Increasing? Gini Coefficients and the Elusive Rise of Elite Universities." *Minerva* 48: 55–72.

Huisman, Jeroen, Norgård, Jorunn. D., Rasmussen, Jørgen. G., and Stensaker, Bjørn. 2002. "'Alternative' Universities Revisited—a Study of the Distinctiveness in Universities Established in the Spirit of 1968." *Tertiary Education and Management.* 8: 315–332.

Jarzabkowski, Paula. 2005. *Strategy as Practice: An Activity-Based Approach.* London: Sage.

Jessop, Bob. 2001. *The Future of the Capitalist State.* Cambridge: Polity.

Kerr, Clark. 2001. *The Uses of the University.* 5th ed. Cambridge, MA: Harvard University Press.

Kyvik, Svein. 2009. *The Dynamics of Change in Higher Education: Expansion and Contraction in an Organisational Field.* Dordrecht: Springer.

Labianca, Giuseppe, Fairbank, James. F., Thomas, James. B., and Gioia, Dennis. 2001. "Emulation in Academia: Balancing Structure and Identity." *Organization Science* 12: 312–330.

Leibfried, Stephan. 2009. *Die Exzellensinitiative. Zwischenbilanz und Perspektiven.* Frankfurt: Campus.

Li, Jun. 2012. "World-Class Higher Education and the Emerging Chinese Model of the University." *Prospects*, 42: 319–339.

Maassen, Peter and Olsen, Johan P. 2007. *University Dynamics and European Integration.* Dordrecht: Springer.

Maassen, Peter and Stensaker, Bjørn. 2011. "The Knowledge Triangle, European Higher Education Policy Logics and Policy Implications." *Higher Education* 61: 757–769.

Martin, Ben. 2012. "Are Universities and University Research under Threat? Towards an Evolutionary Model of University Speciation." *Cambridge Journal of Economics* 36: 543–565.

Martin, Ben and Etzkowitz, Henry. 2001. "The Origin and Evolution of the University Species." *Journal for Science and Technology Studies* 13: 9–34.

Musselin, Christine. 2005. "Change and Continuity in Higher Education Governance? Lessons Drawn from Twenty Years of National Reforms in European Countries." In *Governing Knowledge*, edited by Ivar Bleiklie and Mary Henkel. 65–80. Dordrecht: Springer.

Olsen, Johan P. and Maassen, P. 2007. "European Debates on the Knowledge Institution: The Modernization of the University at the European Level." In *University Dynamics and European Integration*, edited Peter Maassen and Johan P. Olsen. 3–22. Dordrecht: Springer.

O'Shea, Rory, Allen, Thomas, Morse, Kenneth, O'Gorman, Colm, and Roche, Frank. 2007. "Delineating the Anatomy of an Entrepreneurial University: The Massachusetts Institute of Technology Experience." *R&D Management*, 37: 1–16.

Power, Michael. 2007. *Organized Uncertainty: Designing a World of Risk Management.* Oxford: Oxford University Press.

Ritzen, Jo. 2010. *A Chance for European Universities.* Amsterdam: Amsterdam University Press.

Robbins, Keith. 2003. "Universities: Past, Present, and Future." *Minerva* 41: 397–406.

Salmi, Jamir. 2009. *The Challenge of Establishing World-Class Universities.* Washington: The World Bank.

Schuetze, Hans Georg. 2007. "Research Universities and the Spectre of Academic Capitalism." *Minerva* 45: 435–443.

Stensaker, Bjørn. 2015. "Organizational Identity as a Concept for Understanding University Dynamics." *Higher Education* 69: 103–115.

Stensaker, Bjørn and Benner, Mats. 2013. "Doomed to be Entrepreneurial? Institutional Transformations or Institutional Lock-in of 'New' Universities." *Minerva* 51: 399–416.

Teixeira, Pedro, Jongbloed, Ben, Dill, David D., and Amaral, Alberto. 2004. *Markets in Higher Education. Rhetoric or Reality?* Dordrecht: Kluwer Academic Publishers.

Tuchman, Gaye. 2009. *Wannabe U: Inside the Corporate University.* Chicago: University of Chicago Press.

Wildavsky, Ben. 2010. *How Global Universities Are Reshaping the World.* Princeton: Princeton University Press.

Whitley, Richard. 2008. "Constructing Universities as Strategic Actors: Limitations and Variations." In *The University in the Market*, edited by Lars Engwall and Denis Weaire. 23–37. Cochester: Portland Press.

Chapter 8

The Soviet Flagship University Model and Its Contemporary Transition

Isak Froumin and Oleg Leshukov

Some 30 years ago, sociologist Burton Clark sought to illustrate and classify how different national systems of higher education were influenced by three major players: the state, the academy, and the market. In the United States, the market, in terms of students and business interests, was more influential than in other parts of the world. Soviet higher education was as on the other end of the spectrum: a highly state-regulated system, with weak authority by academics and university leaders, with little influence by markets; indeed, within a command economy, the state determined the market. All universities were "cogs" in the central-government machine.

At its outset, the Soviet model of higher education constituted a unique experiment in social engineering. Russian communist leaders regarded higher education as a means of supplying the national economy with skilled employees and scientific research organized to satisfy specific economic demands. It also was a force for nation-building; a mechanism to educate and enculturate political leaders and professionals; and a system intended to support regional, political, and economic needs within Russia's vast geographic boundaries and satellite nations (Kuzminov et al. 2013).

This model emerged after the Revolution of 1917 and constituted a highly structured, mission-driven network of institutions. It placed a special prestige and role among a group of regionally based and Soviet-styled Traditional Flagship Universities outlined in earlier chapters of this book. But these leading national universities were different from those found in other parts of the world. They had a defined leadership role within a regionally coordinated system of postsecondary technical schools and universities. The best and the brightest that graduated from a secondary school went to these regional Soviet Flagships. Under the Soviet model, basic research was largely the confines of the Russian Academy of Sciences, forming the elite research institutions devoid of teaching responsibilities. Most universities were focused almost exclusively on teaching and had no authority to conduct research.

The collapse of the Soviet system and the shift to a new, more market-oriented economic model forced a significant transformation of the Russian higher education system, including the mission, organization, and behaviors of institutions themselves. A lessening of central state control, the dissolution of the industry-oriented education system, and the creation of the new market environment marked its downfall. Consequently, some Soviet Flagship Universities failed to adjust and were, de facto, stripped of their status. Others managed to preserve and strengthen their leadership within the system. The post–Soviet system also included the establishment of new institutions, sometimes in the form of newly merged universities. Many of these newcomers were able to occupy the needed niches by effectively serving a changing labor market. Other existing and newly formed postsecondary institutions floundered, unable to cope with the shifting economic model. On the whole, the post–Soviet higher education system went into a period of uncertainty and chaotic adaptation.

In contrast, the past decade or so has been characterized by a significant return of the state into education policymaking, helping reshape the nation's network of post-Soviet Flagships and other institutions. Striving to improve education quality and research efficiency, the national government undertook a number of reforms, forcing and encouraging mergers and supporting a specific group of leading universities to pursue many of the values of the New Flagship model. Yet, unlike in the Soviet era, there still remains no well-defined higher education configuration.

This chapter explores the historical development of the Soviet and then the new Russian higher education system, and specifically the Soviet Flagship university, its demise, and aspirational resurgence, today heavily shaped by global university rankings.

An important question is whether Russia's leading universities need the state to encourage or force maturation into more globally competitive and socially relevant institutions. Or should it be largely the responsibility of universities themselves? Our view is that there are limits to external state control and influence via funding and central policy directives. More effective university management will relate to internal decision making and institutions pursuing their own academic cultures and mission within an increasingly competitive environment.

The Soviet Higher Education Project

In the aftermath of the Revolution of 1917, the Soviet government did not take long to pursue ambitious reforms that affected all aspects of social life. Higher education was no exception. Over its first ten years in power, the new government pursued various and, at times, contradictory, reform efforts—from attempts to raze the higher education sector to the ground that included limiting the number of admissions or closing and merging tertiary institutions, to an active expansion of the system. The new Russian higher education system came to include a significant redefinition and elevation of the nation's largest, oldest, and the most prestigious universities, including Moscow State University, Saint Petersburg State University, Kazan State University, and others. In the midst of much political tumult, these new Soviet Flagships upheld the academic reputation of Russia by educating the new Soviet elite and by continuing the nation's long history of scholarly research and technical expertise in fields such as mathematics and engineering. This special role for the higher education system emerged in earnest by the 1930s.

As in all sectors of the national economy, higher education had to adhere to strict regulations. The State Planning Committee, a special government agency typical for command economies, calculated the amount of resources that were needed for the development of the Russian economy, including the number and type of trained and educated workers and professionals. Designed initially as a five-year plan in 1928, the objectives included identifying the exact number of university graduates in each study area needed to satisfy the demands of a new Soviet economy, and the number and organization of postsecondary institutions required. It led to the appearance of distinct types of universities, characterized by different missions (Froumin et al. 2014):

- Specialized Sectorial (industrial) Institutions focused on staffing a specific sector of industry, such as aviation and railroads on a national scale and focused on overall national productivity goals.
- Regional Infrastructural Universities established on a territorial-production principle, sometimes the result of separating academic units from other larger, older universities. These universities focused on providing training for teachers, medicine, and similar professions.
- Soviet Flagship Universities offered a comprehensive array of academic programs and degrees, training staff for other higher education institutions (especially in basic sciences), staff for research institutes, and personnel for local managerial elites (economics, history, and law).

This was not the nomenclature in the Soviet era, or today, for categorizing postsecondary institutions. For instance, "Flagship University" is language that was not used historically, or today (thus far) in Russia; instead "state university" or "leading university" is the more common way of identifying the major, research-intensive universities of today. However, this categorization of each higher education sector helps us in the following analysis.

What emerged in the 1930s was a strong, coherent, and hierarchical as well as regional approach to building a system of higher education found in few other nations at that time outside of the United States. But it also imposed significant constraints on the development of higher education, limiting the prerogatives of institutional leaders and faculty to creatively interact with local economies and society in general (Kuzminov et al. 2013; Froumin et al. 2014). The purpose and organization of these three types of institutions related to the centrally identified labor needs of the Soviet state, and focused almost entirely on teaching and creating a rigid and centrally controlled model. By 1954, for example, this included regulations mandating that upon graduating, all young professionals work for no less than three years at specific business or industrial facilities, such as production plants, state-owned and collective farms, hospitals, and schools, depending on the directives issued by the ministry (Decree 1954).

As noted previously, most university faculty did not engage in academic research in any significant way. That was the responsibility of the Academy of Sciences—a similar model found in Germany that invested most of its academic research capacity in the Max Planck and other non-university institutes. In Russia, the Academy supported research centers, laboratories, and design bureaus, with the expressed purpose of meeting most of the scientific research needs of the state. The lack of a significant research role for universities, and a focus largely on teaching, along with their lack of institutional autonomy and ability to innovate, proved a profound weakness in the development of Soviet universities and technical institutions (Johnson 2008, p. 160). However, a select group of Soviet Flagships did have a number of exclusive rights and opportunities to conduct mostly applied research.

Soviet Flagship Universities Over Time

The Soviet Flagship was at the top of the hierarchical higher education system. Most were established before the Russian Revolution, including Moscow State University, St. Petersburg State University, and a number of universities located in the capitals of large republics, such as Kiev State

University. Having retained the academic heritage that they had before the Revolution, these universities continued to provide education of the highest quality and remained as leaders in their respective regional networks of postsecondary institutions—with the exception of Moscow State and St. Petersburg, which formed Russia's only truly national universities.

As originally outlined in the July 1931 Decree of the Council of People's Commissars N 752, "On Reorganizing State," the Soviet Flagships educated students in the fundamentals of natural sciences, physics and mathematics, and the humanities, largely to fill academic positions at other Soviet universities and technical colleges—a prominence they retain in the modern era of Russia's higher education system. They trained staff for research centers affiliated with the Academy of Sciences. These universities also offered education programs not found in other university sectors—for example, there were periods in the history of the Soviet Union when the entire nation had only four faculties of philosophy: at the Moscow, Leningrad, Sverdlovsk, and Kiev universities (Vakhitov 2014).

Another decree by the Council of People's Commissars (the top executive body of the Soviet Union) stated, "Universities must be transformed into the main training grounds for highly skilled professionals, specializing in general research and teaching at higher education institutions and secondary schools." Another decree in 1936 sought to solidify Communist Party control of these institutions. University rectors (equivalent to a university president) had to henceforth be appointed and dismissed by a central government All-Union Committee on Higher Education. Candidates who filled academic departments and regional ministries ("commissars") responsible for higher education also had to be approved in Moscow. The goal was to make sure that university leadership would follow the ideology of the Soviet state. As a result, the professional competency of many university administrators was not a priority—a pattern of party control mimicked eventually by China.

Unlike most other higher education institutions, the comprehensive Soviet Flagships began to offer postgraduate programs in the late 1930s. By 1939, there were 1,200 students attending postgraduate training courses, with some 464 alone at Moscow State University (Avrus 2001). By the end of 1930s, approximately half of all Soviet Flagship University graduates were opting for a career in academia and research (Vakhitov 2014), either within the various higher education institutions or at one of the Academy of Sciences institutions. The Soviet Flagship's central role grew with the rapid growth in the enrollment and in the number of sectorial and infrastructural institutions. As shown in figure 8.1, there were a mere 152 higher education institutions in 1917; ten years later, only 90. But by 1940 the total had climbed dramatically to 481 (Chanbarisov 1988).

Figure 8.1 Number of Higher Education Institutions in the Soviet and Post-Soviet Period.

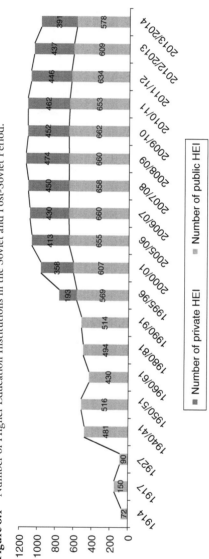

Growth in the number of institutions led to the advent of a great number of new and highly specialized universities. More often than not, these new institutions resulted from separating academic programs from an existing Flagship University by a central. Authority over their management went to a sectorial ministry, such as railroads, electricity, and steel production. For instance, there were six sectorial HEIs that had branched out from the Rostov State University. This included a new university for teacher training, one for communist economics, another for medicine, and another for industrial development.

Throughout the 1930s, new sectorial universities formed national networks with the intent of coordinating programs and meeting national labor needs. A lead university was designated to set curricular and other standards for other sectorial institutions with the same specialization to follow (Kuzminov et al. 2013). For example, the Moscow Institute of Steel headed all the metallurgic institutions in the various Soviet regions; the Moscow Mining Institute headed a similar national network. These leading campuses also provided applied research related to their particular professions or industries (Tasits 2012).

In this era of reform that valued specialization and perceived labor market needs, several faculties of the Moscow State University (e.g., the medical or philology faculty) separated themselves to form new independent institutes. As a result, Soviet Flagships increasingly focused on degree programs such as physics, mathematics, natural sciences, and the humanities. The rapid growth in sectorial universities elevated the regional Flagships as elite, prestigious institutions that generated not merely workers, but the political and academic intelligentsia. However, these institutions still played a larger leadership role in a region, in part because they supplied the faculty and researchers for a growing higher education sector, and because of their special status under the Soviet government.

In the midst of chaotic political reforms under Stalin, special advantages were given to Soviet Flagships. Statutory law gave these universities more flexibility when responding to industry demands for various qualifications and skills—a privilege not accorded the sectorial and infrastructural institutions. In 1934, the head of the ministry responsible for governing education ("the People's Commissariat for Education of the Russian Soviet Federative Socialist Republic") stated that the Flagships were to be major centers of the Soviet scientific thought (Avrus 2001). This allowed senior faculty and graduate students to carry out scientific research, helping to generate the talent that ultimately supported Soviet science and military capabilities during the Cold War (Avrus 2001).

Another privilege granted to Flagships by the late 1930s: the right to determine their own curricula. All of the other educational institutions were obligated to follow the curricula that had been drawn out for their use at the corresponding ministries and departments. Flagships also received additional funding. The average funding standards for student support was over twice as high in these universities as those in the other higher education sectors (Froumin and Povalko 2014).

Especially at the Moscow and Saint Petersburg State Universities, professors at Flagships had high prestige and salaries comparable to that of high-ranking officials. All of this made a career in the academia sphere immensely appealing. Moreover, an educational allowance for housing and other expenses of students and postgraduates was comparable to the average wage across the country. By comparison, financial incentives for professors and students at all the other postsecondary institutions were significantly lower. All of these factors further elevated the prestige of the Flagships and made them highly attractive for the best professors and students.

The Soviet Flagships also became the primary vehicle for enrolling international students from other socialist regimes. In 1946, Soviet universities started welcoming students from partner countries (Avrus 2001). Moscow State University was the first to open its doors to foreigners, closely followed by other major institutions. For a long time, teaching foreign students remained the sole domain of Flagships.

During the Stalin era, the building of a new campus, and its massive and signature Soviet-era main building, for Moscow State University exuded the importance of this leading university and its real and symbolic role in promoting education and the nation-state's devotion to science and learning. Built between 1949 and 1953 during a period of economic hardship, this majestic building demonstrated that higher education was at the top of the government's agenda (Avrus 2001). Similar building programs were launched at other Soviet Flagships.

The new and old Flagships were all located in the capitals of Union republics and autonomous republics, such as Kiev State University and Baku State University (Dmitriev 2013). Each trained the local and national elite and party officials (Froumin and Povalko 2014). Another purpose was to help unite the linguistic, cultural, and territorial development of various peoples who lived in the Soviet Union (Martin 2001). Flagships introduced programs related to the various national languages and devoted resources to studying and supporting regional cultural traditions and practices.

In this way, the Soviet Flagships became a driving force behind the cultural and economic development of their respective regions in a fashion. But it is important to note that not every region had its own Flagship university. The Soviet territorial planning policy dictated that a Flagship University must be created mostly in the capitals of Union republics, in autonomous districts, or other large regions. Comprehensive universities that were located in such regions, such as Moscow, St. Petersburg, and Tomsk Oblast, had the greatest demand among students and could best influence and serve the need for graduates in other higher education sectors. In those regions that lacked comprehensive universities, the center of the education system shifted to sectorial universities.

The Beginning of the Modern Era

At the end of the Soviet era in the 1980s, the government in Moscow eased its central control of the education system. All postsecondary institutions gained a new level of management authority. Soviet administrators attempted to give institutes and universities a more important role in managing their curriculum and programs. At the same time, there was no well-defined policy to guide local campus administration on management and governance. This gave rise to serious challenges on how to adapt to an increasingly market-oriented environment in the midst of limited resources or experience.

In one effort to help guide institutions in this new era, academic leaders in Flagship Universities helped to create special Teaching and Methodological Associations (UMOs). Each association brought together a group of public institutions to develop uniform curricular and pedagogical practices, relying on the expertise and leadership of the regional Flagships. Such associations were created in many fields, including teacher training, medicine, culture and art, information security training, agriculture and fishing technical education, and military training.

Bauman Moscow State Technical University, for example, headed the association responsible for training engineers, while Moscow State University led the UMO responsible for education in social science and humanities fields. The result was an important transformation in the culture of Russian universities into more active participants in education policy making.

The collapse of the Soviet Union accelerated the emergence of the new economic order, include the following: (1) the emergence of market mechanisms and a private higher education sector; (2) initially declining enrollment demand; (3) greater diversification of education programs; (4) liberalization of education programs and an increase of university autonomy; (5) efforts to become more internationally engaged; and

(6) a new recognition of international academic competition and benchmarking, including rankings.

Universities faced unprecedented challenges. The social and economic recession in the country and destruction of the mandatory job placement system resulted in a downturn in enrollments, with particularly significant impact among institutions in remote regions of the country. These circumstances also encouraged inbreeding among the ranks of faculty and administrative staff and a decline in coordination among institutions. Faculty mobility among the universities and cooperation in the area of methodological support—once a strength of the Soviet system—dramatically declined. Instead of a single process for development and approval of educational materials, for example, many independent publishing houses sprang up that published textbooks and other course materials without any review.

Post-Soviet Flagships

Greater autonomy provided an opportunity for institutions to experiment. In the short term, this experimentation led to lower quality and disarray. Under the Soviet system, the state was the primary regulator and consumer of educational services. Now new stakeholders emerged that included not only national and regional governments, but also households, a growing private sector and the academic community itself (Freeman 1984). At the same time, state funding for all higher education institutions declined dramatically. How could the Flagship Universities adapt to this new environment?

Heads of the leading universities sought development strategies. Many of the rectors hired during the Soviet period falsely assumed special administrative and financial rights (Vishlenkova and Dmitriev 2013) as a legacy of their special status under the Soviet government. They had difficulty managing the transition period. Many universities chose to expand low-cost, part-time degree programs; some created branches in other regions and localities. The movement was toward mass, cheap, and low-quality educational programs for students (Kuzminov et al. 2013).

Yet the specialized education programs characteristic of the Soviet era remained, restricting student choice on what they might study and, in turn, their future opportunities for jobs and mobility in a changing economy. Students often faced a narrowly defined and rigid vocational and professional curriculum (Ushakov and Shuruev 1980, Balzer 1993). Enrollment demand continued to decline. Many of the traditional specialized single-discipline degree programs closed at both the Flagship and sectorial universities. This had a particular significant effect on the sectorial institutions, most of which had significant financial problems. They began to look for other sources of income, including degree programs in the social and economics sciences. But this proved overly ambitious. Most did not have the appropriate faculty expertise or the resources to create quality programs (Platonova and Semyonov 2014). This resulted in many sectorial universities closing or merging with other institutions. At one time, they had been leaders in specific areas of training determined by the state; now they had lost their sense of identity and purpose.

The net result was the end of a once well-defined hierarchy of higher education institutions. Throughout this transitory period, two universities maintained a special status: Moscow State University and St. Petersburg State University. A presidential decree in October 1990, "On the Status of Higher Education Establishments," provided Moscow State University broad autonomy in academic and financial management and continued government funding levels (Avis 1992). By 2009, this included separate expenditure lines in the national budget and the status of being "unique scientific and educational complexes, [the] oldest universities of the country with great importance for development of the Russian society." Further elevating the special status of Moscow State and St. Petersburg Universities, new rectors required approval by the president of the Russian Federation; rectors at other universities were elected by faculty and students and approved by the government authority. Moreover, these two institutions gained informal control of accreditation for any new social science and professional programs that allowed them to regulate the offering of programs in these fields at other universities (Ten 2007).

While many of the former Soviet Flagships and sectorial universities struggled, new universities emerged. These included new private institutions organized on the model of universities in the West. The Russian Economic School (Moscow) and the European University in St. Petersburg were examples. New public universities were also were established, including the Higher School of Economics (HSE) in Moscow, modeled on the London School of Economics, with faculties in the social sciences and now with a school of engineering. These new universities pursued graduate education as a significant component in their programs—much more so than the older Soviet universities of the past (Froumin 2012). Shortly after their inception, a number of these new universities had some of the highest enrollments. They quickly attained high levels of research productivity and journal publications relative to their Russian counterparts.

Yet the overall quality of the emerging Russian higher education system was understood to be extremely low, revealed in part by exposure to the academic programs of universities in other parts of the world and by the poor showing of Russian universities in international rankings. By the mid-2000s, Russia's ministry responsible for higher education took action to address these problems, primarily reducing the large number of small institutions with narrowly tailored degree programs by encouraging institutional mergers. The federal government also began to focus funding support on a group of so-called "Federal" universities to be located in different federal districts of the country (Froumin and Povalko 2014). Forty universities merged into nine to create these new federal universities (Froumin and Povalko 2014), with missions that reflected the New Flagship model. According to the Federal Law of the Russian Federation dated February 10, 2009 No. 18-F, the federal universities were to accomplish the following functions:

- Provide for the systemic modernization of the higher and postgraduate vocational education;
- Carry out staff training, retraining, and/or qualification improvement based on the use of modern education technologies for comprehensive social and economic development of the region;
- Perform fundamental and applied scientific research in a wide range of fields and seek ways of bringing the results of intellectual activities to practical application;
- Act as a leading scientific and methodological center.

An example of a Federal university is the Far East Federal University (FEFU). Established in 2011 through the merger of several universities, FEFU is a significant player in the economic development in the Russian region that borders the Pacific Ocean—an historically economically depressed territory characterized by a declining population and an underdeveloped labor market. The new university now draws the best students and teachers in the region: students who at one time looked to escape to more populated and economically developed regions of Russia.

FEFU and a group of other new universities are conscious of international models for quality assurance and desire interaction with other major universities outside of Russia's borders (Froumin and Povalko 2014).

Bolstering the reform movement, the Ministry of Education and Science in 2008–2010 developed a competitive process to choose 29 existing universities that would become "national research universities." The chosen now receive additional financing for basic and applied research, for hiring faculty, and for expanding graduate education, particularly at the master's level. Funding is also for increasing technology transfer, for expanding the interaction with local economies, and for promoting international engagement (MoES 2015). One goal announced by the President of the Russian Federation (No. 599 dated May 7, 2012): at least five Russian universities should be in the top 100 international academic ranking by 2022.

More recently, the Ministry of Education and Science announced a competition to select 15 universities to receive additional funding to support an even more ambitious ranking goal. The "Academic Excellence Project" is for four years, with a total announced budget of 44 billion rubles. These funds can be used for the hiring of new staff, including those with experience abroad; improvement of graduate and postgraduate programs; introduction of new education programs jointly with the leading foreign partners; and implementation of measures to attract foreign students. Figure 8.2 provides the location of these 15 universities.

In part because of these funding initiatives, leading Russian universities are more focused on ways to improve their rankings and have only elements of the more holistic New Flagship University model. They are improving their research productivity and, to some degree, interaction internationally. However, many are struggling to create a relatively new academic culture focused on institutional self-improvement, including improving the quality and character of their teaching, research, and public service missions.

Becoming a Russian Flagship

How might a group of Russia's more entrepreneurial universities adopt key aspects of the New Flagship model?

First, they need to become much more international, not only in their interaction with other universities and academics in other parts of the world, but also in adopting norms and practices of the best universities—many of which are outlined in the first part of this book. This is not an easy task. The legacy of the Soviet higher educational system reinforces a domestic, provincial viewpoint among many academics and university leaders. This is only now slowly beginning to change, in part induced by ministerial funding opportunities and discussion on how to elevate Russia's universities to be both competitive and collaborative with other major universities. This is one reason why there is a need to recruit faculty and students from throughout the world to help change the culture and management capacity of Russian universities.

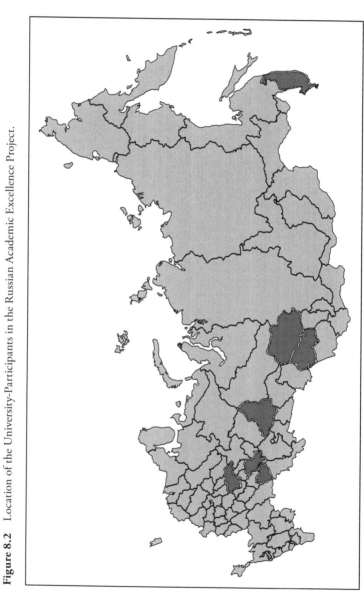

Figure 8.2 Location of the University-Participants in the Russian Academic Excellence Project.

Second, they need resources from the state to pursue these norms and to increase their interaction globally, with relative autonomy to shape their own strategies.

Third, while recruiting some faculty internationally, the top Russian universities need to substantially improve their graduate programs, especially at the PhD level. They need to seek a more significant and well-defined role in preparing the next generations of academics and academic leaders. This should include greater faculty mobility and steps to limit academic inbreeding that characterized the Soviet system (Yudkevich, Sivak, 2015).

Fourth, leading universities aspiring to be New Flagship Universities must continue to build a comprehensive array of academic programs, with quality across the disciplines, and with opportunities for multidisciplinary collaboration among faculty and students. This will require a better alignment of their research and teaching activities, and improved conditions for greater research productivity and engagement with local economies.

Among the Russian universities adopting aspects of the Flagships model, the National Research University Higher School of Economics—Moscow (HSE) offers one of the best examples. HSE has developed internal policy and practices that reflect aspects of the New Flagship model. In a relatively short time, during a period of major societal and economic changes, it is perhaps Russia's more innovative and entrepreneurial university (Froumin 2012). This has included the following internally developed initiatives:

- Opening new programs in the areas that were not covered by other universities;
- Development of a sophisticated system of incentives for the research performance of the teaching staff;
- Introducing teaching in English even in the absence of the favorable regulatory framework;
- Bringing the best foreign scholars to lead research centers on a part-time basis;
- Creating an international advisory council.

These and other initiatives, along with a new management structure, significant funding, and a relatively high level of autonomy granted by the federal ministry, helped create a progressive academic culture that, in turn, has helped attract some of Russia's best students and young and energetic faculty. The HSE example, and analysis of the experience of other Russian universities, indicate that a label given by the state cannot guarantee status as a New Flagship University. It requires the development and maintenance of an internal academic culture devoted to institutional self-improvement.

REFERENCES

Avis G. 1990. "The Soviet Higher Education Reform: Proposals and Reactions." *Comparative Education* 26, no. 1: 5–12.

Avis G. 1992. "Soviet Union Comparative." *Education Review* 36, no. 2: 271–273.

Avrus A. 2001. *Istoriya rossiyskikh universitetov [History of Russian Universities]*. Moscow: Moskovskiy obshachestvenny nauchny fond.

Balzer, H. 1993. "Engineering Education in the Former Soviet Union." *The National Council for Soviet and East European Research*, Georgetown University.

Chanbarisov Sh. 1988. "Formirovanie sovetskoy universitetskoy sistemy [Formation of the Soviet University System]." *Vysshaya shkola*. Moscow.

Clark, B. 1983. *The Higher Education System: Academic Organization in Cross-National Perspective*. Berkeley, CA: University of California Press.

Dmitriev A. 2013. "Pereizobretenie sovetskogo universiteta." *Filosofsko-literaturnyj zhurnal "Logos."* No. 1: 41–64.

Freeman R. E. 1984 *Strategic Management: A Stakeholder Approach*. Boston, MA: Pitman.

Froumin I. "Establishing a New Research University: The Higher School of Economics, the Russian Federation." In *The Road to Academic Excellence: The Making of World-Class Research Universities*, edited by Philip G. Altbach and Jamil Salmi. Ch. 10, 293–321. Washington: The World Bank, 2011.

Froumin I., Kuzminov Y. I., and Semyonov D. 2014. "Institutional Diversity in Russian Higher Education: Revolutions and Evolution." *European Journal of Higher Education* 4, no. 3: *Special Issue: Transformation in Post-Socialist Higher Education Systems*.

Froumin I. and Povalko A. 2014. "Top Down Push for Excellence: Lesson from Russia." In *How World-Class Universities Affect Global Higher Education. Influences and Responses.*" 47–64. Vol. 30. Boston, Rotterdam, Taipei: Sense Publishers.

Johnson M. 2008. "Historical Legacies of Soviet Higher Education and the Transformation of Higher Education Systems in Post-Soviet Russia and Eurasia." In *The Worldwide Transformation of Higher Education*, edited by D. P. Baker and A. W. Wiseman. 159–176. Emerald Group Publishing Limited.

Kouzminov, Y., Semyonov, D., and Froumin, I. 2013. "Struktura vuzovskoi seti: ot sovetskogo k rossiyskomu masterplanu (HEIs Network Structure: From the Soviet to the Russian Masterplan)". *Voprosy obrazovania (Educational Studies)* 4:8–63.

Martin, Terry D. 2001 *The Affirmative Action Empire: Nations and Nationalism in the Soviet Union, 1923–1939*. Ithaca: Cornell University Press.

Platonova D., and Semyonov D. 2014, Program Diversification and Specialization in Russian Higher Education Institutions / Working papers by NRU Higher School of Economics. Series EDU "Education". No. 17/EDU/2014. Available online at: www.publications.hse.ru/preprints/137664991, accessed on January 2015.

Tasits N.2012 *Nauchnaya politika SSSR v 1927–1941 gg.* Raspisanie peremen. Ocherki istorii obrazovatelnoy i nauchnoy politiki v Rossiyskoy imperii—SSSR (konets 1880–kh—1930–egody). Novoe literaturnoe obozrenie, Moscow.

Ten L. 2007. "The Market and Higher School Management in the Recent Period." *Board of Rectors.* 1:105.

Ushakov, G., and Shuruyev, A. 1980 "Planirovanie i finansirovanie podgotovki spetsialistov [Planning and Funding of Specialist Training]." *Ekonomika.* Moscow.

Vakhitov R. 2014. *Sud'by universiteta v Rossii: imperskij, sovetskij i postsovetskij razdatochnyj mul'tiinstitut.* Moskva: Strana Oz.

Vishlenkova E. A., and Dmitriev, A. N. 2013. "Pragmatika tradicii, ili aktual'noe proshloe dlja rossijskih universitetov." In *Soslovie russkih professorov. Sozdateli statusov i smyslov,* edited by I. M. Savel'eva and E. A. Vishlenkova. 61–95. Moscow: HSE.

Sivak E., and Yudkevich M., 2015. "Academic Immobility and Inbreeding in Russian Universities." In *Academic Inbreeding and Mobility in Higher Education. Global Perspectives.* Basingstoke, UK: Palgrave Macmillan.

Decree of the Council of People's Commissars N 752 "On Reorganizing State Universities," dated July 13, 1931.

The Decree of the USSR Council of People's Commissars "On the Higher Education Institution Activities and Management," dated June 23, 1936.

Decree of the USSR Council of Ministers and the CPSU Central Committee, "On Improving the Sorting and Engagement of Highly Skilled and Semi-Skilled Workers," dated August 30, 1954.

Federal Law of the Russian Federation dated February 10, 2009 No. 18-F.

Decree of the President of the Russian Federation No. 599 dated May 7, 2012.

Website MoES (Ministry of Education and Science,) www.минобрнауки.рф/. Accessed in January 2015.

Website RAEP (Russian Academic Excellence Project) www.//5top100.ru//. Accessed in January 2015.

Chapter 9

Epilogue: Reflections on a New Flagship University

Manja Klemenčič

Each higher education system has one or several universities that stand out among the rest in terms of prestige, embodying the hopes of a nation. They are the frontrunners in educating national elites, in attracting the best students and academics, in granting social status, and, increasingly, in gaining resources intended to improve their performance in global rankings.

This book argues that leading national universities, and those that seek such a status, need to articulate and seek a much grander and more sophisticated vision: the New Flagship University. The leitmotif is twofold. One is the profound dissatisfaction with the way university rankings are ordering the global higher education system and distributing rewards and incentives. The other prompts Flagship Universities to seek self-improvement and meaningful engagement with the societies that gave them life and purpose.

Due to the rise in global interdependencies in all spheres of economic and social interaction, leading national universities are expected to be globally engaged and competitive. No longer is it sufficient for a university to be recognized as the most prestigious at home. Now it also needs to compete globally for elite status. And this is how the notion of a World Class University has emerged (Salmi 2009), with university rankings presenting themselves as the powerful instrument to determine the status of universities in this relatively new global competition.

While global engagements are undoubtedly desirable and advantageous, it is the race for global positional goods through league tables that the New Flagship University model seeks to challenge. The argument presented is compelling: by competing for status in global university rankings, the universities are beginning to lose sight of what excellence encompasses and what is relevant. The crude measurements imposed by rankings distort the authentic purposes and missions of universities, which historically focused first and foremost on regional and national relevance. Global engagements of universities, and indeed global prestige, ought not to be conceived as ends unto themselves, but instead as paths toward meaningful engagement in and service to societies. Contesting the universities' competition for global positional goods, indeed, the global university hierarchy, this book calls on universities to rethink and conceptualize their priorities and reconsider the direction of their self-improvement efforts.

In national systems, competition among the leading universities tends to be fierce but confined to the in-group (Marginson 2006), or else there is no competition at all in smaller systems where only one university enjoys a privileged status and captures national pride. Until the emergence of global higher education markets, leading national universities did not really have external pressures to self-improve. Their status was fairly secure and self-reproducing (Marginson 2006). The incentives to improve the quality of their teaching and research programs, and service to society, were internally generated and prompted by the strategic engagements within their higher education systems.

With the global rankings, this situation has changed. The resistance of national Flagship Universities toward external demands has crumbled due to the emergence of the perceived direct link—in the eyes of the governments and the wider public—between status in league tables and the universities' ability to drive national economic growth and development. Governments are expressing demands and offering incentives for their universities to get to the top 100 in the league tables. Hence, the external pressures for universities to self-improve are stronger in the age of globalization, and the directions for self-improvement are skewed toward the criteria applied by the rankings. Within national systems, the status of leading national universities generally still remains unchallenged (they still get the largest part of public funds and best students, and house the best staff), but the governments' demands on expected performance (value for money) are becoming more pronounced.

Contending this trend, the New Flagship model introduces an expanded and comprehensive view of a university's mission, policies, and practices. The model meticulously addresses and expounds on all of the vital functions and operations of a New Flagship University. It is not that all is new in the New Flagship model; many universities are pursuing key components of the profile. Its strength is in providing coherency and a narrative to the array of activities and practices of the best and most influential universities. Rather than claiming prescriptive powers, it lends itself as a tool kit for reflection that both university leaders and policy makers can consider for enabling university self-improvement. The breadth of Douglass's own academic and professional profile is clearly reflected in the depth and the wealth of examples of policies and practices that accompany the disposition of each university policy realm (teaching and learning, research, service, and governance).

The Relationship between the State and Flagship Universities

Douglass is careful to note that the ideals of a New Flagship University play out differently in different national contexts. The contributors of the regional and country chapters also express this proposition. The role of the state in attempting to control and influence the activities of each national Flagship, and the challenges associated with the size and organizational culture, stand out from these empirical chapters. In every national system, the state authorities have always taken a strong interest in their leading national universities and sought to control and steer them. These institutions are key strategic players in the political and economic life of each nation. They play a central role in educating professional and political elites. They have helped organize and develop state institutions. And they are considered among the pillars of national identity-building and are valued for nurturing social cohesion.

The approach of the state toward their Flagship Universities is always one component of a larger national approach for steering a national higher education system. Yet, the treatment of Flagships is typically more controlling and interventionist than for other institutions. Again, this happens precisely because their governments see these universities as central for reaching national, political, economic, and societal goals. They also possess significant symbolic capital, such as prominent public status, visibility, and legitimizing power, for social initiatives and political outcomes. Hence, Flagships certainly enjoy special privileges in terms of funding and symbolic capital granted by the state, but evolving accountability regimes often curb their autonomy. The specific mechanisms of control vary across countries and typically include formal representation of government officials on university governing bodies, accountability and performance standards linked to funding agreements, and a tightly knit web of informal relationships between university personnel and the university graduates holding positions in the state bureaucracy. Of course, ministries are not the only stakeholders taking interest in the affairs of their leading national universities. Business-interest associations, trade unions, and political parties also seek influence and control. In some countries, the election of the rector (or president or vice chancellor) stirs up political party interference and involvement.

The state typically controls the number and geographic spread of universities through financial instruments. In some countries, such as Russia and China, the state provides funding for its version of the Flagship University in different regions, and, in addition, provides competitive funding largely intended to help them compete in global league tables—the proxy for assessing the most productive universities. Within the European Union, national governments tend to provide additional funding for "centers of excellence" within institutions rather than promoting single institutions. They also encourage mergers between institutions to pool resources and boost competitive advantages. This is more in line with the European spirit of egalitarianism and a desire to find a balance between achieving World Class excellence and regional development.

The organization of leading national universities within national higher education systems can be conceptualized as consisting of two approaches: the "corporatist and neo-corporatist" and the "pluralist." The qualification of the original corporatist approach implies that the state has licensed a single university as its Flagship University, providing most of its funding while retaining a high level of control over its governance, academic programs, and deliverables. The neo-corporatist approach implies that the selected university has more autonomy from the state—autonomy being defined as institutions having decision-making competences and being allowed to exercise them independently (Enders, de Boer, and Weyer 2013, 7).

There are two extensions of the corporatist and neo-corporatist approaches. One is when the state grants Flagship status (or its equivalent) to several universities that are functionally complementary, such as in Saudi Arabia, which has a university specializing in petroleum and minerals (King Fahd University of Petroleum and Minerals), in addition to comprehensive universities. Another is a territorially differentiated model, where the state supports a Flagship University in each region, as in the cases of Russia and China. The territorially differentiated system is accentuated in federal systems with strong regional governments where competences over higher education (including funding) have been transferred from federal to regional level. Another variation of the model is ethnically or religiously differentiated systems common in multiethnic and multireligious states with more than one Flagship University, each having a distinct ethnic or religious designation.

In pluralist systems, there are several universities with Flagship status that perform identical functions and compete with each other for resources. As discussed earlier, there is a fierce but closed competition among such universities within a single national system. A variation on the pluralist model is where the government ceases to promote single institutions as Flagships, but rather promotes individual departments, schools, or centers within several institutions. The state-sponsored "excellence initiatives" have been set up within a number of European higher education systems specifically to promote profiling and mission differentiation among universities, elevating a select group of Flagship Universities. It is expected that Flagships will be successful in winning a large part of preferential funding, but not all of the funding and not for every academic area.

These leading institutions are also expected to invest more in areas of excellence and cut down in weaker areas; the latter being, of course, significantly more difficult than the former. The understanding is that not every academic program is of "flagship" quality. Since the league tables continue to push for rankings of entire institutions, it remains unclear whether these excellence initiatives will prevail as the future direction of state steering or we will continue to see stratification of national higher education systems with the Flagship Universities firmly consolidated on the top.

Flagship Universities as Complex Organizations and the Role of University Culture

As argued in this book, New Flagship Universities are generally comprehensive institutions—large in the number of enrolled students and in the breadth of their academic degree programs. The larger they are, the more complex their structures and operations, and the more likely it is that the quality of their subunits varies. The level of professionalization (or corporatization) of the university organization and the governance arrangements vary significantly from one Flagship to another. Even in the more corporate model, the central administrative structures are often too weak to fully manage the fairly autonomous constituent parts.

More corporate governance arrangements, as outlined in the New Flagship profile, make it easier to implement internal quality assurance systems, to advance institutional research, and to boost strategic planning and policy development. These functions are critical for university self-improvement as advocated in this book. Institutional research is, in particular, gaining in importance as university leaders need to manage increasingly complex organizational structures in a rapidly changing environment prompted by globalization, shifting student demographics, technological advancements, decreasing public spending, and increasing market orientation of higher education (Weber and Calderon 2015).

To the meticulous list of features characterizing the New Flagship University model, the book adds the necessary ecology that links the structures, functions, processes and relationships, and defines the dynamics of change—the university culture. Douglass points to academic freedom and autonomy as "inviolable values" (Sporn 1996) and shows how the pressures from rankings and the World Class University frenzy are impacting the orientations of Flagship Universities throughout the globe. Douglass devotes ample discussion on the pragmatic ways for universities to enact social purposes, for example, via service-based learning and promoting public service and collaboration with stakeholders from the local communities. This is linked to a discussion of the governance arrangements, quality assurance, and institutional research that are essential in university self-improvement.

The New Flagship University profile focuses on exploring and articulating the model. What is now needed is a discussion on the less tangible processes for institutions to fully or partially transition to this model. In many institutions, this will require cultivating shared beliefs and the sense of common purpose, and building commitment, engagement, and belonging among students, faculty and staff, and to some degree ministries supportive of the broader vision of a New Flagship. These processes may be driven and managed by university managers and administrators (Sporn 1996; Dill 2012), but there are ample possibilities—largely unexplored—for a bottom-up processes (Klemenčič, 2015).

Symbolic management of a university's organizational culture mapped in some form to the New Flagship model is a new avenue for further exploration: How can the New Flagship University enhance the capabilities of all internal constituencies to imagine, initiate, and pursue the activities important for their own self-formation as well as for the university's societal role, and for their self-improvement, whether through individual or collective action? (Klemenčič, in press). In other words, the question arises how a university enables and strengthens faculty, students, and administrative staff's agency, that is, their self-reflective and intentional action and interaction with the university (Klemenčič 2015). The opportunity for all members of an academic community to influence the university environment toward personal, collective, and societal well being and advancement should indeed be seen as one of the main legitimizing ideas of a New Flagship University.

Many leading national universities have been transformed from serving national needs to competing for global prestige. There is a growing concern over the global competition imperatives resulting from rankings and the preponderance of the World Class University metaphor. Universities are adapting to these imperatives without necessarily reflecting on and scrutinizing the changes in their purpose and mission. Gaining a competitive global ranking has displaced service to society. With the New Flagship University model, we might find a path to a more relevant and thoughtful future. Both higher education practitioners and policy makers will benefit immensely from this comprehensive, persuasively argued, and meticulously evidenced account.

REFERENCES

Dill, D. D. 2012. "The Management of Academic Culture Revisited: Integrating Universities in an Entrepreneurial Age." In *Managing Reform in Universities: The Dynamics of Culture, Identity and Organisational Change*, edited by B. Stensaker, J. Välimaa, and C. Sarrico. Basingstoke, UK: Palgrave Macmillan.

Enders, J., de Boer, H. and Weyer, E. 2013. "Regulatory Autonomy and Performance: The Reform of Higher Education Re-Visited." *Higher Education* 65, no. 1: 5–24.

Klemenčič, M. (in press). "Student Involvement in Quality Enhancement." In *The Handbook of Higher Education Policy and Governance*, edited by J. Huisman, H. de Boer, D. D. Dill and M. Souto-Otero. Basingstoke, UK: Palgrave Macmillan.

Klemenčič, M. 2015. "What Is Student Agency? An Ontological Exploration in the Context of Research on Student Engagement." In *Student Engagement in Europe: Society, Higher Education and Student Governance*," edited by M. Klemenčič, S. Bergan, S. and R. Primožič. Council of Europe Higher Education Series No. 20. Strasbourg: Council of Europe Publishing.

Marginson, S. 2006. "Dynamics of National and Global Competition in Higher Education." *Higher Education* 52, no. 1: 1–39.

Salmi, J. 2009. *The Challenge of Establishing World-Class Universities*. Washington, DC: World Bank Publications.

Sporn, B. 1996. "Managing University Culture: An Analysis of the Relationship between Institutional Culture and Management Approaches." *Higher Education* 32, no. 1: 41–61.

Webber, K. L. and Calderon, A. J. eds. 2015. *Institutional Research and Planning in Higher Education. Global Contexts and Themes*. Abingdon, UK and New York, NY: Routledge.

Appendix 1

Global University Rankings— Variables and Weights

World University Rankings—*Times Higher Education*

First published on September 16, 2010, the *Times Higher Education* World University Rankings attempts to gauge a wide range of what universities do. While the Academic Ranking of World Universities, compiled by Shanghai Jiao Tong University, focuses largely on research performance, the *Times Higher Education* World University Rankings seeks to capture aspects of a larger range of a university' activities—research, teaching, knowledge transfer, and internationalization. The WUR uses 13 calibrated performance indicators grouped in five areas:

- Teaching: the learning environment worth 30 percent of the overall ranking score
- Research: volume, income and reputation worth 30 percent
- Citations: research influence worth 30 percent
- Industry income: innovation worth 2.5 percent
- International outlook: staff, students, and research worth 7.5 percent.

Universities are excluded from the *Times Higher Education* World University Rankings if they do not teach undergraduates; if they teach only a single narrow subject; or if their research output amounted to fewer than 1,000 articles in selected journals between 2007 and 2011, or 200 articles a year. In some exceptional cases, institutions that are below the 200-article threshold are included if they have a particular focus on disciplines with generally low publication volumes, such as engineering or the arts and humanities.

To calculate the overall rankings, "Z-scores" were created for all data sets except for the results of the academic reputation survey. The calculation of Z-scores standardizes the different data types on a common scale and allow fair comparisons between different types of data—essential when combining diverse information into a single ranking. Each data point is given a score based on its distance from the mean average of the entire data set, where the scale is the standard deviation of the data set. The Z-score is then turned into a "cumulative probability score" to arrive at the final totals. If University X has a cumulative probability score of 98, for example, then a random institution from the same data distribution will fall below the institution 98 percent of the time. For the results of the reputation survey, the data are highly skewed in favor of a small number of institutions at the top of the rankings. To compensate for this, WUR recently included an exponential component to increase differentiation between institutions lower down the scale.

Academic Ranking of World Universities ARWU—Shanghai Jiaotong University

Universities are ranked by several indicators of academic or research performance, including alumni and staff winning Nobel Prizes and Fields Medals, highly cited researchers, papers published in *Nature* and *Science*, papers indexed in major citation indices, and the per capita academic performance of an institution. For each indicator, the highest scoring institution is assigned a score of 100, and other institutions are calculated as a percentage of the top score. Scores for each indicator are weighted to arrive at a final overall score for an institution. The highest scoring institution is assigned a score of 100, and other institutions are calculated as a percentage of the top score. An institution's rank reflects the number of institutions that sit above it. In total, more than 2,000 institutions have been scanned by ARWU and about 1,200 institutions have actually been ranked.

Indicators and Weights for ARWU 2013

Figure A1.1   Indicators and Weights for ARWU 2013.

Criteria	Indicator	Weight (%)
Quality of education	Alumni of an institution winning Nobel Prizes and Fields Medals	10
Quality of faculty	Staff of an institution winning Nobel Prizes and Fields Medals	20
	Highly cited researchers in 21 broad subject categories	20
Research output	Papers published in Nature and Science*	20
	Papers indexed in Science Citation Index-expanded and Social Science Citation Index	20
Per capita performance	Per capita academic performance of an institution	10
Total		100

*For institutions specialized in humanities and social sciences such as London School of Economics, N&S is not considered, and the weight of N&S is relocated to other indicators.

QS World University Rankings— Quacquarelli Symonds

The primary goal of the QS World University Rankings is to help students make informed comparisons between their international study options. Since first being compiled in 2004, the rankings have expanded to feature more than 800 universities around the world, with over 3,000 assessed. The top 400 universities are given individual ranking positions; after that, universities are placed within a group, starting from 401–410, up to 701+. The rankings compare these top 800 universities across four broad areas of interest to prospective students: research, teaching, employability, and international outlook. These four key areas are assessed using six indicators, each of which is given a different percentage weighting.

Four of the indicators are based on "hard" data, and the remaining two on major global surveys—one of academics and another of employers—each the largest of their kind. Below is a weighting used in each of the six indicators used:

- Academic reputation 40 percent
- Employer reputation 10 percent
- Student-to-faculty ratio 20 percent
- Citations per faculty 20 percent
- International faculty ratio 5 percent
- International student ratio 5 percent

Appendix 2

Assigned Characteristics of a WCU— "The Challenge of Creating a World Class University," World Bank 2009

- Has an international reputation for its research.
- Has an international reputation for its teaching.
- Has a number of research stars and world leaders in their fields.
- Recognized not only by other world-class universities. for example, US Ivy League but also outside the world of higher education.
- Has a number of world-class departments that is, not necessarily all.
- Identifies and builds on its research strengths and has a distinctive reputation and focus that is, its "lead" subjects.
- Generates innovative ideas and produces basic and applied research in abundance.
- Produces groundbreaking research output recognized by peers and prizes, for example, Nobel Prize winners.
- Attracts the most able students and produces the best graduates.
- Can attract and retain the best staff.
- Can recruit staff and students from an international market.
- Attracts a high proportion of postgraduate students, both taught and research.
- Attracts a high proportion of students from overseas.
- Operates within a global market and is international in many activities for example, research links, student and staff exchanges, and throughput of visitors of international standing.
- Has a very sound financial base.
- Receives large endowment capital and income.

- Has diversified sources of income, for example, government, private companies sector, research income, and overseas student fees.
- Provides a high-quality and supportive research and educational environment for both its staff and its students, for example, high-quality buildings and facilities/high-quality campus.
- Has a first-class management team with strategic vision and implementation plans.
- Produces graduates who end up in positions of influence and/or power that is, movers and shakers such as prime ministers and presidents.
- Often has a long history of superior achievement for example, the Universities of Oxford and Cambridge in the United Kingdom and Harvard University in the United States.
- Makes a big contribution to society and our times.
- Continually benchmarks with top universities and departments worldwide.
- Has the confidence to set its own agenda.

Sources: Jamil Salmi, "The Challenge of Creating a World Class University," World Bank 2009. Alden, J., and G. Lin. 2004. "Benchmarking the Characteristics of a World-Class University: Developing an International Strategy at University Level." Leadership Foundation for Higher Education, London.

References

Alden, J., and G. Lin. 2004. "Benchmarking the Characteristics of a World-Class University: Developing an International Strategy at University Level." Leadership Foundation for Higher Education, London.

Allen, I. E., and Seaman, J. 2013. *Changing Course: Ten Years of Tracking Online Education in the United States.* Wellesley, MA: Babson Survey Research Group and Quahong Research Group.

Altbach, Philip. 2005. "A World Class Country without World Class Higher Education: India's 21st Century Dilemma," *International Higher Education* (Summer 2005).

Altbach, Philip. 2003. "The Costs and Benefits of World-Class Universities," *International Higher Education* (Fall 2003).

Altbach, P. and Balan, J. 2007. *World Class World: Transforming Research Universities in Asia and Latin America.* Baltimore: Johns Hopkins University Press.

Altbach, P., ed. 2011. *Leadership for World Class Universities: Challenges for Developing Countries.* London: Routledge Publishers.

Asian Development Bank News 2001. "Viet Nam to Build Its First World-Class University." http://www.adb.org/Documents/News/VRM/vrm_200107.asp.

Association of Governing Boards 2010. Statement on Board Responsibility for Institutional Governance. Washington, DC: http://agb.org/news/2010-03/statement-board-responsibility-institutional-governance.

Atkinson, Peter M. 2014. "Assess the Real Cost of Research Assessment." World View. *Nature.* December 11: 516 (7530): 145. doi:10.1038/516145a.

Berdahl, R. M. 1998. "The Future of Flagship Universities." Remarks at the Convocation Texas A&M University. October 5.

Bernasconi, Andres 2007. "Are There Research Universities in Chile?," in *World Class World: Transforming Research Universities in Asia and Latin America,* edited by Philip G. Altbach and Jorge Balan. Baltimore: Johns Hopkins University Press.

Bernasconi, Andrés 2012. "Are Global Rankings Unfair to Latin American Universities?" *Inside Higher Education,* October 15. http://www.insidehighered.com/blogs/world-view/are-global-rankings-unfair-latin-american-universities#sthash.XpboINbW.dpbs.

Brint, Steven. 2014. "Co-curricular Learning and the Physical Campus." Remarks at the First Berkeley-Stanford Online Summit, UC Berkeley. March 8.

Bunting, I., Cloete, N. and van Schalkwyk, F. 2013. *An Empirical Overview of Eight Flagship Universities in Africa: 2001–2011*. Cape Town, South Africa: Centre for Higher Education Transformation.

Business Weekly. 2002. "Building Top-Notch Universities." April 24, 2002, Website: http://www.chinadaily.com.cn/chinagate/doc/2002-04/24/content_247215.htm.

Butler, P. and Mulgan, R. 2013. "Can Academic Freedom Survive Performance Based Research Funding," *Victoria University of Wellington Law Review*, 44, November: http://www.victoria.ac.nz/law/research/publications/vuwlr/prev-issues/volume-44,-issue-34/07-Butler.pdf.

Chirikov, Igor 2013. "Research Universities as Knowledge Networks: The Role of Institutional Research, *Studies in Higher Education*, 38, no. 3: 456–469.

Cloete, N., Bailey, T. Pillay, P. Bunting, I., and Maassen, P. 2011. *Universities and Economic Development in Africa*, Higher Education Research and Advocacy Network in Africa (HERANA) Centre for Higher Education Transformation, Cape Town, South Africa: http://chet.org.za/books/universities-and-economic-development-africa-0.

Douglass, J. A. 1998. "Shared Governance at the University of California," CSHE Research and Occasional Papers, CSHE.1.98 March. http://cshe.berkeley.edu/shared-governance-university-california-historical-review.

Douglass, J. A. 2000. *The California Idea and American Higher Education: 1850 to the 1960 Master Plan*. Stanford University Press, 2nd edition 2007. http://www.sup.org/book.cgi?book_id=3189.

Douglass, J. A. 2007. *The Conditions for Admission: Access, Equity, and the Social Contract of Public Universities*. Stanford University Press. http://www.sup.org/book.cgi?book_id=5558%205559.

Douglass, J. A. 2009. "Higher Education's New Global Order: How and Why Governments Are Creating Structured Opportunity Markets," CSHE Research and Occasional Papers Series, December. http://cshe.berkeley.edu/publications/publications.php?id=348.

Douglass, J. A. 2009. "The Race for Human Capital," in *Globalization's Muse: Universities and Higher Education Systems in a Changing World*, edited by J. A. Douglass, C. J. King and I. Feller. Berkeley: Public Policy Press.

Douglass, J. A., and Thomson, G. 2010. "The Immigrant's University: A Study of Academic Performance and the Experiences of Recent Immigrant Groups at the University of California." *Higher Education Policy*, 23, 451–474: http://www.palgrave journals.com/hep/journal/v23/n4/pdf/hep201018a.pdf.

Douglass, J. A. 2012. "China Futurisms: Research Universities and Leaders or Followers?" *Social Research: An International Quarterly*, 79, no. 3: 639–688.

Douglass, J. A. and Zhao, C.-M. 2013. "Undergraduate Research Engagement at Major US Research Universities," Research and Occasional Paper Series, Center for Studies in Higher Education, CSHE.14.13.

Eaton, Judith. 2004. "The Opportunity Cost of the Pursuit of International Quality Standards," *International Higher Education* (Summer 2004).

Eggins, Heather 2010. *Access and Equity: Comparative Perspectives*. Rotterdam, Netherlands: Sense, p. 12.

Estermann, T., E. Benntot Pruvot, and A. L. C. Laeys-Kulik 2013. *Designing Strategies for Efficient Funding of Higher Education in Europe.* Brussels: European Association of Universities.

Felden, J., 2013. *Global Trends in University Governance.* Education Working Paper Series, The World Bank.

Fong, Pang, and Linda Lim 2003. "Evolving Great Universities in Small and Developing Countries," *International Higher Education* (Fall 2003).

Frazer, Malcolm 1994. "Quality in Higher Education: An International Perspective," in *What Is Quality in Higher Education?*, edited by Diana Green. 101–111. London: Society for Research into Higher Education, 1994.

Franzoni, C., Scellato, G., and Stephan, P. 2011. "Changing Incentives to Publish." *Science*, 333 (August 5): 702–03.

Furco, A. 1996. "Service-Learning: A Balanced Approach to Experiential Education." *Service Learning.*

Gornitzka, A. 2013. "Channel, Filter or Buffer? National Policy Responses to Global Rankings," in *Global University Rankings: Challenges for European Higher Education*, edited by T. Erkkilä. Basingstoke: Palgrave Macmillan.

Hazelkorn, E. 2011. *Rankings and the Reshaping of Higher Education.* London: Palgrave Macmillan.

Hazelkorn, E. 2014. "University Rankings Schizophrenia? Europe Impact Study," *University World News,* no: 343 (November 14): http://www.universityworld news.com/article.php?story=20141113071956625.

Hollister, R. 2013. "The Engaged University—an Invisible Worldwide Revolution." Tisch College of Citizenship and Public Service: http://activecitizen .tufts.edu/about/dean-rob-hollister/publications-and-presentations/the -engaged-university-an-invisible-worldwide-revolution/.

Huisman, J. 2008. "World-Class Universities." *Higher Education Policy*, 211: 1–4.

Hobbs, Arthur. 1997. "World Class University and Cultural Diversity," www.math .tamu.edu/~arthur.hobbs/3d.html.

Jackman, W. Robert and Randolph M. Siverson. 1996. "Ratings the Rating: An Analysis of the National Research Council's Appraisal of Political Science PhD. Programs." *PS: Political Science and Politics*, 29, no. 2 (June 1996): 155–160.

Jiang, Xueqin. 2001. "China's Top 2 Universities Try for 'World Class' Status." *The Chronicle of Higher Education.* www.chronicle.com/weekly/v48/i17/17a03301.htm.

Kehm, B. 2013. "Global University Rankings—Impacts and Unintended Side Effects." *European Journal of Education.* 49, no. 1 (March): 102–112.

Kerr, C. 1963. *Uses of the University.* Cambridge, MA: Harvard University Press.

King, R. 2011. *Universities Globally: Organizations, Regulation and Rankings.* Cheltenham: Edward Elgar.

King, Christine 2003. "World Class?" http://education.guardian.co.uk/world class/story/0,14048,1085324,00.html.

Knobel, Marcelo, Tania Patricia Simoes, and Carlos Henrique de Brito Cruz. 2013. "International Collaborations between Universities: Experiences and Best Practices," *Studies in Higher Education*, 38. no. 3 (2013): 405–424.

Lee, Gilton 2000. "Brain Korea 21: A Development-Oriented National Policy in Korean Higher Education," *International Higher Education* (Spring 2000).

Lee, E., and Bowen, F. 1971. *The Multicampus University: A Study of Academic Governance*. Carnegie Commission on Higher Education. New York: McGraw-Hill.

Liu, N. C., Wang, Q., & Cheng, Y. Eds. 2011. *Paths to a World-Class University. Global Perspectives in Higher Education*, 43. Rotterdam: Sense Publishers.

Locke, W. 2011. "The Institutionalization of Rankings: Managing Status Anxiety in an Increasingly Marketized Environment," in *University Rankings. Theoretical Basis, Methodology and Impacts on Global Higher Education*, edited by J. C. Shin, R. K. Toutkoushian, and U. Teichler. 201–228. Dordrecht: Springer.

Ma, W. 2007. *The Trajectory of Chinese Doctoral Education and Scientific Research*. Berkeley: Center for Studies in Higher Education, CSHE.

Ma, W. 2008. "The University of California at Berkeley: An Emerging Global Research University." *Higher Education Policy*, 211, 65–81.

Marginson, S. 2008. "Ideas of a University for the Global Era." Paper for seminar on Positioning University in the Globalized World: Changing Governance and Coping Strategies in Asia. Centre of Asian Studies, The University of Hong Kong; Central Policy Unit, HKSAR Government; and The Hong Kong Institute of Education, December 10–11, The University of Hong Kong.

Marginson, S. 2011. "Higher Education in East Asia and Singapore: Rise of the Confucian Model." *Higher Education*, 615: 587–611.

Marginson, S. 2013. "University Rankings and Social Science." *European Journal of Education*. 49, no. 1 (March): 45–59.

Marope, P. T. M., Wells, P. J., Hazelkorn, E. eds. 2013. *Rankings and Accountability in Higher Education: Uses and Misuses*. Paris: UNESCO Publishing.

Marshall, J. 2014. "Hollande Pledges €2 Billion for Excellence Initiatives." *University World News*, February 12, no. 307: http://www.universityworld news.com/article.php?story=20140212135224632

Mohrman, Kathryn 2005. "World-Class Universities and Chinese Higher Education Reform," *International Higher Education* (Spring 2005).

Mok, K. H 2011. "Enhancing Quality of Higher Education: Approaches, Strategies and Challenges for Hong Kong," in *Quality in Higher Education: Identifying, Developing and Sustaining Best Practices in the APEC Region*, edited by Neubauer, Deane and John N. Hawkins. Singapore: APEC Secretariat.

Mowery, David C., Richard R. Nelson, Bhaven N. Sampat, and Arvids A. Zeidonis. 2004. *Ivory Tower and University-Industry Technological Transfer Before and After the Bayh-Dole Act*, Stanford, CA: Stanford University Press.

National Research Council. 1995. *Research-Doctorate Programs in the United States: Continuity and Change*. Washington, DC: National Research Council.

Nerad, M., and Evans, B. 2014. *Globalization and Its Impacts on the Quality of Ph.D. Education: Forces and Forms in Doctoral Education Worldwide*. Rotterdam, The Netherlands: Sense Publishers.

Ngok, Kenglun and Weiging Guo. 2008. "The Quest for World Class Universities in China: Critical Reflections," *Policy Futures in Education*, 6, no 5.

Niland, John 2000. "The Challenge of Building World Class Universities in the Asian Region," Online opinion Australia's e-journal of social and political debate. http://www.onlineopinion.com.au/view.asp?article=997.

Ordorika, Imanol and Pusser, Brian. 2007. "La máxima casa de estudios: The Universidad Nacional Autónoma de México as a State-Building University." In *World-Class Worldwide: Transforming Research Universities in Asia and Latin America*, edited by Philip Altbach and Jorge Balán. 189–215. Baltimore: Johns Hopkins University Press.

Postiglione, G. 2011. The Rise of Research Universities: The Hong Kong University of Science and Technology. In *The Road to Academic Excellence: The Making of World-Class Research Universities,* edited Philip G. Altbach and Jamil Salmi. 63–100. Washington: The World Bank.

Proctor, Lita M. 2005. "Presentation to the President's Commission of the Future of FSU," Website: http://www.fsu.edu/~future/proctor.html.

Proulx, R. 2005. "Criteria for Ranking Universities with Affiliated Components." In Liu, Nian Cai, ed. 2005. Proceedings of the First International Conference on World-Class Universities WCU-1 Shanghai: Shanghai Jiao Tong University.

de Rassenfosse, Gaétan and Williams, R. 2015. "Rules of Engagement: Measuring Connectivity in National Systems of Higher Education. *Higher Education.* Published online March: http://link.springer.com/article/10.1007/s10734-015 -9881-y#page-1

Rutschow, E., and Schneider, E. 2011. "Unlocking the Gate What We Know about Improving Developmental Education." Manpower Demonstration Research Corporation, New York City.

Schalkwyk, F van. 2014. "University Engagement as Interconnectedness." *University World* News, December 19, 2014. Issue No: 348: http://www.university worldnews.com/article.php?story=20141218053615504.

Schulze-Celven, T. 2015. "Liberalizing the Academy: The Transformation of Higher Education in the United States and Germany." CSHE Research and Occasional Papers Series, January.

Shattock, M. 2013. "University Governance, Leadership and Management in a Decade of Diversification and Uncertainty." *Higher Education Quarterly*, 67, no. 2: 217–233.

Stensaker, B. and Vabø, A. 2013. "Re-Inventing Shared Governance: Implications for Organizational Culture and Institutional Leadership." *Higher Education Quarterly*, 67, no. 2: 256–274.

Salmi, Jamil, and Alenoush Saroyan 2007. "League Tables as Policy Instruments: Uses and Misuses." *Higher Education Management and Policy* 19, no. 2: 31–68.

Thoenig, J.-C. and and Paradeise, C. 2014. "Organizational Governance and Production of Academic Quality: Lessons from Two Top U.S. Research Universities." Pending publication *Minerva*.

Tijani, Ibikunle H. 2013. "Developing World Class Universities in Nigeria: Challenges, Prospects and Implications." Paper delivered at the 2nd FUNAI Leadership Development Seminar, Federal University Ndufu-Alike Ikwo, Ebonyi State, Nagieria, June 5.

Tinto, V. 2003. "Learning Better Together: The Impact of Learning Communities on Student Success." In Promoting Student Success in College, Higher

Education Monograph Series, pp. 1–8. Syracuse, NY: Syracuse University. Retrieved September 22, 2009, from http://faculty.soe.syr.edu/vtinto/Files /Learning%20Better%20Together.pdf.

Trow, Martin. 1976. "Elite Higher Education: An Endangered Species?" *Minerva* 14, no. 3 (Autumn): 355–76.

Verba, S., Shcolzman, K. L., and Brady, H. 1995. *Voice and Equality: Civic Voluntarism in American Politics.* Cambridge, MA: Harvard University Press.

Vest, C. 2005. "World Class Universities: American Lessons," *International Higher Education* (Winter 2005).

Volkwein, Fredericks J., Ying Liu, and Woodell, James. 2012. "The Structure and Functions of Institutional Research Offices," in *The Handbook of Institutional Research*, edited by Richard D. Howard, Gerald W. McLaughlin, and William E. Kight. San Francisco: Jossey-Bass.

Wang, Yingjie. 2001. "Building the World-Class University in a Developing Country: Universals, Uniqueness, and Cooperation." *Asia Pacific Education Review*, 2, no. 2.

Ware, M, and Mabe, M. 2012. *The STM Report: An Overview of Scientific and Scholarly Journal Publishing.* International Association of Scientific, Technical and Medical Publishers, The Netherlands: http://www.stm-assoc .org/2012_12_11_STM_Report_2012.pdf.

Watson, D., Hollister, R., Stroud, S., and Babcock, E. 2013. *The Engaged University: International Perspectives on Civic Engagement.* International Studies in Higher Education. New York: Routledge Press.

Wende, M. C. van der. 2009. "European Responses to Global Competitiveness in Higher Education." Research and Occasional Paper Series, No. 7, 2009. Berkeley: Center for Studies in higher Education, University of California: http://cshe.berkeley.edu/european-responses-global-competitiveness-higher -education.

Wende, M. C. van der 2014 (forthcoming). "On Mergers and Missions: Implications for Institutional Governance and Governmental Steering," in *Global Outreach of World-Class Universities: How It Is Affecting Higher Education Systems. Centre for World-Class Universities.* Jiao Tong University, Shanghai. Sense Publishers.

Williams, R., de Rassenfosse, G., Jensen, P., and Marginson, S. 2013. "The Determinants of Quality National Higher Education Systems." *Journal of Higher Education Policy and Management*, 35, no. 6 (2013): 599–611.

Yudkevich, M., Altbach, P., Rumbley, L. (eds). 2015. *Academic Inbreeding and Mobility in Higher Education.* Basingstoke, UK: Palgrave Macmillan.

Contributors

Andrés Bernasconi, PhD, is associate professor and vice-dean at the School of Education of the Pontificia Universidad Católica de Chile, and director of its Center for Research on Educational Policy and Practice. He holds degrees from the Pontificia Universidad Católica de Chile, Harvard University, and Boston University.

Daniela Véliz Calderón in associate researcher at the Center for Research on Educational Policy and Practice CEPPE, in Santiago, Chile (http://www.ceppe.cl/). Her research interests relate to the academic profession, internationalization, equity, and gender. She has a PhD in Higher Education from the University of Maine and an MA in Student Development in Higher Education from the same university.

John Aubrey Douglass is senior research fellow—Public Policy and Higher Education at the Center for Studies in Higher Education (CSHE), University of California—Berkeley. He is the author of *The Conditions for Admissions, The California Idea and American Higher Education*, and coeditor of *Globalization's Muse: Universities and Higher Education Systems in a Changing World*.

Tatiana Fumasoli is a researcher and assistant professor at the Department of Education, Faculty of Educational Sciences, University of Oslo. Previously she was a postdoctoral fellow at ARENA Centre for European Studies, University of Oslo. She received her PhD from the University of Lugano (Switzerland) with a thesis on strategy of higher education institutions. Her main interests are university management and the role of political and social actors in higher education governance and policy. Her work has appeared, among others, in *Higher Education, Minerva, Higher Education Policy, International Journal of Public Administration*, and with reputed international publishers.

Isak Froumin is professor of Education and academic supervisor, Institute of Education, National Research University Higher School of Economics—Moscow, and the author of more than 250 publications. His current key research interests are development of higher education systems, higher education differentiation, university and school governance.

John N. Hawkins is codirector of the East West Center's Asian Pacific Higher Education Research Partnership and professor emeritus of Social Sciences and Comparative Education at the Graduate School of Education, University of California, Los Angeles. He has served as president of the Comparative International Education Society and editor of the *Comparative Education Review*. His latest publications include *Changing Education: Leadership, Innovation, and Development in a Globalizing Asia Pacific*, and *Policy Debates in Comparative, International and Development Education.*

Manja Klemenčič is fellow and lecturer in Sociology at the Department of Sociology, Faculty of Arts and Sciences, Harvard University. She researches, teaches, advises, and consults in the area of international and comparative higher education, with particular interest on the implications of contemporary higher education reforms on students. She is editor in chief of *European Journal of Higher Education*, thematic editor of the section "Elite and Mass Higher Education in the 21st Century" of the *International Encyclopedia of Higher Education Systems and Institutions*, coeditor of the book series "*Understanding Student Experience in Higher Education*" (Bloomsbury) and serves on the Governing Board of the *Consortium of Higher Education Researchers* (CHER) and *Global Forum on Improving University Teaching (IUT)*.

Oleg Leshukov is a junior research fellow, Laboratory for Universities Development, Institute of Education, National Research University Higher School of Economics—Moscow. His current key research interests are development of regional higher education systems, national-regional relationships in governance of higher education.

Bjørn Stensaker is professor of higher education at the University of Oslo. He has a special research interest in governance, organizational change, and quality assurance in higher education, and he has published widely on these issues internationally.

Index